MODERN AMERICAN HISTORY ★ A Garland Series

Edited by
FRANK FREIDEL
Harvard University

COUNSEL
AND ADVISE ★ A Political Biography
of Samuel I. Rosenman

Samuel B. Hand

Garland Publishing, Inc.
New York & London ★ 1979

Library of Congress Cataloging in Publication Data

Hand, Samuel B   1931–
    Counsel and advise.

    (Modern American history)
    Includes bibliographical references and index.
    1. Rosenman, Samuel Irving, 1896–1973.   2. United
States—Politics and government—1933–1945.
3. United States—Politics and government—1945–
1953.   4. New York (State)—Politics and government—
1865–1950.   5. Presidents—United States—Staff—Biography.   6. Judges—New York (State)—Biography.
I. Title.   II. Series.
E748.R73H36   973.917'092'4 [B]   78-62383
ISBN 0-8240-3632-8

All volumes in this series are printed on acid-free,
250-year-life paper.
Printed in the United States of America

Contents

                                                                page

Foreword   vii

Preface   ix

 1. Excelsior   1

 2. Securing Counsel   21

 3. Impolitic Judges v. Judicial Ambitions . . .   37

 4. New Deals and Political Dealings   57

 5. Sixty Centre Street   75

 6. "Sammy the Rose"   97

 7. For the Record   111

 8. Fortuitous Phrases   125

 9. Politics of Reorganization   147

10. The Palace Guard   171

11. The End of an Epoch   187

12. Working with Truman   199

13. Attorney at Law   227

Footnotes.   247

Index   353

Foreword

The appearance of a full biography of Samuel I. Rosenman has long been delayed, obviously because of the excellence and success of Rosenman's own memoir. *Working with Roosevelt* is not only one of the most readable and perceptive of the wide array of New Deal memoirs; it is also the finest account and analysis of the way in which Franklin D. Roosevelt's speeches took shape. Indeed it is the indispensable book on presidential speech writing. But there is much that is interesting and even vitally important about Judge Rosenman that the memoir, with its focus entirely upon his relationship to Roosevelt, did not touch. Hence the importance of Samuel B. Hand's *Counsel and Advise*, which for the first time places Rosenman's contributions to the New Deal and World War II in their larger context, and above all adds an account of Rosenman's equally vital contribution to President Harry S. Truman's Fair Deal.

Quite possibly the most notable of Rosenman's many achievements was the way in which he encouraged Truman during his first months in office to reaffirm the long-range liberal goals of his predecessor. Truman had just moved into the White House from a Senate seething with hostility toward Roosevelt and these objectives, and with the exception of Rosenman was surrounded by advisors of equally conservative bent. Truman was obviously ambivalent. Within his family and among intimates he was sometimes less than complimentary in his view of Roosevelt, yet he had supported most New Deal legislation. Rosenman's remarkable role was, after having been so close to Roosevelt, to win the confidence of Truman and to serve as the bridge between the New Deal and the Fair Deal. What he had expected to be temporary service for Truman stretched into a year. It was Rosenman who drafted the 21-point message to Congress of the fall of 1945 which set forth what Truman later proudly hailed as the outline of the Fair Deal.

From the outset, working for Al Smith through the New Deal and Fair Deal to minor service for President John F. Kennedy, Rosenman stood in the liberal, reform tradition. He was one of those who made his contributions from an eastern European Jewish heritage and an upbringing in New York City. Despite his spectacular record at Columbia Law School, he was graduated at a time when young men of his background were inadmissible to prestigious law firms. It was not only a sign of changing times but also of the way Rosenman, working with great political leaders, helped bring about change, that in 1964 he was elected President of the Association of the Bar of the City of New York.

There is much noteworthy in Hand's biography concerning Rosenman's career as a lawyer and judge, and his continuing role in New York politics. Of special interest is the analysis of Rosenman's editing of the *Public Papers* of Roosevelt, and his organizing and reorganizing of government agencies during World War II. During the war, Rosenman seems to have been a counterweight on the homefront to the more conservative James F. Byrnes. Altogether this is an important study of a figure of lasting significance.

Frank Freidel

Harvard University

Preface

This biography had its inception in 1957 when I proposed Samuel I. Rosenman as the topic for my doctoral dissertation at Syracuse University. Despite the zeal with which I asserted its feasibility to my advisor, I possessed no particular intellectual or personal commitment to the subject. It was, I now recognize, an instance of a graduate student asserting himself simply because it seemed possible to do so. I suspect my advisor, Oscar T. Barck, recognized that then, but he allowed me to pursue the biography anyway. During the almost twenty years that intervened since the dissertation was completed I have regretted neither of our decisions.

In the course of my research I met with Judge and Mrs. Rosenman on many occasions, and although they had never seen me until I brought them news of my proposed biography they were generous with their time and Job-like with their patience. For an extended period they allowed me to research in their home and in the Judge's law offices. They also supplied some uninhibited comments on my work. One of my most prized possessions is an exegesis of their copy of my dissertation. Although I have not always accepted their suggestions, I am keenly aware that they saved me from many blatant errors and plausible but incorrect assumptions. They also occasionally shifted my perspective. It was an awesome experience to have the Judge confront me with massive documentation and forceful testimony suggesting I had reached a dubious conclusion.

Judge Rosenman maintained a noteworthy career until his death in 1973, and the biography required continual updating. The periodic release of new material by the Roosevelt and Truman Libraries necessitated occasional reassessments of conclusions reached earlier. Materials released after 1967, however, have tended to either re-inforce prior judgments or to reflect material I had viewed earlier in the possession of the Judge.

Although my sources are indicated in the notes (I assume this is the most effective way to indicate in-debtedness) I owe special thanks to the Roosevelt, Tru-man, Association of the Bar of the City of New York, Syracuse University, and University of Vermont Libraries. The Truman Library and the University of Vermont gener-ously made funds available to support the research. I cannot possibly mention all the archivists, librarians, and colleagues who assisted me, but the late Philip Brooks was so special that not to single him out would be an act of ingratitude.

My deepest appreciation is to Harriet, my wife since before I first proposed the biography, who has probably read it as often as I have.

Chapter One

EXCELSIOR

On the morning of October 17, 1928, Samuel Irving
Rosenman emerged from a Manhattan apartment house, settled
himself and a collection of bulging suitcases into a waiting taxi and motored to a Hudson River pier. A Hoboken
Ferry was loading passengers and Rosenman boarded promptly. Then after entrusting the care of his suitcases to
a fellow-passenger, he sought out Franklin D. Roosevelt,
the Democratic nominee for Governor of New York State.

Although Rosenman had served seven years in state
government, and in his capacity as Legislative Bill Drafting Commissioner was closely associated with the New York
political leadership, he and the gubernatorial candidate
had never met. Roosevelt had not been active in New York
legislative politics since having served two terms as a
Senator from Dutchess County prior to the First World War.
His subsequent political efforts had been directed almost
exclusively to national concerns. Admittedly unfamiliar
with many of the intricacies of more recent New York affairs, he had appended Rosenman to his campaign staff as
a resource man for such background information. There
was, however, no assurance that Rosenman's services would
be solicited during the campaign.

Louis Howe, Roosevelt's principal aide, had earlier
suggested that Roosevelt link his own campaign to that of
Alfred E. Smith, the Democratic Presidential candidate.
Smith had been a highly popular New York Governor and Howe
hoped that by campaigning on a "never mind me, vote for

Al basis," Roosevelt could associate himself with recent
state developments without having to speak of them in any
detail.[1] The strategy seemed tailored to Roosevelt, but
he also prepared for the contingency that he might deviate
from it, and inquired if either Maurice Bloch, his campaign manager, or Belle Moscowitz, Smith's principal aide,
could suggest someone steeped in recent New York legislative developments who might be made available to him
for the duration of the campaign. Both Bloch, as representative of the party machinery, and Mrs. Moscowitz, as
spokesman for the Smith intellectuals, recommended Sam
Rosenman. Roosevelt sent word that their man was to be
added to his staff.[2]

        Belle Moskowitz received the word and carried it
to Rosenman. Had Rosenman possessed the power of prophesy
he would have exulted at the move. As it was, however,
he accepted the assignment without enthusiasm. Personally
dedicated to the Smith program and skeptical of Roosevelt's
commitment, he had, although only thirty-two years old,
already achieved enviable personal success under the aegis
of the Democratic Party. Demonstrations of his continuing
loyalty and usefulness would be credits toward even more
substantial rewards.

        The youngest of five children of Jewish immigrants
Sol and Ethel Paler Rosenman, Sam had been born in San
Antonio, Texas on February 13, 1896. Less than half a
dozen years earlier, Sol had immigrated to New York City
from the Ukrainian district of Kamenets-Podalski. Arriv-
ing without his family but with some small capital, he
established a cork business with a fellow Kamenets emigré
as partner. Quickly despairing of this particular route
to affluence, he renounced the cork industry and joined
his older brother Isaac (Ike) as a storekeeper-peddler in
San Antonio, Texas. Jewish peddlers had been a prominent
part of the Texas landscape for almost as long as the
Alamo, and Sol, like multitudes of his predecessors,
prospered.

San Antonio was then a city of almost fifty thousand persons with a well established Jewish community.
Not only were there no legal restrictions upon Jews, but
it appeared, at least to one schooled by life in the Jewish pale, that other more subtle disabilities were absent
as well. Such privileges as sharing the racial prejudices
of the region's dominant white community, for instance,
were extended and accepted as a birthright. Relations
between San Antonio's Jews and Gentiles were less strained
than were relations within the Jewish community; for a
spirit of resentment had developed between those who had
adopted a reformed branch of Judaism and those who professed orthodoxy. Furthermore, the San Antonio reform
movement consisted in large part of the descendants of
German Jews while orthodoxy tended to be more attractive
to the Yiddish-speaking Russian and Polish immigrants.
Thus the split not only involved ritual, but also took
on the coloration of an antagonism between the native-
born and older arrivals and the more recent immigrants.[3]

Sol was not a profoundly religious man, and despite
orthodox proscriptions to the contrary, one of his first
acts in America was to clip his beard and earlocks. In
the new country, to be clean shaven would be a business
asset. Ethel was still in Kamenets when she learned of
this transgression and it shamed her deeply. She and her
four children had remained rooted to the old country less
because of economic pressures than because Ethel feared
that once they left they would also abandon cherished
ways. Sol's beard came to exemplify her dilemma. Although she regarded its discarding as near apostasy, she
could never persuade him to grow it back. Ethel was finally convinced that family opportunities in America out-
weighed the inevitable deprivations in tradition that life
there would bring, and after five years of separation the
Rosenman family was reunited in San Antonio. Once in
Texas, Ethel resigned herself to her family's rejection
of orthodoxy. Insisting throughout the rest of her life
upon her own personal observances of Jewish dietary law,

she made little effort to convince her family to maintain
her ways. Sam was born the year after his parents were
reunited. He was their youngest child and the only one
born in the United States.

Sol's career as a Texas peddler eventually became
more picturesque than profitable. Perched atop a horse-
drawn wagon, he roamed through the countryside displaying
his wares to farm families increasingly lured away from
him by the wider selections and cheaper prices of the
burgeoning mail order companies. By 1905 prospects in
Texas no longer seemed attractive to Sol, and after establishing an older son in a general store, he moved the
rest of his family to the lower Harlem district of Manhattan where he set up another son in a pants manufactory.
The general store proved more successful than the New York
enterprise and eventually Sam's older brothers returned
to Texas to also operate general stores while Sol and
Ethel remained in New York with Sam and his sister. The
three-store chain was sufficiently prosperous to provide
all the Rosenmans with substantial middle class comforts.

Sam was nine when his family arrived in New York
City. Lower Harlem, populated largely by immigrant Jewish families of the small entrepreneurial class, possessed
a different tone from the San Antonio neighborhood. The
school was larger and brought Sam into contact with more
children. In San Antonio, everyone, no matter how poor,
lived in a house with a yard. The Rosenman home had been
quite commodious. In New York, however, everyone seemed
to live in a tenement, and Sam had to learn about crossing
streets. The weather was cooler and this was a good thing
except that during the summer Sam was no longer able to
continue with his fishing. Finally, and this may have
given Ethel secret comfort, the hot tamale vendor had been
replaced by the kosher delicatessen. Only in subsequent
years, when Sam was to become aware of his larger environment, would New York City's more cosmopolitan character
influence him. Its most direct influence was through the
public school system.

The New York school system found in Sam an already serious student. His initial faith in the primacy of education was nurtured by an unremitting record of academic success. After elementary school he attended Townsend Harris High School, a special unit within the city system which admitted only abler students for an accelerated program. From Townsend Harris, Rosenman moved on to the City College of New York. Despite winning some coveted freshman academic awards, City College was a disappointment to him. He commuted to school and failed to experience any sense of college life. CCNY, he concluded, didn't seem like a "real college," and after the rigors of Townsend Harris even the course work was a letdown. Columbia College, on the other hand, had dormitories and seemed "more like what a college should be." Besides, Sam had already decided upon a law career, and he assumed Columbia provided a superior preparatory program than the city college. After his freshman year he transferred to Columbia College where he continued to harvest academic triumphs--receiving scholarships for his junior and senior years--and immersed himself in other undergraduate activities as well. These included the debate team, the presidency of his social fraternity, and a part as a chorus boy in the 1915 Columbia Varsity Show.

Despite these successes, his undergraduate years were "very unhappy" ones. "In those days Jews were social outcasts at Columbia." Fraternities were religiously segregated, for instance, and Phi Epsilon Pi, the fraternity over which Sam presided, was founded by Jewish students ineligible for Christian houses. While apparently resigned to his inferior status, he developed "little love for Columbia." More than half a century after his graduation, and "in spite of the social changes at the College since" then, he had not rid himself of "deep dislike and resentment."[4]

Despite these dissatisfactions, Columbia instruction had a profound intellectual impact. Professor Carleton Hayes was especially influential and Rosenman later cred-

ited the experience of studying the social legislation of
Germany, New Zealand and Australia under this historian
as the basis for his own developing political philosophy.
Of at least equal consequence, however, was that "during
his younger years he was never subjected to the influence
of people of big business."

    In June, 1915 he graduated summa cum laude and Phi
Beta Kappa. That September he entered Columbia Law School
and at the conclusion of the year was named an editor of
the *Law Review*. In April 1917 the United States entered
World War I, and, after completing his second year courses,
Rosenman enlisted as a private in the army. Eventually
reaching the rank of first lieutenant, he spent all but
the first few months of his military service at Camp
Merritt, New Jersey, processing troops for overseas assignment. When in November 1918 the war ended, Rosenman
learned that he would not receive his own discharge until
the summer. Eager to resume his law studies, he secured
the consent of Harlan F. Stone, Dean of the Law College,
to re-enroll that February. After arranging his military
duties for night hours, the Lieutenant commuted by trolley
car and ferry from Camp Merritt to the Columbia campus in
Manhattan daily. He maintained this regimen until his
discharge in August, 1919, and shortly thereafter was
awarded his LLB degree. Admitted to the New York State
Bar in January, 1920, he took his first professional employment as clerk to a prosperous and elderly Manhattan
attorney.

    During the spring of that same year he met his fu-
ture wife, Dorothy Reuben. Dorothy, pretty and possessed
by a lively social conscience, was then director of the
Temple Emmanuel nursery school. Unlike her future husband, her roots in the United States extended back some
generations. It was a source of pride that her mother's
uncles had fought in opposing armies during the Civil War.
Sam and Dorothy first met at a picnic and within a few
months the meeting blossomed into a serious romance. The
fledgling lawyer was determined, however, not to marry

until his income was large enough to support a family in
a respectable manner; he and Dorothy agreed to consider
themselves engaged, but not to disclose this fact outside
their immediate families. Despite Mrs. Reuben's pronounced
lack of enthusiasm for such secret understandings, it persisted for several years until Sam had significantly expanded his law practice.[5]

With precisely this objective, Rosenman entered
politics. Although he first registered as a Republican,
a careful assessment of the local situation suggested
little personal opportunity in Republican ranks, so he
joined the Monongohela Democratic club. In 1921, while
still an anonymous member, he resolved to promote his
legal career by campaigning for Assemblyman from the Eleventh District. The district, despite the dominance of
Tammany Hall in city politics, had been Republican ter-
ritory for fifteen years. In the 1920 election, incumbent Fred Nichols had amassed the largest plurality in
its history,[6] and no one among the local Democratic luminaries, most of whom had recorded defeats in earlier campaigns, was particularly anxious to run. Rosenman turned
the situation to his advantage by soliciting the support
of Joseph Shalleck, the Monongohela president.

Joe Shalleck, an extravagant personality whose reminiscences were doubtless colored by subsequent events,
recalled that as club president he had come to appreciate
that the newly enacted women's suffrage amendment was destined to alter the local political environment. The then-
dominant hard-drinking, rough-speaking leadership was too
limited in appeal and therefore must either be replaced
or allied with the young, clean-cut, articulate, college-
trained group that was then emerging in politics. Rosenman appeared as a prototype of this new breed. "You probably won't get elected the first time," Shalleck recalled
advising him, "but you ought to get your name before the
voters." An important drawback was that the candidate
would be required to finance his own campaign. Shalleck
estimated it would cost about $200 for advertising, and

Rosenman, "a fifty-dollar a week lawyer," agreed to bear
the expense. A short time later Shalleck introduced
Rosenman to District Leader Jimmy Hines as a potential
candidate for the assembly seat.[7]

It was unwritten law that the district leader picked
the district candidates and at that moment Jimmy Hines
needed Rosenman or someone remarkably like him at least
as much as Rosenman needed the district leader. Hines
had recently returned to politics after a tour of duty
as an army officer in France to discover that Tammany
Grand Sachem Charles F. Murphy regarded him as unreliable.
Boss Murphy had taken advantage of his absence to set up
a rival district organization, and Hines was forced into
a struggle to maintain his control.[8] Hines, doubtless
aware of the advantage to his own position if a Democratic
Assemblyman were elected from his district, recognized
Rosenman as an admirable candidate and readily assented
to his nomination.

As a former army officer and a Jew in a district
containing a sizeable Jewish population, Rosenman possessed obvious political assets. Most important was his
status as an honor graduate of both Columbia College and
Columbia Law School. The university was set like a wedge
piercing the heart of the Eleventh District, and it provided a source for much of the district's social and intellectual leadership. As an alumnus, Rosenman could be
expected to draw support from the normally Republican
campus community. His electioneering tactics befitted
his status. Instead of the usual street corner meetings
and torchlight parades, the Rosenman campaigners concentrated upon doorbell ringing and letter writing. The
candidate selected Milton Kupfer and Dorothy Reuben as
his principal campaign assistants. Kupfer was Rosenman's
closest friend and had been a fellow *Law Review* editor
at Columbia. Under his direction, friends from the University circulated among the Columbia graduates in the
neighborhood and systematically solicited votes for their
fellow "alum." Dorothy organized a group of women to ring

doorbells, distribute posters, and induce members of the
electorate to write personal letters to their acquaintances in the candidate's behalf.[9]

The substance of Rosenman's platform was taken bod-
ily from the platform of the Democratic candidate for
Mayor, John F. Hylan. As a local candidate with no public
record of his own, Rosenman saw no alternative but to look
to the head of his ticket. Following Hylan's lead, the
aspiring assemblyman advocated a five-cent subway fare
and improved transportation facilities. Compensation for
war veterans and "a seat for every school child" were
other planks upon which the Democratic candidates built
their campaign. Rosenman's own contributions were to
label his opponent a "do-nothing legislator," to promise
advocacy of increased social legislation, and to work toward repeal of the anti-socialist Lusk Laws.[10]

The final election results showed Rosenman with a
600 vote plurality over the Republican incumbent. The
third place candidate polled more than 700 votes.[11] Continuing to represent the Eleventh District until after
the 1926 legislative session, Rosenman conducted four
subsequent campaigns to retain his seat. None were as
close as his first one. His plurality never again fell
below 2,000 and in 1925, his last Assembly campaign, it
rose to over 5,500.[12]

In January, 1922, when Rosenman first arrived at
the state capitol, both the executive and the legislative
branches of government were dominated by the Republican
party. Governor Nathan Miller had defeated the incumbent
Alfred E. Smith in the Republican landslide of 1920, and
both houses of the State Legislature possessed their almost perennial Republican majorities. Rosenman served
out the session in the obscurity customarily reserved for
freshman legislators. During his second term, however,
he emerged as an active leader in the business of the
State Assembly. In large part this was made possible by
the return of Alfred E. Smith to the Governor's office.

Smith, whose prior experience as minority leader and
speaker of the State Assembly had brought him an awareness of some of the special problems of that body, was
distressed over the dearth of Democratic members able
enough to explain the Governor's program on the floor.
The dilemma was compounded by a Republican leadership
more able and experienced in debate and content to rele-
gate itself to the less rigorous tasks of criticism.
Smith aides acted to promote the legislative fortunes of
the Governor by advancing Democratic assemblymen with
the greatest potential regardless of the more usual sen-
iority considerations. Rosenman was marked for such preferment.[13] Always an able and conscientious student, he
devoted himself to intensive study of the outstanding
state issues as well as the relatively minor business of
the Assembly. Ideologically Rosenman might be best described as both a reflection and instrument of a legislative trend which since before the First World War had
operated to transform the New York State Assembly from
a virtually insurmountable obstacle to a laboratory for
legislative experimentation. Displaying an understandable
bias, Frances Perkins has written that:

> The extent to which this legislation
> marked a change in American political atti-
> tudes and policies towards social responsi-
> bility can scarcely be overrated. It was,
> I am convinced, a turning point; it was not
> only successful in effecting practical reme-
> dies but surprisingly, it proved to be suc-
> cessful also in vote getting.[14]

Rosenman was a firm adherent of the philosophy that state
power be extended to effect improvements in living and
working conditions. As the possessor of the technical
skills required to translate legislative intentions into
effective legislation, he became a most prolific drafter
of bills. His skill, rare in even the most august representative assemblies, was especially prized by the New

York State Legislature, a body which seldom--at any single
session--boasted an awesome array of learned members.

His activities relating to housing are illustrative
of his bill-drafting abilities. It was common practice
at that time for a landlord to refuse renewal of leases
at existing rentals. The tenant was then given the option of signing a short-term lease at an increased rate
or of seeking other quarters. There existed, however,
almost no possibility of renting similar quarters at previous rates. Even under normal conditions new construction would not have kept pace with the rapidly expanding
population; the problem was intensified by a curtailment
of construction during the war.

The issue had become so acute by 1920 that Governor
Al Smith, completing his first term in office, called a
special session of the State Legislature. While Smith
believed that the long-range solution was to help provide
additional construction of low and medium priced housing
units, he also supported action to provide immediate relief for the estimated one hundred families facing evic-
tion.[15]

One of the rent laws passed in the September, 1920
special session attempted to maintain the existing rent
level by prohibiting increases at the time of lease re-
newals. This was acknowledged to be temporary rather
than permanent legislation.[16] The law was in effect when
Rosenman became a member of the State Legislature, and
by that time its inadequacies were apparent. The constitutionality of the act had been upheld by the courts,
but in the course of the litigation its provisions had
been interpreted so as not to apply to any new leases entered into after the date of the law's enactment.[17] A
practical effect of this ruling was that families which
entered into original leases after September, 1920, were
left unprotected.

In May, 1923, Rosenman moved to amend the original
rent laws to include these unprotected groups as the 1920
legislators had intended. He proposed a bill which would
protect all renters entering into leases after September,
1920. The proposed act would run concurrently with the
original rent law. Both were due to expire in February,
1924.

Upon its passage by the State Legislature, the
Rosenman bill became the target of attack by the United
Real Estate Owners Association, the most powerful real
estate lobby in the state. This organization not only
criticized the wisdom of the measure but also denied its
constitutionality. Association spokesmen asserted that
if Governor Smith signed the bill into law the Association would attack it in the courts, where they were certain it would be declared unconstitutional.[18] These assertions did not fall upon deaf ears, for Governor Smith
also entertained doubts as to the constitutionality of
the Rosenman bill. "You can't go on indefinitely," the
Governor said, "invoking the police power of the State to
permit tenants to virtually fix their own rents. I realize I started a lot of this, but we can carry it too far
and destroy the whole thing." He concluded with the
warning, "A bill of this nature might be the means of
threatening the stability of the whole rent law system."[19]

The Governor did not deny the desirability of this
particular law, but rather feared the consequences of its
possible court invalidation. At an open hearing prior to
gubernatorial action, constitutional issues were stressed
by opponents of the bill. One such individual told the
Governor: "The measure if signed, might be the means of
having the rent laws declared unconstitutional. The rent
laws are working very well now, and I believe in letting
well enough alone."[20]

Rosenman also appeared at this hearing to testify
in behalf of his bill,[21] and it was his cause which finally prevailed. One June 2, 1923, Al Smith signed the

measure into law, alleging that his original doubts as to the constitutionality of the act had been allayed. If a housing emergency still existed, its provisions could not be construed by the courts as an undue exercise of the state's police powers. "Recent investigations show that the housing emergency still affects rentals, and that new tenants are especially subject to the unreasonable rent increases."[22]

The passage of the act did not end the opposition to it. The United Real Estate Owners Association, true to its word, continued to protest the constitutionality of the new law and threatened litigation. Through its chief spokesman, Stewart Brown, the organization maintained that there was no longer a housing emergency, and there were "thousands of empty apartments at rents that tenants can pay, but don't want to pay."[23] Rosenman, who insisted his measure was both constitutional and desirable wrote to Brown: "It is only because the Rosenman law prevents you from taking advantage of the emergency that you are opposed to it."[24]

In October, a legal suit involving a landlord who maintained that the Rosenman Act was an invasion of his constitutional rights came before the State Supreme Court. The landlord's attorney argued that there was no longer a housing shortage and that his client therefore should not be restricted by the act in any leasing arrangements with his tenant. Rosenman, as attorney for the tenant, argued that the emergency still existed, and that, therefore the measure was a legitimate exercise of the state police power. The court held in favor of the tenant and the Rosenman Act prevailed.[25]

Encouraged by this initial success, Rosenman began to press for even more comprehensive housing legislation. A criticism of the rent laws was that while they prohibited a landlord from raising rents, they permitted him to decrease service and to neglect maintenance of his tenants' apartments.[26] Discussing this aspect of the housing laws, Rosenman wrote that it should be "remembered that these rent laws formed a new kind of legislation without precedent in the history of either the state or the nation." He thought they were effective as far as they went, but also conceded that the criticism was valid. He hoped to alter this situation through additional state intervention.[27]

Early in 1924, however, advocates of rent control received an unexpected setback. State Supreme Court Justice Isidor Wasservogel ruled that, since the courts had already decided that tenants not in possession of their apartments when the original 1920 rent laws were passed were not entitled to the protection of the law, he was bound to apply a similar ruling to the Rosenman Act. The Rosenman Act, he declared, did not apply to persons who entered their apartments after June, 1923, the date the law went into effect.[28]

Rosenman was irate. He declared the judicial decision "clearly violated the intention of the Legislature, of myself ... and of Governor Smith... The interpretation of the Rosenman Act by Justice Wasservogel is in my opinion erroneous." At the same time Rosenman announced he would introduce legislation that would "repeal this decision."[29]

Additional legislation was unnecessary, as other Justices subsequently interpreted the Rosenman Act in a manner more in keeping with the intention of its author. In May, 1925, New York's highest court resolved all such controversy by affirming an Appellate Division decision that the act applied to leases entered into after its enactment. If there had ever been any doubt as to the meaning of the 1920 rent law, the Court of Appeals, asserted, the Rosenman Act had put it "beyond the realm of controversy."[30]

This proved the last major victory by rent control advocates during the 1920's. The rent laws, including

the Rosenman Amendment, were extended for two more years
in 1924,[31] and again in 1926,[32] but their scope was diminished rather than expanded. Rosenman, along with
others who shared his social conviction, was now forced
to struggle to maintain those controls they had already
won. The opposition successfully argued that such legislation was no longer necessary as the housing emergency
had lessened.

By no means were all of Rosenman's efforts in the
Assembly devoted to rent laws or similar remedial legislation. Among his most controversial bills were those
advocating greater dissemination of birth control information.[33] Rosenman managed to secure committee hearings
on this taboo subject for the first time in New York State
history, but persuaded very few legislators to give this
issue serious thought. One colleague, with a particularly
large family suggested the bill might be strengthened by
making its provisions retroactive. Even then, however,
he could not dare vote for it. Margaret Sanger, who had
previously met only with disappointment in having such
bills introduced--one legislator withdrew after being
warned "it would do me an injury that I could not overcome for some time," while another feared rousing "levity
from his associates,"--labeled Rosenman's efforts as
"courageous" and drew solace from the belief that even
though the bills were defeated "the atmosphere was clar-
ified."[34]

Among the Assemblyman's most visionary bills were
those he introduced while acting as legislative spokesman
for Robert Moses' plan for an extensive state park system.[35] Moses, who was then legislative representative of
the State Association, a small but vocal civic group,
conducted Rosenman on frequent tours along the barren
shore of Long Island in the area of what today is Jones
Beach. He displayed an eloquent enthusiasm during these
walks which overcame Rosenman's original skepticism and
induced the young assemblyman to lend his vigorous support
to the project.

Many bills which Rosenman introduced in the Assembly were presented simultaneously in the Senate by Nathan Straus, Jr.[36] Included among these was one which attempted to legislate a maximum eight-hour working day for women and minors. The sponsors believed the eight-hour day no longer to be a theoretical dream but a crying necessity.[37] Their fellow legislators, however, did not agree. Another unsuccessful bill which was introduced under their aegis would have amended the State's Workman's Compensation laws so that any establishment which employed two or more persons would be included under its provisions. Other measures providing for amendment to Workman's Compensation were introduced at the same session, but it was "generally admitted that the Straus-Rosenman bills are the most drastic."[38]

Rosenman's frequent proposals were not only unacceptable to conservative Assembly leaders such as Edmund Machold, the Republican speaker, but were also often regarded as too radical by many of his Democratic brethren. His pursuance of an independent course of action in the introduction of legislation, however, did not lead him onto the road of party irregularity. His voting record revealed his support of bills, which though usually less comprehensive than his own versions, were in his opinion the best measures obtainable from the legislature at the time. These latter measures were with some few exceptions those receiving official Democratic endorsement.

His efforts earned him high praise from the Citizens Union, which regarded him as one of the Assembly's "most useful and independent members." One of the four among fifty-seven legislators whom the Union rated as excellent, he was described as a "capable and essentially well fitted legislator with an excellent record of votes and other activities."[39] Moses' New York State Association described him as: "One of the few members of his party in the Assembly capable of explaining and supporting the party program [and] most promising of the new men on the Democratic side."[40] Of even greater significance was the fact

that Democratic leaders were also increasingly impressed
by Rosenman's activities. He was observed as a scholarly
and personable individual with a voting record quite acceptable to party regulars and possessed of a unique tal-
ent in devising and interpreting legislation.

In 1926 Rosenman was favored with a choice between
two opportunities. The first came about as a result of
the decision of Nathan Straus to retire from the State
Senate. Both Straus and Jimmy Hines regarded Rosenman
as Straus' logical successor, and Hines went so far as
to publicly commend this "champion of the rentpayers" as
the most desirable candidate. Rosenman, however, was more
attracted by the second opportunity; an appointment to
the Legislative Bill Drafting Commission.[41] After soliciting and obtaining Democratic designation for the position,[42] his appointment was made official, when, as part
of a non-statutory but long standing agreement among the
politicos to keep the Commission bi-partisan, Republican
legislative leaders agreed to abide by the selection of
the State Democratic Organization.[43]

Rosenman's reasons for preferring the Commission
appointment over an Assembly or Senate seat were largely
economic. A commissioner's salary was set at $5,000, well
above the legislature's $2,500 level. In addition the
position did not require reelection nor attendance in
Albany except during legislative sessions. The indirect
advantages of the office were even more compelling. Because of the specialized nature of their work, Bill Drafting Commissioners develop an expertise highly prized in
legal circles and are often called upon in their private
professional capacity to assist in such activities as
drawing up codes for municipalities, counties, and even
private corporations. The fees received from this type
of law practice are frequently large ones.

So far things had gone pretty much according to
plan, and Rosenman's political efforts had helped establish his professional reputation within a relatively

short time. He had graduated from clerkship to a shortlived partnership with Susan Brandeis and Benjamin Kirsch
and then with Leonard Biel. By September, 1924, his
practice was sufficiently remunerative to permit him to
support a wife "in a respectable manner," and he and
Dorothy Reuben married. The Bill Drafting Commissioner-
ship promised to lead to even larger financial success.

     Although personal and professional considerations
had dictated that he seek the job, its political consequences were to have far greater impact. Bill Drafting
Commissioner was the first of many roles which cloaked
Rosenman in anonymity. His writing and research talents
were rewarded with legislation adopted in the areas of
government reorganization, home rule amendments, and
grade crossing elimination.[44] As is true in all law-mak-
ing bodies, however, these were adopted under the name
of their legislative sponsor rather than that of their
draftsman. On slow days the Albany correspondents no
longer filed stories of Rosenman's plans for remedial
housing legislation, nor was he mentioned in accounts of
Albany politics. He was a superbly efficient but unpublicized craftsman.

     It was during this period of relative obscurity that
Rosenman established the foundation upon which he built
his subsequent public career. Aside from legal experience,
especially valuable to him was an opportunity to deal with
the practical problems of government reorganization with
which his office was continually involved. Furthermore,
in his anonymous but key position, Rosenman soon became
a member of the outer fringe of the inner circle of Governor Smith's "kitchen cabinet." He had earlier developed an association with Robert Moses and Belle Moskowitz,[45]
and he also maintained a close working relationship with
Maurice Bloch, Democratic leader of the Assembly. On
several occasions he had contributed towards Governor
Smith's speeches.[46] By 1925 Smith was already the front-
running candidate for the 1928 Democratic presidential

nomination, and some of Rosenman's efforts took the form of compilation of background material that Smith might use in the forthcoming contest.

By September, 1928, Smith had secured the presidential nomination, and he, along with other leading New York Democrats, prevailed upon Franklin D. Roosevelt to accept the gubernatorial spot in an attempt to strengthen the state ticket. Shortly thereafter "legislative expert" Rosenman was "loaned" to the gubernatorial candidate for the duration of the campaign.

The Bill Drafting Commissioner faced his temporary charge with some ambivalence. Most young men would have been overjoyed at this assignment, and, Rosenman viewing it as a personal opportunity, was quite pleased. Ideological considerations, however, left him less sanguine. He had never met Roosevelt, and, in fact, had seen him only once before. While the gubernatorial candidate had the reputation of being a liberal, his new assistant had his doubts.

> Despite his reputation, I did not know
> the full extent of Roosevelt's liberalism
> when I first met him. Indeed I was a bit
> afraid after the work I had done on some
> of Smith's programs, Roosevelt was going
> to be a letdown for me and all Smith liber-
> als. I knew Roosevelt's family and cul-
> tural background; and I was skeptical.[47]

Gratified, however, at this unique opportunity, Rosenman collected material he thought he might use in his new assignment, and methodically sorted it according to subject matter into red manila envelopes which he in turn stuffed into several suitcases. Then on that very warm morning of October 17, 1928, Sam Rosenman took the bulging suitcases by taxicab to a pier in lower Manhattan, boarded the Hoboken Ferry, sought out the candidate and shook hands with Franklin Delano Roosevelt for the first time.

Chapter Two

SECURING COUNSEL

That morning Franklin Delano Roosevelt began his
first gubernatorial campaign trip. The ferry carried the
candidate and his associates across the Hudson River to Hoboken, New Jersey, where they boarded the Erie Railroad and
proceeded north and west on a political pilgrimage through
New York State. The tone for the campaign was already
set. In accepting the nomination Roosevelt had proclaimed
himself "a disciple in a great cause" pledged to "consolidate and make permanent the great reforms which will for
all time attach to the name of Alfred E. Smith." Calling
for even further "progress", he envisioned the day when
"the businessmen of the Nation as well as the political
leaders will look to Albany for business efficiency..."[1]

For the first few days of the campaign Roosevelt
exclusively utilized "never mind me, vote for Al" tactics
and attacked anti-Catholic prejudice. Except for the
usual amenities he failed even to acknowledge Rosenman's
presence. The Bill Drafting Commissioner was not disturbed. Campaigning with a candidate he did not much
respect, he had steeled himself to excess baggage status.
He had a "detached indifferent feeling" toward his assignment and was "going along just to do a chore." Maurice
Bloch, distressed over Roosevelt's tactics, telegraphed
Rosenman to "tell the candidate that he is not running
for President but for Governor, and tell him to stick to
state issues."[2] Rosenman, disinclined to show the telegram to Roosevelt, would have been content to remain a
supernumerary throughout the campaign had the candidate

not switched tactics on his own initiative. In Buffalo,
Roosevelt announced he intended to speak on labor issues
and Rosenman selected from his suitcases several folders
thick with material on the subject and presented them to
the candidate. After a cursory reading Roosevelt returned
the material and announced he was leaving to meet with
some local political leaders. "Knock out a draft of what
you think I ought to say tomorrow night and let me have
it in the morning," he told the startled Rosenman. "We'll
go over it again tomorrow."[3]

Rosenman spent a sleepless night arranging, interpreting, explaining and rearranging his voluminous statistics. At breakfast he presented his handiwork to the
candidate. The Commissioner had amassed an impressive
array of arguments and supporting data calculated to demonstrate that, despite Republican opposition, the Democratic party had achieved an enviable record of labor
legislation. He had not, however, supplied an effective
campaign address, and Roosevelt proceeded to give him a
lesson in "how to pull a speech together and pep it up."
The lesson lasted through the morning, and the initial
draft was extensively revised. Ultimately, it provided
the basis for the eventual speech and the former supernumerary was inexplicably delighted when after all the
cutting and rephrasing, many of his original sentences
and even some of his paragraphs remained.

That evening as the candidate delivered his address,
Rosenman responded as a novice playwright on opening night.
Standing at the rear of the auditorium, he nervously
mouthed each word. "When the applause came...he was more
uplifted than the speaker." He never tired of this experience, nor did he in later speeches ever quite lose
the excitement of that first occasion.[4]

The Buffalo address was not a spectacular success.
It was, however, sufficiently effective to persuade Roosevelt to employ Rosenman in the composition of the major
speeches throughout the remainder of the tour. Rosenman's

worker who would disappear after
n.[8]

ay provided one of the closest contests
ry. Roosevelt defeated his Republican
Ottinger, by only 25,000 of the over
cast. The victory celebration was further
overwhelming defeat of Al Smith, and his
State in his race-for the presidency.
d Hoover's victory a "defeat for liberal-
isappointment could not erase his sense
tation at Roosevelt's success.[9] Despite
ticism, Roosevelt's cause had become his

month Rosenman, along with Lieutenant
Lehman and other state leaders[10] journeyed
, Georgia. They gathered at Roosevelt's
ork out a legislative program and discuss
ntments with him. The conferees were both
xious. There had been a great deal of
to the role Al Smith would play in the new
and it was generally assumed that the in-
would retain not only the Smith policies,
incipal Smith aides.[11] Rosenman regarded
action most likely and assumed along with
ommentators that his own role in the Warm
nce would be to learn the nature of any
ation and then prepare it for the forth-
of the New York legislature.[12]

he conference it became increasingly appar-
velt was going to name his own staff. For
a Lieutenant Governor was admitted into
and soon afterwards Robert Moses resigned
ost of Secretary of State.[14] It was ex-
hanges in the Governor's staff were occur-
ecause certain members wanted to step
of the members reputed to be staying on

long and successful
with great detail in
published seven year:
recital of activitie:
most romantic account
along country roads i
nights and early morn
growing intimacy, res
date. When the polit
City for the final we
delighted and signifi
tourage. He then met

Howe, who had re
the campaign, had alre
velt's service, and wa
supporter. The price
that his role as Roose
not be subverted. For
an *alter ego* than as a
the intrusion of new pe
His resentment transcen
a genuine fear that som
Franklin."[6] Roosevelt
"Louis can be difficult
anyone else have a dire

Rosenman was never
From the time of his ini
an equal to the long-tim
to the circumstances of
access to the candidate.
that access and a less tl
Howe and Rosenman resulte

did not really like
liked me less the m
to do. However, du
1928 he was friendl
wardly, for I am su

a temporar
the campai

Election d
in New York hist
opponent, Albert
4,200,000 votes
tempered by the
loss of New York
Rosenman regarde
ism," but this
of personal exa
his initial ske
own.

Later tha
Governor-elect
to Warm Springs
invitation to w
political appoi
jubilant and an
speculation as
administration,
coming Governor
but also the pr
this course of
the political
Springs confer
proposed legis
coming session

During t
ent that Roose
the first time
the cabinet,[13]
from the key
plained that
ring "mainly
aside."[15] On

long and successful career as a ghostwriter is chronicled
with great detail in *Working With Roosevelt*,[5] a memoir
published seven years after the President's death. His
recital of activities during the 1928 campaign is an almost romantic account of speeches composed while bouncing
along country roads in chartered buses, of sleepless
nights and early morning conferences, and finally of
growing intimacy, respect, and admiration for the candidate. When the political caravan filed back into New York
City for the final week of the campaign, Rosenman was a
delighted and significant addition to the Roosevelt entourage. He then met Louis Howe for the first time.

Howe, who had remained in New York City throughout
the campaign, had already spent sixteen years in Roosevelt's service, and was his most devoted and selfless
supporter. The price Howe demanded for his loyalty was
that his role as Roosevelt's most influential advisor
not be subverted. For many years he had served more as
an *alter ego* than as a subordinate, and he bristled at
the intrusion of new personalities to share his functions.
His resentment transcended mere jealousy for he possessed
a genuine fear that someone might mislead his "beloved
Franklin."[6] Roosevelt was well aware of this trait.
"Louis can be difficult," he once confided, "He can't let
anyone else have a direct line through to me."[7]

Rosenman was never willing to work through Howe.
From the time of his initial labors he regarded himself
an equal to the long-time Roosevelt intimate, and owing
to the circumstances of the campaign trip enjoyed direct
access to the candidate. He insisted upon maintaining
that access and a less than cordial relationship between
Howe and Rosenman resulted. Louis, Rosenman has written:

> did not really like me from the start...and he
> liked me less the more work Roosevelt gave me
> to do. However, during these campaign days of
> 1928 he was friendly enough to me at least out-
> wardly, for I am sure he considered me only

a temporary worker who would disappear after
the campaign.[8]

Election day provided one of the closest contests
in New York history. Roosevelt defeated his Republican
opponent, Albert Ottinger, by only 25,000 of the over
4,200,000 votes cast. The victory celebration was further
tempered by the overwhelming defeat of Al Smith, and his
loss of New York State in his race-for the presidency.
Rosenman regarded Hoover's victory a "defeat for liberalism," but this disappointment could not erase his sense
of personal exaltation at Roosevelt's success.[9] Despite
his initial skepticism, Roosevelt's cause had become his
own.

Later that month Rosenman, along with Lieutenant
Governor-elect Lehman and other state leaders[10] journeyed
to Warm Springs, Georgia. They gathered at Roosevelt's
invitation to work out a legislative program and discuss
political appointments with him. The conferees were both
jubilant and anxious. There had been a great deal of
speculation as to the role Al Smith would play in the new
administration, and it was generally assumed that the incoming Governor would retain not only the Smith policies,
but also the principal Smith aides.[11] Rosenman regarded
this course of action most likely and assumed along with
the political commentators that his own role in the Warm
Springs conference would be to learn the nature of any
proposed legislation and then prepare it for the forthcoming session of the New York legislature.[12]

During the conference it became increasingly apparent that Roosevelt was going to name his own staff. For
the first time a Lieutenant Governor was admitted into
the cabinet,[13] and soon afterwards Robert Moses resigned
from the key post of Secretary of State.[14] It was explained that changes in the Governor's staff were occurring "mainly because certain members wanted to step
aside."[15] One of the members reputed to be staying on

was Edward G. Griffin, Smith's legal advisor,[16] and Rosenman was caught unprepared when Roosevelt suggested he replace Griffin as Governor's Counsel.

The offer was flattering, but not an unqualified opportunity. Although the position carried a $10,000 salary, a substantial increase over that of Commissioner, it would provide Rosenman with less opportunity for his own thriving law practice. Rosenman's personal income and corresponding sense of economic security had risen substantially since his appointment as Bill Drafting Commissioner and he could well afford the appointment as Counsel. His principal objection was the nature of the job.

Under Smith the Counsel had been little more than a sinecure, and Rosenman, on the eve of his thirty-third birthday, found the prospects of mere timeserving unappealing. Even the urgings of such respected political associates as Belle Moskowitz failed to convince the reluctant Bill Drafting Commissioner to assent to the post.

The issue was still unresolved when shortly after Rosenman's return from Warm Springs he wrote Roosevelt he had "started on the work which you assigned me," and assured the Governor-elect that if he had "anything in mind where I can be of service please call on me."[17] Roosevelt, who could be quite literal-minded when the occasion demanded, took Rosenman at his word. Before the end of the month, the *New York Sun* announced Rosenman's appointment as Counsel. He would, the newspaper reported, continue his duties as Bill Drafting Commissioner until after the legislative session, at which time he would assume his new post.[18]

Pressured and confused by the announcement, Rosenman hurriedly phoned Roosevelt. The Governor-elect was his most charming self. There was, he assured Rosenman, really no reason for concern. It was just that he had

decided not to wait any longer for a decision. "I" he
laughingly explained, "made up your mind for you."[19]
Having no other option remaining, Rosenman graciously
concurred.

In reminiscing over the incident Rosenman has written, "As time went on I was very thankful that he [Roose-
velt] had not waited for me to make up my mind." His
fears that his functions would be ceremonial were rapidly
dispelled, and he remained as Counsel, "---and loved it-
--" until nearly the end of Roosevelt's Governorship.[20]

Roosevelt was equally thankful that Rosenman accepted the position. The Counsel's technical skills, legislative experience and point of view not only made him
the principal administrative aide to the Governor but
also provided a vital link between the Smith and Roosevelt administrations. Rosenman's availability enabled
Roosevelt to continue and expand the Smith program without having to turn to either Smith or Smith's principal
aides for frequent and publicized assistance--an important
factor in helping explain the emergence of Roosevelt rather than his predecessor, the titular head of the National
Democratic party, as New York State's leading Democrat.

Once assuming office, Rosenman transformed the
Governor's Counsel into a formidable administrative and
advisory agency. Political analysts did not readily
discern this change, and the bulk of early press reports
concerning Rosenman's activities are limited to functions
previously associated with his office. Prominent among
these was criminal investigation. The new Counsel, as
had his predecessor, assumed the duties of pardons clerk,[21]
reviewed all requests for extradition, and undertook
special investigations of unusual or irregular problems
in criminal law which had been brought to the attention
of the Governor. These ranged from the review of a mandatory life sentence given an habitual shoplifter,[22] to
a spectacular investigation of the still unresolved disappearance of State Supreme Court Justice Joseph Force
Crater.[23]

Although Albany news accounts referred to Rosenman with increasing frequency as the enlarged role of his office became more apparent, he never developed into a prime news item. Heavily indebted for this relative anonymity to the unspectacular day-to-day nature of his work, it was precisely the profusion of routine detail to which the Counsel attended that provided the most impressive measure of his assistance to Roosevelt. If the Governor's office be likened to a machine, Rosenman functioned as one of the central gears: a highly tooled instrument maintaining continuity and motion. The most precise movements were observed only indirectly, through reciprocating motion. Erratic performance was discernible throughout the machine.

Exercising influence in spheres neither previously nor since associated with the Counsel's office, Rosenman organized and selected personnel for statewide committees;[24] researched and prepared gubernatorial messages ranging from health programs,[25] to the regulation of employment agencies,[26] and when local governments sought permission to increase their bond issues, delegations traveled to Albany to confer with the Governor's Counsel.[27] It was also Rosenman who prepared memoranda on proposed constitutional amendments so that in Roosevelt's words "we should be ready to take a stand on them one way or another."[28]

While Governor, Roosevelt instituted the policy of having weekly luncheon meetings with selected members of the State Legislature. Also in attendance at these luncheons--popularly dubbed the turkey cabinet since turkey was invariably a menu item--was the Lieutenant-Governor and the Governor's Counsel. Conceived as a means to better acquaint the Democrats with details of the executive program, Rosenman's special task at these sessions was to provide background and explanations for some of the more technical aspects of proposed legislation.

These meetings are usually credited with producing
a more enlightened and tightly organized Democratic legislative minority than would have otherwise existed.
Some Roosevelt associates became so enchanted by the turkey cabinet that, when as President, Roosevelt encountered
a rebellious Congress, Rosenman suggested that the President might obtain tighter control through instituting the
weekly sessions as a regular Washington practice.[29]
Roosevelt disregarded the suggestion as being rooted in
nostalgia rather than current political reality.

In New York State the Governor is constitutionally
required to accept or reject within thirty days all bills
passed by the State Legislature. Since it is both the
privilege and custom of the Legislature to pass the vast
bulk of its laws during the closing meeting of each session, the Governor is in reality forced to review and
decide upon all the work of that body within thirty days.
In 1931 it ammounted to approximately 1200 bills,[30] of
which the Governor vetoed one-third.[31]

The Counsel's task upon these occasions was to lead
a small staff through an imposing maze of legislative
handiwork and to advise which bills merited approval. He
also prepared detailed memoranda on those proposed laws
he considered unacceptable. The Governor usually vetoed
bills as inconsistent with administrative policy or of
doubtful constitutionality. Rosenman also searched for
more subtle deficiencies. He was quick to spot a bill
so poorly drafted as to be inadequate to fit the purpose
for which it was passed. He was equally adept at uncovering innocuous looking bills which Albany solons occasionally pushed through in the confused closing minutes
of a crowded session and which were conceived to do other
than that which was immediately apparent.

Rosenman thrived on this activity and at the time
described it as "not only a real joy, but an actual inspiration." Once the thirty day period was concluded
Roosevelt vacationed at Warm Springs. His Counsel would

find relaxation among a hoard of routine details and the
mass of correspondence which invariably accumulated during
the final weeks of the legislative session.[32]   After completing these chores, Rosenman and his family would de-
camp from Albany.

Maintaining apartments in both Manhattan and Albany,
the Rosenmans resided in the state capital during legislative sessions and Manhattan for the rest of the year.
After the conclusion of the 1930 session, however, the
advantages to this semi-migratory arrangement seemed out-
weighed by other considerations.   Principal among these
were two sons; James Saul born in 1927 and Robert in 1931.
With resources inadequate to maintain two homes with all
the advantages they hoped to provide their children, they
decided to give up their Albany apartment.   A less important concern was the increasingly complex logistics involved in the migrations.   The Counsel, who as a general
rule served as a model of composure during trying professional circumstances, was prone to perform out of character during analogous domestic situations.   Noting at the
conclusion of their 1933 vacation that "it was the first
time Sam had even been on hand when the family Rosenman
decamped," Dorothy confided to the Roosevelts that "the
experience somewhat disturbed" his "judicial calm."[33]

During early 1931, the Counsel lodged at an Albany
hotel, but this arrangement was shortlived.   The Roosevelts, who apparently deplored solitary living by their
friends invited Sam to move in with them at the Executive
Mansion and the Counsel accepted the offer.

An almost inevitable by-product of this boarding
arrangement was Rosenman's enhanced political stature and
influence.   His unofficial proximity to Roosevelt's person distinguished him further from other subordinates.
Similar to Howe contemporaneously,[34] and Harry Hopkins
in future years, being privy to confidences and present
for most conferences was socially unavoidable and seldom
questioned.   Physical proximity does not in itself assure

active participation, and in some instances Rosenman observed matters as an interested bystander. On most issues,
however, he contributed significantly. The struggle over
waterpower development provides an important instance of
the latter.

Governor Roosevelt, like Governors Charles Evans
Hughes and Alfred E. Smith before him, advocated harness-
ing the latent power of the St. Lawrence River under
state control to provide cheap electricity for private
consumers. Roosevelt also believed the state should maintain the power sites rather than grant or lease them to
private utilities. In 1929, the utility lobby was among
the strongest in operation. Assembly Speaker Edmund
Machold was an official of one of the largest power companies in the state; Senator Warren T. Thayer, Chairman
of the Senate Committee on Public Service, was in the pay
of still another utility.[35] These Republican legislative
leaders agreed to the state's nominal ownership of power
sites, but insisted they be rented to private companies
under long term leases. Rates would be regulated by the
Public Service Commission.

Roosevelt opposed this plan. He preferred the state
develop power through its own plants and then sell the
power to private companies for transmission to consumers.
He also opposed rate regulation by the Public Service
Commission and instead advocated consumer rates determined
through contracts negotiated between the state and the
private company transmitting the power. Proponents of
the Roosevelt plan received a severe setback in the spring
of 1929 when three major upstate utilities announced a
proposed merger. The new company, the Niagara Hudson,
would be the only power utility in the St. Lawrence area.
As the sole potential purchaser of waterpower, it would
be in a position to force favorable contractual agreements
from the state.

Alarmed over the situation, the administration resorted to indirect attack. Attorney General Ward, as a

Republican, was selected as the immediate target. On
June 27, a Thursday, Rosenman completed the final draft
of a letter from the Governor to the Attorney General
requesting Ward investigate the proposed merger in order
to determine whether it was forbidden under existing state
laws.[36] As directed by Rosenman, the letter was not
mailed until Saturday afternoon. The text of the letter
was released immediately after its posting and well in
advance of Sunday morning newspaper deadlines.[37] Although
the Attorney General did not receive his formal instructions until Monday morning, he, along with other newspaper
readers, learned about his assignment from press reports.

The purpose of these maneuvers was to dramatize the
power issue and simultaneously embarass the only elected
Republican in the Executive branch. If Ward found the
proposed merger legal, and--though perhaps contrary to
the public interest--it certainly was legal, this would
help identify the Republican party still further with an
unpopular alliance with the private utility interests.
If he found the merger illegal, he would provide additional ammunition for the Roosevelt forces while cutting
himself off from the Republican party leadership.

The Attorney General attempted to straddle the issue with a long and detailed report of his subsequent investigation without any finding in law. Rosenman thereupon prepared new instructions. Released in the same
calculated manner as the previous letter, they specifically requested Ward's legal opinion.

The Attorney General tersely replied that having
"already become familiar with the contents of your letter
as published yesterday in all of the Sunday papers, I am
prepared to answer it immediately." Since it was, he declared, his "duty to state the law as it exists, not as
I or anyone elso would wish it to be," he was compelled
to report that in his opinion the merger "did not violate
existing state law."[38]

The Governor announced he was dissatisfied with the report and was ordering Rosenman to restudy the situation and submit his own finding.[39] Roosevelt, of course, had no intention of further contesting the legality of the merger, and Rosenman never submitted a formal report.[40] The incident, however, had served its purpose, for the heightened publicity had brought forth greater public interest in the power struggle. That September the *Nation* magazine devoted an issue to waterpower with New York State's Counsel to the Governor a principal contributor.

The Rosenman article provided its national audience with a brief history of the power struggle in New York and then moved on to an explanation of the Governor's then current position on the issues. Roosevelt opposed state regulation through the Public Service Commission because it would be "ineffective and unsatisfactory." The Commission, he alleged, followed a complicated and outworn evaluation procedure which operated to the benefit of the private utilities. Rather than this, he favored a contractual arrangement that would grant the companies eight per cent on capital investment. Operating expenses would be determined by fixed rules. Abandoning attacks upon the legality of the merger, Rosenman conceded it would put the state at a contractual disadvantage, but, he went on to assert, "if fair contracts cannot be obtained New York State will transmit its own power."[41]

In subsequent publicity efforts Rosenman echoed the Governor's insistence that state transmission of power might prove "the only way to deal firmly with the distribution problems."[42] This threat and public opinion were sufficient to wrench a compromise from Republican legislative leaders, and in January 1930, the legislature granted the Governor authority to appoint a survey board to investigate and report on power development on the St. Lawrence River. Roosevelt hailed the legislative action as marking "a red letter day" in the history of the state, and then wrestled for over six months with the problems of selecting the survey board personnel. The Governor's failure to announce even reasonably prompt appointments gave Republicans, such as Hamilton Ward, opportunities to chide Roosevelt for delay and later to attack him for inaction.[43] Finally in mid-August, after resolving such problems as getting Al Smith to agree on what basis he would agree not to accept an appointment to the Commission,[44] the Governor announced his appointments. The Commission met for the first time the following month and submitted its final report the following year; well after the 1930 gubernatorial elections.

The 1930 election was not a close contest. Republican gubernatorial candidate Charles H. Tuttle, a former United States District Attorney, unsuccessfully attempted to make Tammany Hall scandals the major issues of the campaign. Rosenman had anticipated this, and advised it would be poor policy to answer such charges as it would give them added publicity.[45] Roosevelt appreciated but hardly required such advice, and eventually countered Tuttle's charges of Tammany corruption with recitations of his administrative achievements.

Rosenman, who had been collecting and preparing campaign materials since the previous Spring, thought it appropriate to emphasize waterpower. Republican state leaders also recognized the issue as an important Roosevelt asset, and their willingness to permit the creation of the St. Lawrence River Development Commission was dictated, at least in part, by the hope that such cooperation would blunt its effectiveness as a campaign issue. Furthermore, in addition to its appeal within the state, "waterpower" possessed a traditional attraction to progressives throughout the nation. Out-of-state Roosevelt adherents such as Felix Frankfurter advised Rosenman there was no better issue upon which Roosevelt might stake a popular fight.[46]

Although the principal issue, waterpower was hardly the only Democratic asset,[47] and Rosenman contributed materials for a series of nine pamphlets elaborating the

outstanding "accomplishments" of the Roosevelt administration. Other than waterpower, these included old age security, farm relief, labor legislation, and public housing.[48] In later years Rosenman looked upon these activities as evidence of Roosevelt's "mature and consistent
social philosophy." With a fair degree of success he has
since attempted through his literary activities to label
this period the "Genesis of the New Deal."[49]

During the final month of the campaign the Counsel
accompanied Roosevelt on a swing through the state and
assumed the major share of speechwriting burdens. A desperate last minute influx of national Republican leaders
highlighted and forced Roosevelt to reply to repeated
charges of Tammany corruption, but achieved little else.
That November Roosevelt was reelected with, up to then,
the largest plurality in the history of the state.

Soon after election day, the struggle over hydroelectric power resumed. In January, 1931, the St. Lawrence Power Development Commission advised the Governor
that the state should undertake the development of the
river, and that the rates to be charged by the transmission companies should be fixed by contract rather than be
left to regulation by the Public Service Commission. The
next logical step was to establish a St. Lawrence Power
Authority with authority to undertake the necessary construction and negotiate for the eventual distribution of
the power. In March, a bill embodying these suggestions
was introduced in the Assembly. A key provision empowered
the Governor to appoint the members of the proposed Authority, which in addition to hydroelectric development was
also to concern itself with the related problems of commerce and navigation along the St. Lawrence. The bill
passed the Assembly and was sent on to the Senate for
further action.

In the meantime Rosenman drafted amendments to en-
large the authority of the proposed agency which the Governor hoped the Senate would append to the Assembly ver-

sion of the bill.[50] Roosevelt suggested to John Knight,
the President Pro Tem of the Senate, that seven such
amendments be adopted. Knight, rejecting all of them,
instead proposed to remove the Governor's appointive power
and grant it to the Legislature. His amendment providing
for this also specified that the original membership of
the Authority would consist of members of the St. Lawrence
Power Development Commission which had been appointed by
the Governor the previous year.

The administration viewed the lodging of such appointive power with the Legislature as tantamount to
granting it to private utility interests, and Rosenman
applied himself to the task of creating what would appear
an articulate and spontaneous grass roots reaction against
the Knight amendment. The Counsel proceeded to telephone
Democratic leaders throughout the state and instructed
them to get "resolutions from civic groups and associations interested in water power approving the Governor's
stand and disapproving the action of the legislature."
He went on to assure the local leadership that if they
sent those resolutions to Albany, "we will get publicity
on same." To promote prompt and accurate responses these
phone calls were followed up by "Personal Confidential"
letters in which statements on waterpower were enclosed
to guide the drafting of resolutions.[51]

Senator Knight was unprepared for the subsequent
"spontaneous reaction" against his proposed amendment.
The Republican leader claimed it "nothing short of amazing...that Governor Roosevelt should object to the naming
in the bill of the commission which he himself appointed."[52]
The Senator's efforts to minimize the potential significance of the bill were futile. Conflagrant public
opinion and the threat of a Roosevelt radio address split
Republican Senate ranks sufficiently to defeat the Knight
amendment by three votes. Afterwards the Senate unanimously passed the Assembly version of the bill.

With this victory Roosevelt exhausted his opportunities for constructive statesmanship in St. Lawrence power development. Actual construction could not begin until after the United States and Canada completed a treaty, then being negotiated, over rights to the St. Lawrence River. Political considerations precluded President Herbert Hoover from cooperating with the New York Governor, and Roosevelt was permitted no share in the negotiations. On July 18, 1932, he, along with the general public, learned a treaty had been signed. By then Roosevelt, who had just received the Democratic nomination for the presidency, had directed his energies elsewhere.

The Hoover treaty was eventually shelved by the United States Senate and a similar agreement was not ratified until 1954. Three years after that, Rosenman, in the capacity of Counsel to the New York Power Authority, concluded negotiations for the hydroelectric transmission.[53]

Chapter Three

IMPOLITIC JUDGES V. JUDICIAL AMBITIONS

Tammany Hall has frequently been an issue in New
York City and statewide elections. Its endorsement brought
the services of the single most potent political machine
in the state. Conversely the taint of Tammanyism alienated large segments of the electorate who found much to
resent in the organization's urban base and scandal-stained
history. Designated officially as the New York County
(Manhattan) Democratic Committee, Tammany limited neither
its influence nor activities to Manhattan. For although
other counties maintained officially autonomous Democratic
organizations, Manhattan's earlier development and financial supremacy often made it advantageous to operate under
Tammany leadership. In statewide elections, Tammany support was prerequisite to Democratic success. In New York
City elections, its endorsement was usually tantamount to
election.

Samuel I. Rosenman was a Tammany protégé. He had
been sponsored by Tammany in his races for the Assembly,
in his advancement to Bill Drafting Commissioner, and in
his introduction to Roosevelt.

Franklin D. Roosevelt's associations with Tammany
were more circumspect as befitting an upstate politician.
As a freshman Senator from Dutchess Couty, Roosevelt first
tasted political fame as one of a small group of Democratic mavericks who blocked the election of William Sheehan,
a Tammany-dictated choice for United States Senator. With
the rise in his own political horizons, Roosevelt became

increasingly tolerant of Tammany activities, especially
when they paralleled his own interests. By 1918 Boss
Murphy considered him as a possible gubernatorial candidate, and two years later agreed to assist him to gain
the vice-presidential nomination. After Roosevelt's
crippling poliomyletis attack, he asserted his claim to
political prominence through nominating addresses at the
1924 and 1928 Democratic National Conventions--in behalf
of Tammany Sachem Al Smith. Also in 1928, Roosevelt was
persuaded to run for Governor by Smith and formally nominated by New York City Mayor James "Jimmy" Walker.

        Both Rosenman and Roosevelt had given and received
much from the Tammany Tiger, and each felt the additional
need of the New York County machine to realize their further ambitions: Roosevelt the White House, Rosenman the
New York State Supreme Court. For Roosevelt, contempla-
tion of securing nomination and election to the presidency
over the opposition of his own state's single largest
Democratic machine was a political nightmare. Yet Rosenman's more modest personal ambition was even more dependent upon Tammany favor. He would have to be elected from
a judiciary district composed of New York and Bronx counties. Without Tammany support this seemed an impossible
dream.

        John F. Curry, the New York County Democratic
leader and Grand Sachem of Tammany Hall, however, became
a bitter opponent of both Roosevelt and Rosenman. Overt-
ly hostile to the ambitions of both men, he provided the
leadership for intraparty opposition. By no means the
most astute of Tammany leaders,[1] Curry reigned during a
period in which the organization faced problems whose
solutions would have been elusive to far abler men. The
Great Depression exerted unprecedented pressure upon the
city machine. Finances were weakened and requests for
patronage and job aid increased to such levels as could
never be satisfied by normal Tammany resources. It should
have been apparent to Curry that it was political suicide
to break with Roosevelt and deprive his organization of

access to huge and ever-increasing state and ultimately
national resources. He nonetheless insisted upon and persisted in the break until long after its consequences had
been made obvious.

The Tammany-Roosevelt split grew from Curry's con-
ception of patronage responsibilities. Regarding the
measure of services rendered to Tammany as an almost exclusive qualification for holding public office, Curry
not only selected candidates of marginal ability and dubious integrity, but also possessed neither the competence nor the desire to curb their excesses.[2] These became so flagrant that early in 1929, reform elements in
New York City demanded Governor Roosevelt take official
action against delinquent officials. Roosevelt was slow
to act, and Republican leaders condemned his delay as
evidence of subservience to Tammany.

Roosevelt was confronted with one of the major political dilemmas of his life. If he conducted a wholesale
removal or even investigation of the allegedly delinquent
officeholders, he would jeopardize future support from
Tammany Hall. This would be costly to him in the 1930
gubernatorial campaign and could foreclose all hope for
the party's 1932 presidential nomination. On the other
hand he could not continue to ignore the situation without tarnishing his image as a progressive statesman. This
also could prove disastrous to his 1932 hopes. The problem was significant enough to warrant close attention by
almost all the Governor's principal aides, but Rosenman,
who with the exception of Roosevelt stood to lose the most
from a Tammany-Roosevelt fissure, was the aide most personally and officially involved in the subsequent proceedings.

Having closer personal and public contact with the
New York machine than any other member of the Governor's
circle, Rosenman was a logical liaison between Roosevelt
and Tammany. The function was neither designated nor
consciously designed, and Rosenman attributed it to his

being more accessible than Roosevelt. It was, for instance, much easier to reach the Counsel than the Governor
by telephone. Once Rosenman had delivered the message
the function would feed upon itself. Roosevelt in turn
"would naturally take it for granted that I [Rosenman]
was going to call and give his decision to the people who
had talked with me."[3] Curry, who would often use Rosenman to carry confidential messages to the Governor, also
grew accustomed to receiving replies through him, "especially the unpleasant kind of message, such as that he
[Roosevelt] was not going to follow Curry's recommendation for some political appointment."[4] Liaison between
Roosevelt and Curry provided Rosenman with additional
prestige and possibly influence. It was not, however, a
very enviable situation for an aspiring judge whose personal interest was in maintaining good relations with two
individuals who were fast growing apart.

A further and related complication was that Roosevelt invariably relied upon his Counsel for assistance in
answering allegations of misconduct by state and local
officials. Theoretically, such charges might require investigations of members of either political party from
all regions of the state. In practice, however, the vast
preponderance of charges and subsequent investigations
involved Tammany luminaries.

The earliest such instance was in 1929 and resulted
from the collapse of a New York City bank. An investigation produced evidence that a Smith-appointed Superintendent of Banks had accepted bribes from the defunct bank's
president and the Superintendent was subsequently indicted in criminal court.[5] Also involved in the scandal
was Tammany General Sessions Judge Francis X. Mancuso.
Mancuso had served as Chairman of the bank's board of
directors, and while not charged with criminal offenses,
questions of his judicial propriety had arisen. The Governor was adverse to suggestions that he summarily dismiss
Mancuso from office, and instead submitted an independent
report of the banking failure[6] to a joint committee re-

presenting the City Bar and the New York County Lawyers
associations. The committee was to study the report, conduct further investigations, and ultimately make suggestions as to possible punitive action.[7] To insure that
he was constantly in touch with the committee's proceedings, the Governor assigned his Counsel to sit in on
them.[8] After the committee had concluded its hearings,
but before it presented its formal conclusion, Mancuso
resigned his judgeship. Roosevelt then appointed Amadeo
A. Bertini as Mancuso's successor. Bertini's most apparent qualifications were his boyhood friendship with Jimmy
Walker and his Italian ancestry.[9]

From this incident there can be discerned the pattern to which Roosevelt generally adhered after subsequent revelations of misconduct in office in New York
City. Whenever an official was accused of gross impro-
prieties, and public opinion and the duties of office
required gubernatorial action, Roosevelt empowered or permitted the establishment of an agency independent of the
executive to make an investigation and present its findings to the Governor. In this way, before Roosevelt was
forced to implement his removal powers, the individual
concerned would have the opportunity to either refute
the charges or save himself, the Governor, and the Democratic party further embarassment by resigning. Since
any guilt was directed against the individual and not the
organization, Roosevelt would select successors from among
Curry-sponsored candidates.

Almost simultaneous to this resolution of the Mancuso affair, the administration was confronted with the
disclosure of additional judicial scandals.[10] The most
spectacular was the mysterious disappearance of Supreme
Court Justice Joseph Crater; but the Ewald case was the
most troublesome. City Magistrate George F. Ewald was
accused of having purchased his office from a Tammany
district leader, Martin J. Healy. The circumstances sur-
rounding the affair suggested that while purchase of judicial office was highly irregular it was not highly un-

usual, and a clamor was raised for the investigation of
the entire New York City administration.

Fearful that such an investigation would have an
adverse effect upon Democratic returns in the 1930 elections, the administration resorted to delaying tactics.
When the Socialist Party requested the Governor institute
a Moreland Act investigation, Roosevelt countered with
the argument that the Governor lacked the authority; since
municipalities could not be investigated under the Moreland Act. Republicans, ably seconded by the press, then
demanded the Governor convene a special session of the
State Legislature to grant him the necessary authority.[11]

Roosevelt and Rosenman discussed this possibility
with Republican legislative leaders who took the occasion
to attack the Governor for allegedly blocking an inquiry
of the New York City administration, but denied they were
interested in a special session of the Legislature.[12] The
Democrats were overjoyed. "Sam Rosenman and I," Roosevelt
revealed, "almost fell over backwards...when [Republican
leader] Knight read his statement to the press...We opened
our mouths to protest but realized what a fool break it
was and kept quiet."[13]

Their reprieve was shortlived. Evidence against
Ewald and Healy was presented to Thomas C. T. Crain, the
District Attorney of New York County. This elderly Tammany sycophant so bungled his assignment that he not only
failed to secure indictments, but intensified existing
suspicions of his own integrity. The Governor's office
was soon beseiged with protest; Roosevelt and his Counsel
were forced to the reluctant conclusion it had become
necessary to supercede Crain in the investigation. The
Governor thereupon directed the convening of an extraordinary grand jury. Selecting his favorite scapegoat,
Attorney General Hamilton Ward, to direct the inquiry, he
specifically limited it to the Ewald Case. As in the
Mancuso instance Rosenman maintained close surveillance

over the progress of the investigation,[14] and prior to
the release of the grand jury findings Ewald resigned.

This time the Governor and his Counsel announced
their decision to extend the investigation to include a
review of the entire Magistrate Court system. Unwilling
to provide such an opportunity to Hamilton Ward, they instead directed the Appellate Division of the First Judicial District to conduct the investigation.[15] An independent Democrat and former Court of Appeals Justice,
Samuel Seabury, was selected by the jurists to direct the
inquiry,[16] and thus marked the beginning of the end of
the era of the Curry-Walker Tammany Hall.

The 1930 election campaign, despite Republican efforts otherwise, diverted public attention from Tammany
scandals to other issues, and the Democrats emerged from
the contest in control of all statewide offices. Even
Hamilton Ward was denied reelection as Attorney General.

The Rosenmans celebrated the victory with a Carib-
bean vacation cruise. It was a "grand trip," and Dorothy
assured the Governor that during the course of their
voyage they had continued their Tammany investigations.
But despite having searched "the Seas far and wide,...
looked beneath banana trees and tobacco plants,...and
searched through the alleys and bazaars of Panama": they
had been unable to locate missing Judge Crater. However,
by "reclining on one deck chair for fourteen days, and
by the conservation of energy at every port, and by the
steady consumption of bananas between and following every
meal Sam managed to gain at least twenty pounds." The
captain, Dorothy reported, was going to "roll him off the
boat" when they arrived home.[17]

The Counsel, who doubtless disembarked in some less
spectacular manner, was greeted upon his return with a
request from Samuel Seabury for authority to permit an
investigation beyond the Magistrates Court.[18] There had
been vocal sentiment demanding a broader investigation

for some time, but Seabury had uncovered hitherto unsus-
pected irregularities which made it difficult to dismiss
such demands as an overreaction. The administration made
no immediate response to the request, but in March, 1931,
almost two months after the Seabury-Rosenman meeting, the
investigator was invited to Albany to discuss the matter
further with the Governor and his Counsel.[19] The following week, Rosenman dispatched a commission authorizing
Seabury to conduct an investigation into charges brought
against District Attorney Crain.[20]

     This limited extension of the investigator's juris-
diction hardly satisfied those demanding an inquiry of
the entire New York City administration. Among the most
active and vocal in this group were two New York City
clergymen, the Reverend John Haynes Holmes and Rabbi
Stephen S. Wise. Within a week after announcement of
Seabury's extended authority, these two civic leaders re-
presenting the City Affairs Committee, made an unscheduled
St. Patrick's Day call upon the Governor to present him
with a 4,000 word document charging Irish-Catholic Mayor
James J. Walker with negligence and incompetence in office.

     Rosenman duly instituted a study of the Holmes-Wise
charges, and the public was assured that the Governor and
his aide would give them "paragraph by paragraph consideration."[21] When Tammany stalwarts contended the Governor
lacked the authority to remove the Mayor, Rosenman promised to "search law books for all legal precedents to the
situation."[22] Despite the assurances of a long and detailed examination of both the charges and the removal
procedure, an early and persistent rumor alleged that the
Governor and his Counsel felt the clergymen had "not made
out a case that will stand up in court."[23] Walker, who
was requested to answer the charges, contended that the
attacks upon him were part of a Communist plot; the first
step in a master plan to undermine American institutions.
Father Coughlin, the Detroit radio priest, appeared in
New York to lend his vigorous support to Walker in this
encounter with subversion.[24]

The Governor required almost six weeks to frame his official reply to the Holmes-Wise charges; during which time Rosenman was widely publicized as its principal architect. News articles elaborating upon his activities as "Roosevelt's law book" were now frequently accompanied by his photograph. Originally captioned "he advises on Walker,"[25] this same photograph was to reappear in subsequent issues of some upstate journals with more appropriate captions substituted to report more recent events. This practice persisted over a period of twenty years, endowing Rosenman, at least to the eyes of some upstate readers, with an enviably prolonged youth.

On April 28, 1931, the reply was released. "I do not," the Governor reported, "find sufficient justification in these documents as submitted [by Holmes and Wise] to remove the Mayor of the City of New York or to proceed further in the matter of these charges." Immediately after the Governor made his decision public, the Counsel wired its full text to Holmes, Wise, and Walker.[26] With that gesture he hoped to bring the troublesome Walker affair to an end.

Raymond Moley has labeled this Walker decision as Roosevelt's "worst blunder" in his dealings with the Tammany scandals, and Louis Howe, who shared this opinion, "was merciless" in holding Rosenman responsible.[27] Subsequent events supported the belief that the reply was ill-advised. The previous month (March 1931) Republican majorities in the State Legislature had established a joint legislative investigating committee specifically empowered to inquire into the New York City administration and the courts within its geographic area. Samuel Hofstadter, the sole Republican Senator from New York County, was appointed committee chairman and Samuel Seabury was selected as counsel. It was hardly likely that this investigation would be terminated because the Governor refused to entertain the Holmes-Wise charges. Neither did it seem shrewd politics to turn the initiative over to partisan political opponents. If Roosevelt and Rosenman hoped to maintain Tammany support by merely refusing to take the leadership in any investigation, they were soon disappointed.[28]

Another dubious element of the Governor's action was the truculent tone of his reply to the clergymen. While many citizens regarded Holmes and Wise as courageous crusaders in the cause of clean government, Roosevelt and Rosenman considered them meddlesome dilettantes in practical politics.[29] From their viewpoint the incessant and over-zealous activities of the clergymen tended to blur the broader perspectives of state government, not to mention political ambitions. Circumstances had forced the administration to accept Tammany corruption as an issue, and now it feared that through the constant prodding of men such as Holmes and Wise, it would escalate into the major issue. The administration attempted to emphasize that corruption was not a New York City or even a Democratic monopoly, and Rosenman gravely reported that he generally received two or three complaints each week against officials. He had, he revealed, investigated a number of these complaints pertaining to upstate cities and had verified some reported irregularities.[30]

Attempts to demonstrate that the Governor and his staff were confronted with a number of problems, of which political corruption in New York City was not the most urgent and only one aspect of a larger corruption issue, did nothing to dissuade the minister and the rabbi. They continued to inundate the Governor's office with telegrams and messages whenever they felt he was not acting in proper haste. Roosevelt was as impatient with the clergymen as they were with him. Neither he nor his Counsel appreciated their sense of urgency and righteousness, and official replies to the clergymen were frequently so curtly phrased as to constitute rebuke.[31]

The fervor of Holmes, Wise, and more moderate civic group spokesmen was not dampened by the Governor's admonitions, but rather fired by subsequent events. Con-

current with the establishment of the Hofstadter Committee,
the Governor signed into law a bill providing for the addition of twelve State Supreme Court Justices to the Second Judicial Department. Brooklyn was the most populous
county in the Second Department, and the bill was sponsored by the Kings County Democratic Organization or, as
it was more commonly referred to, the McCooey machine.
To assure the creation of the new judgeships "Boss" John
H. McCooey, Sr. had negotiated a special understanding
between Republican and Democratic politicos. The specific terms of that understanding became apparent from the
judicial nominating conventions preceding the 1931 general
elections. Both major parties endorsed identical slates
for the new offices: five Republicans and seven Democrats,
one of whom was McCooey's son John, Jr.

Despite the fact that bipartisan dealings are not
exceptional in New York City politics and usually accepted
under the guise of a nonpartisan judiciary, this particular arrangement aroused citizens already suspicious of
their courts. An independent slate of judicial candidates
running under the banner of "No Deal Party" vied against
the major party nominees, and an association of lawyers,
the *Lex Amici*, demanded the Governor call a special session of the legislature to repeal this "most recent judicial deal."

Delegated to answer the *Lex Amici*, Rosenman allowed
the situation might call for redress, but thought a special legislative session would be "an exceedingly inappropriate remedy even assuming that the legislature would
pass any repealing legislation." The twelve judges had
been added to the Second Judicial Department because of
a desperately overcrowded court calendar. It would, the
Counsel alleged, be inappropriate to repeal this legislation since "the methods of nomination had no bearing
on the necessity of the judgeships." The Governor may
have personally condemned the methods by which the selections were dictated, but there was no constitutional
basis for his interference. The remedy Rosenman con-

cluded, lay with the voters on an independent ticket.[32]
Although he did not make the point publicly, Rosenman
realized the voters could not be expected to apply that
remedy.

He had done his job well. While disassociating
Roosevelt from the selection process, he had also indicated the Governor would make no effort to unmake McCooey's
judges. The *New York Times* viewed the episode as another
challenge to Roosevelt's ambition for the presidency.
As the "front-running" aspirant he was constantly being
forced to choose "the right horn of each two horned dilemma." His most recent choice had been made by his legal advisor, and it had enabled him to emerge unscathed
from "the latest situation which was supposed to give
him embarassment."[33]

The next dilemma was not so simply resolved. On
December 30, 1931, Samuel Seabury presented formal charges
against Tammanyite Thomas Farley, Sheriff of New York
County. Farley had deposited in various banks sums far
in excess of his declared income, and was also accused
of protecting professional gamblers and knowingly appointing incompetent assistants. Seabury advised the Governor
that Farley was "unfit to hold the office of Sheriff and
that to permit him longer to do so would be a grave injustice and an affront to the citizens of this [New York]
County."[34]

Although Roosevelt and Rosenman had been expecting
such charges, their presentation occurred at a singularly
inopportune time. The next few months were to be decisive for the personal ambitions of both men. Even without the Farley complications, they would no longer be
able to sidestep what was up to then the most perplexing
of the Tammany scandals. With the presidential primary
season fast approaching, Roosevelt would soon have to
announce his candidacy, and to assure success it was essential he avoid any appearance of subservience to the
New York machine. Neither would it serve his purpose to
further alienate Tammany.

Seabury had confronted Roosevelt with another two horned dilemma, and Roosevelt instinctively designated Rosenman his agent in the affair.[35] Ultimate decisions were, of course, made by the Governor, but matters such as those relating to the review of testimony and day to day negotiations were conducted by the Counsel. Correspondence relating to Farley was routed through Rosenman's office, and it was his, rather than Roosevelt's signature, that appeared on communications between the State and the principals in the Farley affair.[36]

It was a unique circumstance for Roosevelt to deny himself any publicity attendent upon his office, and in this instance his reticence was dictated by obvious political considerations. By trying to identify the Governor's Counsel, rather than the Governor himself, with the Farley dilemma, Roosevelt hoped subsequent decisions might be perceived as matters of procedure rather than policy; determined solely by existing law and not by political considerations. Both Tammany and the good government elements were, however, too sophisticated to indulge themselves in such legal fiction.

Rosenman, nevertheless, adhered to his predetermined role throughout the Farley proceedings. As a member not only of the Governor's official family but also of his household, Rosenman never before or since enjoyed such prolonged intimate association with Roosevelt. They revealed to him as much as he was ever to learn of the processes of Roosevelt's mind, and provided him with other advantages as well. The after dinner hour, he later reflected, offered the most favorable opportunity for insinuating personal views.[37] It was presumably on one such occasion that he brought his personal ambition to the Governor's direct attention.

On the day before Seabury had presented his charges against Farley, State Supreme Court Justice George V. Mullan died. His death created a vacancy in Rosenman's home judicial district, the First Department, and the

Counsel revealed he hoped the Governor would appoint him
to fill that particular vacancy. In all likelihood it
would be Roosevelt's last opportunity to reward him with
a cherished seat on the state branch. To strengthen his
cause, Rosenman also encouraged mutual friends to intercede in his behalf.

At first blush this appeared a simple favor, well
within Roosevelt's power and interest to bestow. Upon
closer examination it was not quite any of these things.
The Governor's appointee would be an interim selection
holding his commission only until a full fourteen year
term justice could be selected in November, 1932, the
next general election.

Normal political practices dictated that the Governor's appointee receive his party's subsequent nomination, and under normal circumstances Roosevelt's choice
would become a Democratic judicial candidate in November.
It was, however, within Curry's power to deny that nomination and render Roosevelt's appointment almost meaning-
less. Of greater concern if Tammany insisted upon its
own candidate, was that the act of appointing Rosenman
would in itself exacerbate Tammany-Roosevelt relations.
Not only did John Curry insist upon a Tammany-sponsored
candidate, but the Bronx boss, Ed Flynn, put forth his
own proprietary claims to the appointment as well.

In an effort to maintain intraparty harmony, judgeships in the First Judicial Department were designated as
belonging to either Manhattan or the Bronx depending upon
the borough affiliation of the most recent incumbent.
Justice Mullan had died while a resident of Manhattan,
and Curry reasoned the new appointee should also be a
resident of that borough. He and his Tammany organization were willing to support any of a number of candidates
whose names the Tammany chieftain submitted, through
Rosenman, to the Governor. Roosevelt delayed making any
announcement for over two months and Curry's list of acceptable candidates grew with each passing day. It was

always an uncomfortable moment for Rosenman when the increasingly anxious Tammany leader presented him with a
new roster of candidates; especially as Rosenman himself
never made that list.[38]

Ed Flynn argued that Mullan had been originally
elected from the Bronx, and that although he had subsequently moved to Manhattan, the judgeship would still be
considered the property of the Bronx. Flynn, whose loyalty to Roosevelt was incontrovertible, had been growing increasingly restless under Tammany domination. The population of the Bronx had almost doubled since 1920, and
it demanded a proportionately larger share of state and
city patronage. In Flynn's own words "a great coolness
developed between Tammany Hall and the Bronx organization."[39] He contended that his borough possessed only
eight of the thirty-six judges then sitting in the district, and to appoint another judge from Manhattan would
worsen an already inequitable situation. Charles B.
McLaughlin, a popular and efficient Bronx district attorney, was his announced candidate.[40]

Given such circumstances, Roosevelt could hardly
have cavalierly granted Rosenman his wish. But there
were also more personal reasons for his reticence. Reluctant to release a key aide at such a crucial moment,
he was also dubious as to whether a state judgeship was
a laudable enough ambition for his Counsel. Believing
the New York State judiciary to be a "rather sordid de-
pressive Court Bench," Roosevelt feared that someone with
Rosenman's "fine mind and understanding" would be "very
much out of place with some of the 'atmosphere'."[41] He
hoped to entice Rosenman away from such judicial ambitions with what, to Roosevelt, appeared more attractive
alternatives. He suggested, for instance, that should
he fail to win either the presidential nomination or the
election, he and his youthful aide would establish a law
partnership,[42] but the ever practical Rosenman regarded
the possibility of Roosevelt's early return to private
life too remote to warrant serious consideration.

The aspiring presidential candidate then asserted
that if he went on to Washington he would want Rosenman
to go on with him. Rosenman, however, preferred to remain in New York for he "dreaded the intrigues and personal jealousies of the Capital."[43] Having had a preview
of such conditions in Albany where Louis Howe had been
his principal nemesis, he feared that in Washington, where
the stakes were much higher, Howe could be joined by
others. Rosenman would also in other ways be more vulnerable to attack on the national than on the state level.
On state matters he was an acknowledged expert; in national
affairs an untested neophyte. He doubted his own qualifications for a federal post, but possessed great confidence
in his abilities to perform the duties of a state judge.
Roosevelt finally agreed to appoint Rosenman to the vacant judgeship. He stipulated, however, that he would
not announce the appointment until the final day of the
then current legislative session.

Although paramount to Rosenman, the judicial maneuvering was secondary on Roosevelt's own scale of priorities. Holmes and Wise almost predictably chided the
administration for insufferable delay over dealing with
the Seabury charges,[44] and on January 23 Rosenman set
February 1, as the deadline for Farley's reply.[45] That
same January afternoon the Counsel participated in a
ceremony by which Roosevelt formally declared his candidacy for the Democratic nomination as President.[46]

Farley was not intimidated, yet his explanation
that he had earlier stored a fortune in a little tin box
and since deposited those funds in various banks hardly
rebutted the Seabury charges. Still Farley refused to
follow the precedent set by other suspected Tammany officials by resigning, and on February 11, Rosenman notified the principals that the Governor would hold a public
hearing on February 18.[47]

The hearing took place as scheduled. The Counsel
seated alongside the Governor, compiled voluminous and

detailed notes which he later arranged in the form of a
catechism to serve the Governor. Roosevelt's final decision drew liberally from the Rosenman memorandum and his
conclusions were those reached by his Counsel. On February 24, 1932, the Governor issued an order removing
Thomas Farley as Sheriff of New York County.[48]

The Tammany scandals had forced Rosenman into choosing sides between Roosevelt and the Manhattan political
organization. It was a decision he had hoped never to
have to make. Despite the prospects of an imminent judicial appointment, Tammany Hall held an even greater influence than Roosevelt over the ultimate fulfillment of
Rosenman's ambitions. Without the machine's endorsement
he could never hope to gain election to the bench. He
continued to remain, nevertheless, as one of the Governor's principal advisors throughout most of the "pulling
and hauling of Tammany and Seabury." His loyalty, as
Raymond Moley described it, was a "tribute to his devotion to Roosevelt."[49]

On March 11, the final day of the 1932 legislative
session, Governor Roosevelt formally nominated Rosenman
to the court by sending his name to the Senate for confirmation. Describing the nomination as one of the most
unselfish acts of his life, "because I am cutting off my
right arm," Roosevelt affirmed he knew no one better
fitted for the judicial post. This appraisal of Rosenman
came "from first-hand knowledge, because during the past
three years Mr. Rosenman has been of very intimate and
essential help to me in the conduct of this administration." He would, he speculated, miss the nominee's wide
knowledge of law and liberal social viewpoint.[50]

The Senate treated the nomination as an occasion
for encomiums. Republican Majority leader George Fearon
moved for unanimous consent to immediate confirmation.
Affirming there was "no middle aisle" in the upper chamber when Rosenman was concerned, Fearon commended the
nomination as a credit to the Governor and predicted it

would receive the approval of the people. Senator Hofstadter, in what may rank as one of the more ironic
speeches from the Senate chamber, seconded Fearon's motion.   Governor Roosevelt had rendered "a unique service
...in giving this man to the judicial machinery of the
State," and it was "especially fortunate," Hofstadter
thought, to have Rosenman ascend the bench at "a time
when the judicial process is being tested as never before,"   Then, after further remarks and at the suggestion
of Democratic Leader John J. Dunnigan, Rosenman was given
a "rising vote." As presiding officer, Lieutenant-Governor Lehman took "great pleasure in announcing that the
nomination had been confirmed, unanimously." Dorothy
Rosenman, who viewed the proceedings from the visitors
gallery, could hardly conceal her pride.[51]

        The *New York Times* labeled Rosenman "A Good Appoint-
ment" and attributed his rapid rise (he was 36) to "industry and ability." Citing it as a "personal and not a political appointment," the newspaper expected that Tammany
would nonetheless acquiesce to it.[52] Rosenman had made
no attempt to reconcile Curry to his appointment, but
Roosevelt had wasted no time in efforts to placate political leaders. Acting upon the suggestion of Curry, he
appointed John E. Sheehy, a personal friend of the Tammany leader, to succeed Thomas Farley.[53] Ed Flynn, who
had admitted Rosenman's qualifications but scored his
appointment as an injustice to the Bronx, would designate
Rosenman's successor as Counsel.[54]

        There was, however, no immediate need for a succes-
sor as Rosenman had agreed to stay on until after the
thirty-day bill signing period. By mid-April he had disposed of the 825 measures requiring gubernatorial attention and prepared to assume his judicial duties in New
York City. Just prior to departing Albany he penned a
note to the Governor. He was grateful "not only because
you have enabled me to reach a life's ambition so early
in life, but also because you think I am worthy of it and
capable of carrying it on." Never before in Rosenman's

life "were three years of work so full of real pleasure and inspiration." He hoped Roosevelt would consider this letter as his "God-speed...on the road which seems so clear ahead of you and is yours by right." Rosenman also hoped he would "be allowed to help along the road."[55]

Chapter Four

NEW DEALS AND POLITICAL DEALINGS

Milton Kupfer was Sam Rosenman's closest friend. A
fellow *Law Review* editor at Columbia, he had managed Sam's
first election campaign and been best man at his wedding.
Now that Sam was to become a Judge, Milton was to partic-
ipate in the installation ceremony.

Over two hundred friends and associates of the
Rosenmans crowded into a flower banked courtroom of the
New York County State Supreme Court building to witness
the proceedings. Victor Dowling, a retired Appellate
Division Justice congratulated the Bar, the bench, and
the community on Rosenman'a appointment. Assembly Minority Leader Irwin Steingut presented judicial robes in behalf of the State Legislature, and Columbia law classmates
provided an ivory gavel. Mrs. Roosevelt affirmed that
her husband's "admiration for Justice Rosenman's ability
was surpassed only by his feelings of warm friendship for
him," and the ubiquitous Senator Hofstadter was "thrilled
at a pride quite our own at this honor." It was reserved
to Kupfer, however, to speak with the greatest enthusiasm
and grandest ambition for his friend. When the "voices
of everyone here sounding this morning are hushed," he
predicted, "the words of Judge Rosenman and the work that
he will do will go echoing through the corridors of
time."[1]

Kupfer's extravagant predictions paralleled Rosenman's fondest hopes. To become a judge had been Rosenman's
"life ambition," not because he was content with lesser

political office, but because he aspired to influence the
application and interpretation of the law. He could not
expect to exercise profound influence from the court to
which he had been initially appointed, but there were
other, higher tribunals, for which his experience and
writings would ultimately qualify him. His future direction seemed fixed. Had someone suggested ascending the
bench would not mark his most decisive professional act,
Rosenman would have been incredulous. Nonetheless he had,
in fact, edged towards a very different career earlier
that very same month.

During a leisurely after dinner conversation with
Roosevelt, the Counsel had broached the subject of the
presidential aspirant's need for advisors. Rosenman
would soon be leaving for the court and acknowledged his
own inadequacies for assisting a presidential candidate
on a wide range of national issues. Just as he had been
recruited in 1928 to assist in the state campaign, he
now volunteered to recruit a body of "experts" to undertake similar tasks on the national level. Roosevelt was
acutely aware of his own lack of a broad program, or even
an informed opinion on many matters upon which presidential candidates were assumed to be expert, and welcomed
suggestions.

Rosenman thought they "ought to get some people
together to discuss the national problems of today, and
see whether we can come up with some answers or at least
some good intelligent thinking, pro and con, and some new
ideas." He did not know exactly how the group would
operate and thought "we'll have to feel our way as we go
along." In the past such groups had consisted principally
of national political and business leaders, but Rosenman
opposed an advisory staff drawn from these elements.
"They all seem to have failed to produce anything constructive to solve the mess we're in today." They were
also too readily identified with the national depression.[2]
He hoped to utilize university faculties. Lindsay Rogers,
among other academicians, had been consulted by Al Smith

in the 1928 national campaign,[3] and both Rogers and his
fellow Columbia faculty member Raymond Moley, had ably
assisted Governor Roosevelt when called upon for special
assignments in the past.

Moley had repeatedly suggested he would like to
help in the pre-convention campaign, and Rosenman wanted
to utilize his services. "He believes in your social
philosophy and objectives," Rosenman told Roosevelt, "and
he has a clear and forceful style of writing. Being a
university professor himself, he can suggest different
university people in different fields." The Counsel exhausted his argument and then asked the Governor, "Is
that all right with you?" Roosevelt nodded his assent
to both the grand scheme and Moley, and Rosenman began
by phoning the Columbia University public law professor
and inviting him to Albany to discuss the plan further.[4]

Moley was enthusiastic, and after the Albany conference prepared a roster of academicians he thought capable and willing to assist Roosevelt. The list was
brought to Rosenman's New York apartment where Moley,
Rosenman, and Basil O'Connor, a close friend and former
law partner of the Governor, combed over it; name by name
and subject by subject. Almost without exception, the
proposed experts were affiliated with Columbia University,
but none of the triumvirate thought this a limitation.
"At the beginning at least [they] had no money to pay the
travel or living expenses of a professor" and Rosenman
had instructed Moley that "this necessarily meant we
could include only men living in the city who could come
to the many conferences I [Rosenman] anticipated on a
five-cent subway fare."[5] Moley's candidates all met this
prerequisite, and they, in combination with the three
conferees ultimately formed the core of Roosevelt's brain
trust.[6]

The task of organization, however, had just begun.
The day following the original screening, Moley proceeded
to parade his experts through the Rosenman apartment.

Rexford Tugwell came first. On subsequent evenings
Lindsay Rogers, Adolphe Berle, Howard McBain, and Joseph
McGoldrick were among the callers. Others were requested
to submit specific memoranda, but were never invited to
become members of the continuing group. Within two weeks
after initiating the brain trust, Rosenman received his
formal appointment to the Supreme Court.

Although there was over a month between Rosenman's
appointment and his assumption of judicial office, he was
too occupied with the work of the thirty-day bill signing
period to provide assistance to Roosevelt in other areas.
His temporary absence from the councils of the brain
trust was not a serious loss, for during this period Moley
learned to work in more direct contact with the Governor
and demonstrated his value by authoring one of Roosevelt's
most effective speeches.[7] Even before Rosenman assumed
his judicial duties, Moley was providing the day-by-day
supervision of the newly created advisory council. This
arrangement did not alter when Rosenman returned to New
York City. Although as judge he continued his official
association with Roosevelt and devoted his evenings and
weekends to the work of the advisory corps, Moley retained
its direction. Rosenman has suggested that this arrangement persisted because Moley's time was not as restricted
as his own,[8] but as Rosenman had already acknowledged his
lack of familiarity with many of the subjects requiring
exploration by the group, it was only natural that its
leadership would eventually be assumed by someone other
than himself. He retained, however, his role as principal
liaison between Roosevelt and the newly created brain
trust.[9]

Along with Moley and O'Connor, the Judge made frequent trips to Albany to discuss programs and introduce
Roosevelt to new recruits. Rosenman regarded these meetings as the group's major contribution.

It was not [its] purpose...to try to
work out any blueprints for the future and to

lay them down for the Governor to accept or
reject. This is not the way Roosevelt functioned. Sometimes we differed among ourselves.
Then our arguments pro and con would be "bat-
tered out" before him, discussed and debated.
New lines of thought would be stimulated. It
was the kind of "homework" in governmental
thinking which Roosevelt enjoyed, which he
used a great deal in the White House, and
from which he always profited. Out of it
his own thinking was drawn into sharper focus. Sometimes it knocked down newly formed
ideas of his own; sometimes it opened up entirely new avenues which would later broaden
into action.[10]

By mid-Spring of 1932, months before the public was
alerted to its existence, this advisory staff had become
a powerful force in the development of Roosevelt's campaign, so much so, that a few weeks before the Democratic
convention Roosevelt assigned Moley the critical responsibility of preparing an acceptance speech. Basing his
draft upon consultation and memorandum from other brain-
trusters, Moley submitted it to Roosevelt early in June
and soon afterwards left for the nominating convention in
Chicago. He was joined there by O'Connor, Tugwell, and
Berle, but they were only spectators to the proceedings.
The job of corralling and retaining delegate votes was
in the capable hands of Howe, Farley, and Flynn. Roosevelt remained in Albany, and confident of success, invited the Rosenmans to the Executive Mansion to celebrate
his selection as Democratic nominee.

The convention proceedings did not go as smoothly
as the Roosevelt forces had hoped. An unrepentant Tammany Hall and its candidate, the still popular Al Smith,
demonstrated hostility towards the Governor's candidacy
and it took two days of voting and four long ballots before Roosevelt was able to muster the necessary two-thirds
majority. During some of that time, the Judge worked

nervously over the acceptance speech. Moley seldom composed perorations to his speech drafts,[11] and Roosevelt
had been unsuccessful in his own efforts at composition.
Rosenman's contribution, four short paragraphs, gained
the casual acceptance of the chief and was appended to
the address without comment. The overwhelming concern
of that particular moment was not the contents of the
acceptance speech, but whether Roosevelt would receive
the opportunity to deliver it, an occasion for which he
had made elaborate plans.

Once nominated he revealed those plans. He was
going to fly to Chicago and deliver his acceptance before
the assembled delegates. The decision to have the nominee
address the convention was extraordinary, but to fly there
was even more so. Dorothy Rosenman, knowing that the
Judge would accompany Roosevelt, was moved to tears at
the nomination. Excited by events and simultaneously ter-
rified by the thought of her husband flying,[12] she barely
regained her composure in time to attend a press conference through which Roosevelt revealed his flight plans
and passenger list. The Judge, Roosevelt announced while
smiling broadly at Dorothy, would follow to Chicago by
tricycle.[13]

Left behind, Dorothy continued to ponder the hazards
of air travel, but also worked to assuage Al Smith's bit-
terness. Reports were circulating that the now thoroughly
unhappy warrior would give vent to his disappointment by
continuing to oppose Roosevelt's candidacy,[14] and Mrs.
Rosenman contacted Justice Bernard Sheintag, a close
friend of Smith's to get him to intercede with Smith in
behalf of the Democratic presidential nominee. It was
her contention that precipitous action would not only
embarass Roosevelt, but might also be regretted by Smith
at some later date. Sheintag had been closely associated
with the unsuccessful candidate since 1911. Since then
he had enjoyed a steady but unspectacular rise in local
politics. In 1930, after once passing over his candidacy,
Governor Roosevelt had appointed him to the State Supreme

Court.[15] Convinced of the wisdom of maintaining a semblance of harmony between Smith and Roosevelt, Sheintag
agreed to intercept the train carrying Smith home from
the Chicago convention, and on the ride into New York
City he successfully impressed upon Smith the advisability of doing nothing further to interfere with Roosevelt's
candidacy.[16]

The problem of maintaining harmony seemed at times
to be as difficult inside as outside the Roosevelt councils. While Mrs. Rosenman was acting out her role as
peacemaker in New York, her husband had become a center
of controversy in Chicago. Once Roosevelt secured his
party's endorsement, his acceptance speech gained new
significance. Louis Howe requested that he be forwarded
a copy for study, and Rosenman relayed the request to
Grace Tully, a Roosevelt secretary, who read the entire
speech over the telephone to a Chicago stenographer. When
the nominee's plane reached the convention city, an agitated Raymond Moley informed Rosenman that Howe was violently dissatisfied with the speech.[17]

Howe did not demur at its philosophy, but simply
insisted it would not do. Moley later recorded that Howe
had launched into a "fearful tirade" which reached its
climax in the shout "Good God, do I have to do everything
myself? I see Sam Rosenman in every paragraph of this
mess." Moley tried to placate him with assurances that
"Rosenman had really very little to do with the writing
of the speech." Despite Moley's insistence, Howe refused
to believe that Moley could have "perpetrated" it. "I
don't expect Sam to understand, but you'd know it would
go fine under the trees at Hyde Park and be a complete
flop at a convention." His unalterable conclusion was
"(1) that the speech was unsuitable and (2) that it was
unsuitable because Sam had worked on it."[18] Howe had
decided that the only solution was to write a draft himself, and he was already pressing it upon Roosevelt when
Rosenman learned of its existence. The Judge made no effort to intervene.

Roosevelt was not anxious to use the Howe speech, but neither did he want to wound his oldest and most devoted lieutenant. His solution was to substitute the first page of Howe's alternative for that of the Moley version. The rest, except for some deletions he and Rosenman had made during the flight from New York, was read as previously intended. This compromise, divulged only during the course of Roosevelt's delivery, seems to have satisfied everyone.[19]

Howe's fear that Rosenman's contribution would mar Roosevelt's convention appearance was the most spectacular misjudgment of his career. Rosenman's peroration not only provided Roosevelt with the most memorable portion of this speech, it also provided American political literature one of its most memorable paragraphs. At first appearance it was but another call to action:

> I pledge you, I pledge myself, to a new deal for the American people. Let us all here assembled constitute ourselves prophets of a new order of competence and courage. This is more than a political campaign; it is a call to arms. Give me your help, not to win votes alone, but to win in this crusade to restore America to its own people.[20]

As might be expected, the delegates greeted the speech with thunderous applause. More significant was a syndicated cartoon by Rollin Kirby which appeared the following day. Portraying a figure which viewers readily identified as the subject of Edwin Markham's celebrated poem "The Man with the Hoe," the cartoon was hardly a portrait of a man "dead to rapture and despair, a thing that grieves and never hopes." To the contrary, Kirby's figure gazed hopefully at an airplane flying overhead, presumably the one in which Roosevelt had flown to Chicago. Emblazoned on its wings were the words "New Deal."[21] The cartoon stirred the imagination of the public and publicists alike, and the expression "New Deal" has since

become synonymous with Franklin Delano Roosevelt. No one
was more surprised than Judge Rosenman himself at having
stumbled upon the most potent political slogan of his
generation.[22]

During the subsequent campaign, the brain trust
continued its attempts to develop and enunciate a national policy. To accentuate its separateness from the regular Democratic organization it set up its own headquarters in New York City's Roosevelt Hotel. The National
Committee located its offices in the Biltmore, a block
south. Although there were obvious overlappings of functions, there were also large areas in which each group
could operate independently. Rosenman "was not at close
range to the campaign after the delivery of the acceptance
speech,"[23] but Moley, nevertheless, thought the arrangement helped maintain an uneasy separation between Rosenman and Howe. Moley regarded this rivalry as "the single
factor that might have disrupted the course of events."[24]
Roosevelt probably would not have agreed. It is more
likely he would have given his vote to the Seabury-Walker
affair.

Under the direction of Samuel Seabury, its relentless Counsel, the Hofstadter Committee had continued hearing testimony and uncovering irregularities in the New
York City administration. In June, 1932, just prior to
the Democratic National Convention, Seabury presented
Governor Roosevelt with charges against Mayor James J.
Walker along with a request the mayor be removed from
office.[25] Roosevelt delayed acting until after his nomination, and then he moved none too quickly. Despite
Tammany's Chicago opposition, he still hoped for its support in the general election. Continued inaction on the
charges, however, was impossible. Public opinion often
appeared more concerned with what the candidate had to
say about Jimmy Walker than what he had to say about
Herbert Hoover. In August, following the Farley precedent, Roosevelt scheduled a public hearing on the charges.

Although judicial propriety precluded Rosenman from taking any official part in the proceedings, he possessed far more than an academic interest in their outcome. Fear for Roosevelt's future did not exhaust his concern, for in order to remain in judicial office past December, it was essential Rosenman obtain Tammany endorsement at a forthcoming judicial nominating convention.[26] The very things that had brought him judicial preferment, his assistance to and friendship with Roosevelt, had become political liabilities in his dealings with the New York County organization. They would become even greater liabilities if the Governor further alienated Tammany in his handling of Walker.

While maintaining his loyalty to Roosevelt, Rosenman simultaneously attempted to demonstrate his friendship toward the Manhattan machine. He served as an Assistant Grand Marshal at a Tammany June Walk,[27] and appeared among the Tammany sachems during a patriotic rally.[28] At the funeral of Mayor Walker's brother, he, of all the scores of politicians present, was seated alongside of John Curry.[29] But superficial displays of camaraderie were insufficient to placate the increasingly hostile Tammany Hall.

Rosenman's judgeship had become hostage to Mayor Walker's fortune. Almost simultaneous to the commencement of hearings on the Seabury charges, reports began circulating that Judge Rosenman would not receive redesignation.[30] Jimmy Hines confirmed these rumors, when two weeks before the convention, he revealed he could not support Rosenman's candidacy since he was already committed to a candidate of John Curry.[31] Rosenman's only hope for nomination lay in a rapprochement between Roosevelt and Curry forces. Yet Walker's evasive replies at the public hearing only widened the breach. It became irreparable on the evening of September 1, when James J. Walker abruptly ended the hearings by resigning as Mayor of New York City.[32]

Soon afterwards, the Democratic presidential nominee left New York on a nationwide campaign tour. Any
lingering hope for Rosenman's nomination collapsed with
his departure. Flynn offered his support at the convention, but the Bronx organization lacked sufficient votes
to secure the nomination, and "in view of the refusal of
those in control of the convention to support him, Judge
Rosenman declined what would be an empty honor."[33] On
September 29, Roosevelt made an ineffectual last minute
effort at assistance and telegraphed Curry from his campaign train. Not wishing to "interfere in wholly local
matters," he nonetheless reminded the Tammany leader of
Rosenman's "long service to the party," and that he had
abundantly proved his fitness for the Supreme Court.
Roosevelt concluded with his "wholly personal hope that
Rosenman will receive the designation tonight."[34]

At separate conventions that same evening, the
Democratic and Republican parties nominated candidates
for judges in the First Department. State Senator John
J. McNaboe delivered the principal nominating address for
the Democrats. As ranking minority member of the Hofstadter Committee he had earned the reputation as the
committee's most persistent critic. That evening, however, he nominated its Republican chairman, Senator
Samuel Hofstadter, as a Democratic candidate for the Supreme Court. Hofstadter, he explained, "was especially
qualified from every point of view," and especially in
view of his work on the "great committee." Hofstadter
was subsequently nominated by acclamation. Also designated that evening was Aron Steuer, a 33 year-old city
court magistrate whose name had been among those Curry
had submitted to Governor Roosevelt as a possible successor to Justice Mullan. Being the son of Max Steuer constituted his most visible claim to a Supreme Court judgeship. Incumbent Justice Richard P. Lydon and Municipal
Court Justice Thomas A. Leary completed the slate.[35]

Roosevelt may have been amazed by the convention
choices, but he could hardly have been surprised at his

Counsel's rejection. Nevertheless he cabled Rosenman to
express his personal disappointment. Significantly the
future President reminded the shunned jurist that "I have
a long memory and a long arm for friends."[36] Rosenman
remained silent, but Ed Flynn condemned the convention
proceedings. He regretted the failure to "redesignate
Justice Rosenman," but was even more indignant that the
Bronx candidate, Charles B. McLaughlin, had been passed
over.[37] Compounding the offense was the disclosure that
the Republican convention had selected a judicial slate
almost identical to the Democrats. In a twenty-minute
meeting the Republicans had designated Hofstadter, Steuer,
Lydon, and Municipal Court Justice George L. Genung.[38]

Bipartisan approval for incumbent justices was normal procedure, so Justice Lydon's joint endorsement had
been anticipated. Similar preference for Hofstadter and
Steuer, however, made both parties suspect. The *Sun* labeled the nominations as "one of the most amazing deals
in the political history of the city."[39] Some irate citizens demanded that Seabury, presumably the Hofstadter
committee, investigate the proceedings.[40] Other more
placid souls reflected that with the Hofstadter nomination Tammany had reached "new heights of political cyni-
cism,"[41] and one report credited Jimmy Walker with having
"dictated" the nomination from Europe.[42] The New York
bar associations declared Hofstadter and Steuer to be unfit for judicial office and sponsored an independent judicial ticket to oppose their candidacies.[43]

When questioned as to his motives, Curry commented
"We were pleased to nominate Senator Hofstadter." The
more verbose Republican State Chairman William Kingsland
Macy attributed the Aron Steuer nomination to the esteem
in which he held Aron's father, Max. As for Hofstadter,
Macy assured the press he had no prior knowledge of Tammany endorsement and indignantly called upon the Senator
to repudiate it.[44] The *Times* was not impressed with Mr.
Macy's indignation. It believed that Hofstadter's Tammany endorsement had deprived the Republicans of a cam-

paign issue, and that was the reason Macy wanted him to
repudiate it. Neither was the *Times* impressed with the
Bar associations' call for independent judicial candidates.
It saw no detriment to the bench if Hofstadter were elected and regarded assertions by some lawyers that they
would have supported him if there had been no deal "as
amusing as is Mr. Macy's indignation."[45]

Regarding Rosenman's rejection as the most significant aspect of the affair, the *Times* interpreted it as
notice that while Tammany "may be supporting Mr. Roosevelt for President, it intends to be complete master of
the situation in New York City." The rejection also led
observers to question whether Tammany would go along with
him on the state level where several ardent Roosevelt
supporters were candidates.[46] The question was answered
at the state nominating convention. There Curry, along
with Brooklyn Boss McCooey, who had also denied a Roosevelt appointee judicial redesignation, fought against the
gubernatorial nomination of Herbert Lehman. Lehman was
able to overcome this opposition, but not until Al Smith
and Roosevelt combined efforts to assist him.

Despite Roosevelt's intervention on the state level,
he was unwilling to oppose Tammany in New York City.
"To interfere in the proceedings there," Roosevelt wrote,
"would not only have been against precedent but against
my personal policies."[47] As Democratic presidential candidate he hoped to assure against further schism in Democratic ranks. Rosenman respected his wishes by disassociating himself from any further activities in the judicial
campaign. The Independent Judges Party selected its slate
without soliciting Rosenman's candidacy and campaigned
without his aid. Apart from his respect for Roosevelt's
"personal policies," Rosenman regarded the independent
cause as impractical. With the citizens of New York City
voting in an abnormally large number of major contests,
he doubted it would be possible to generate enough public
concern over judicial contests to secure an independent
victory.[48]

Although the Independent Judges Party received a
large protest vote, it fell far short of victory, and
Hofstadter, the special target of the independents and
least successful of the bipartisan candidates, rode into
office with over sixty per cent of the votes. Of far
greater importance to Rosenman, and the country at large,
was that Roosevelt and Lehman had also been victorious in
their contests. Had Rosenman possessed prescience, he
might have taken additional satisfaction from the fact
that his own rejection by Tammany marked the point of
no return in John F. Curry's march toward political
oblivion.

The months following November comprise an ignomini-
ous period of United States history. Denied the confidence of the electorate and frustrated in attempts at
collaboration with the President-elect, Herbert Hoover
presided impotently over a nation plunging deeper into an
economic depression already unparalleled in its intensity.
Rosenman, like most Roosevelt associates, assumed implic-
itly that the incoming administration would provide new
and very real opportunities for rapid recovery. He was
not, however, among those associates who regarded their
own presence in Washington as essential to that success.
In December, after Rosenman completed his abortive term
as justice, Roosevelt reiterated the offer to accompany
him to Washington, and Rosenman again refused. Among
those more anxious to make the trip were a number of his
colleagues from the brain trust.

Rosenman questioned the wisdom of positioning members in Washington. Without questioning individual qualifications for administrative office, he doubted the
group could continue to function with members holding
such posts. In later years it became more obvious that
"there is something about administrative power along the
Potomac that excludes the concept of anonymous helpfulness which was the basis of the success of the original
brain trust."[49] When Rosenman expressed this sentiment
in 1932, however, Roosevelt chose to ignore it. Besides,

unlike Moley and Tugwell, Rosenman had special reasons
for wanting to remain in New York. Governor Lehman had
privately assured him of reappointment to the Supreme
Court, and during what amounted to a six month interim
from judicial responsibilities, Rosenman combined an exceedingly lucrative law practice with active participation in state politics. His most publicized efforts were
directed toward preparing for the termination of prohibition.

Long on record for favoring repeal, he had, as an
assemblyman, denied the eighteenth amendment ever accurately reflected the public will, and professed that prohibition demonstrated the need for a system whereby the
United States constitution could be amended only through
direct vote. He was certain that if such a requirement
had existed in 1919, the eighteenth amendment would never
have been ratified.[50] When, in 1933, New York established
a commission to formulate a state liquor control plan in
anticipation of loosening prohibition restrictions and
eventually repeal, Rosenman accepted the position of commission counsel.[51]

Among the controls advocated by the commission were
a number intended to preclude the reestablishment of the
saloons that had prevailed during the pre-prohibition
era. To this end the commission advocated regulations
such as requiring that alcoholic beverages be served only
at tables.[52] Restrictions of this sort met with particular resistance from New York City legislators, and
the counsel was delegated the commission's principal in-
termediary with Tammany leaders in working out a serviceable compromise.[53] Despite his recent difficulties with
the New York organization, the former Judge effected an
amicable compromise. The final plan provided for the
creation of a State Liquor Control Board to regulate the
licensing of dealers and the sale of alcoholic beverages,
and while the proposals governing sales were not as rigid
as originally advocated, they did provide some protection
against pre-prohibition type saloons. To assure maximum

legislative support, the commission counsel presented
the plan at separate conferences of Republican and Democratic legislators to permit "last minute" resolution of
any final objections. The commission plan was introduced
to the legislature on April 9, two days after the national
beer and wine act had gone into effect, and was passed
with only nominal opposition.[54]

Rosenman's shepherding activities sparked speculation that he would chair the Liquor Control Board; a rumor he publicly repudiated.[55] Non-judicial public service
had become an avocation rather than a vocation, and,
after completing work on the liquor commission, he assumed
the counselorship of a quasi-public mortgage corporation.[56]
From Governor Lehman's personal view, however, he was most
useful during the Governor's first bill signing period.

Acting unofficially but otherwise in a similar capacity as for the Roosevelt administrations, Rosenman
directed the legislative review and advised on final dis-
positions.[57] In subsequent years he occupied a less
prominent but still important place in the bill signing
process. After Lehman reappointed him to the bench and
through 1936, the Governor established a practice of for-
warding thirty or forty bills at a time for the Judge's
recommendations. When work on these bills had been completed Rosenman would return them to Albany in return for
a new batch, and the process would continue throughout
the thirty day period. This arrangement was abandoned
after 1936 when Rosenman began devoting more time to assignments from Roosevelt and correspondingly less to
those from Governor Lehman. Their personal relationship
deteriorated as a consequence.[58]

The persons and events touching upon the 1932 judicial election supply it with a generous portion of irony.
Rosenman's steadfast ambition for a judgeship should have
precluded the pursuit of a more financially remunerative
legal career; yet Curry's refusal to consent to this ambition virtually guaranteed Rosenman an income in excess

of any judicial salary in the nation. For upon reluctantly stepping down from the bench, he became the recip-
ient of an enviable number of requests for his legal services. Many of these were a direct consequence of the
establishment of a National Recovery Administration.[59]

Whatever doubts exist as to whether the 1933 National Recovery Act contributed to the country's overall
economic recovery, there should be no doubt it proved a
boon to the legal profession. The act required that various industries possess codes of fair competition, and
business leaders turned en masse to attorneys for aid in
their formulation. For prospective clients desiring the
services of an attorney reputed to possess great political
influence, and prospective clients were wont to desire
this, Rosenman was an admirable choice. Able to provide
the satisfaction of being enrolled under the banner of
the N.R.A. by an intimate of the President, he was also
equipped to render sound legal advice. "Acutely conscious
that many of his clients would not have given such [large]
retainers to a lawyer less close to the President's ear,"
Rosenman earned within a few months, an income far in excess of a justice's annual salary.[60]

Quickly establishing himself as a spokesman for the
N.R.A., and priding himself as a "business lawyer" at a
time when the views of the New Deal and the business community seemed to coincide, his statements carried the
endorsement of both camps. "The competition" he asserted,
"which wins because of greater efficiency, greater skill,
[and] greater economy is the kind we all strive for."
Unfortunately, existing competition relied upon "sweated
labor, unfair trade practices, [and] false and misleading
advertising." Rosenman was certain that adherence to the
codes of fair competition then being established would
curtail those practices "which after many years have succeeded in crippling modern business." Neither should
employers fear guarantees of the right of collective bargaining. Once employees possessed that right, he predicted, racketeering in labor unions would disappear. Con-

sumers might disapprove of price fixing, but closer reflection revealed it to be in the ultimate public benefit
even if it did not appear to be in the immediate consumer
interest. As counsel for over a dozen large New York department stores, he described price cutting as "the greatest evil which has brought misery to American Business
and which the N.R.A. was enacted to prevent."[61]

Whether or not these sentiments conformed to Rosenman's personal beliefs, it was his professional obligation to argue in the interests of his clients. Furthermore, zealous advocacy might justify his large retainers.
Though it is difficult to discover his private views, it
is readily apparent that, despite the large retainers, his
ardor to resume a judicial career had not diminished, and
in July, 1933, Lehman appointed Rosenman to fill the
judiciary vacancy created by the death of Justice Henry
L. Sherman.[62]

As in the previous year, the press applauded the
appointment. The *Times* declared that during Rosenman's
short tenure as a judge he had displayed learning, impar-
tiality, and ability. "Here is at least the case of one
man so fitted to serve in a judicial capacity that his
nomination and election ought to be beyond question."
The *Times* feared, however, that despite his qualification,
he might again be passed over by Tammany.[63]

Such fears were unfounded. The Democratic First
Judicial Department nominating convention bestowed its
unanimous endorsement. Further evidence of Tammany's
eagerness to atone the previous year's oversights was the
redesignation of Charles B. McLaughlin, who had also received a Lehman appointment. A third Lehman appointee,
Edward R. Koch, incumbent Philip J. McCook, and Denis
O'Leary Cohalan completed the slate.[64] Rosenman's personal satisfaction with the convention results was tempered by his anxiety over the forthcoming campaign. Nineteen thirty three was one of those interludes when, even
in New York City, Tammany endorsement was not tantamount
to election.

Chapter Five

SIXTY CENTRE STREET

Sixty Centre Street in Manhattan is a seven story granite structure which serves as a courthouse for the Supreme Court of the State of New York.[1] Located approximately midway between Chinatown and the Bowery, the building comprises an undersized square city block, and, despite its pseudoclassical appearance, blends easily with the more functional architecture of the government office buildings which surround it. Within the Sixty Centre Street chambers, judges routinely dispense quantities of justice--measured in litigations and sums of money involved--in excess of any comparable state court in the nation. The quality of justice is more difficult to measure. There is general agreement that disinterested and legally competent jurists are essential components of quality, but in the selection of judges these hardly ever serve as exclusive criteria. Assuming political experience to be of advantage in preparing for the bench, Rosenman subscribed to the view that, other things being equal, preference should be given to candidates with political experience.

The 1933 election provided a generous portion of such candidates. Not that it was unusual for judicial candidates to possess political experience; quite the contrary. What made 1933 unusual was the abundance of candidates and the existence of genuine electoral contests. The situation had developed from efforts of anti-Tammany elements to wrest the Mayor's office from Tammany control; in the course of which, the judiciary was

subordinated directly to the mayoralty campaign. From
Rosenman's view the situation was fraught with peril;
peril precipitated by the intransigence of John Curry.

Curry had dissipated Tammany's almost absolute
power to elect its nominees by insisting upon personally
selecting all Democratic candidates. During 1932, Ed
Flynn's protégé Joseph V. McKee, (Bronx) as President of
the New York City Board of Aldermen, had assumed the
duties of Mayor after Walker's resignation. Despite
McKee's popularity and apparent competence, Curry refused
to permit his mayoralty candidacy and instead chose Sur-
rogate Judge John P. O'Brien (Manhattan) as the 1932
Democratic standard bearer. As in the instances of Rosenman and McLaughlin, McKee's rejection had occasioned some
Democratic and public censure.

O'Brien was elected without difficulty, but while
completing the final year of Walker's term, demonstrated
a general ineffectiveness. Curry, nonetheless, insisted
upon O'Brien's renomination and secured it over the strong
protests of Ed Flynn and reform minded elements within
the Democratic party. The Bronx boss used this opportunity to break with Curry and help organize the Recovery
Party, which endorsed McKee for Mayor. The Democratic
schism enhanced chances for Republican success, but some
optimistic Republicans had sensed victory even before
McKee's candidacy.

Jimmy Walker's resignation had not ended Seabury's
activities, and he discerned in the 1933 elections an
especially favorable opportunity to drive the tarnished
Tammany machine from office. Seabury, his aides, and
elements of the Independent Judges Party of the previous
year formed the nucleus of a group which allied itself
with the Republican Party to produce a Fusion Party ticket.
Its candidate for Mayor, a colorful Republican ex-congress-
man, Fiorello H. LaGuardia,[2] proceeded to conduct a
spirited and well received campaign.

Encouraged by the reception accorded its mayoralty
candidate the Fusion Party decided to also endorse candidates for lesser offices. Included among these were
judicial candidates for the First Department. At a special nominating convention it endorsed McLaughlin, McCook,
and three others, one of whom, George Trosk, had served
as Seabury's principal assistant.[3] There was some disappointment over the failure of Seabury's group to designate Rosenman, especially since the rejected candidate
possessed important friends within the Fusion element and
Seabury had himself criticized Tammany for its rejection
of Rosenman the previous year. Critics accused Seabury
of engineering the nominations in order to secure a judicial nomination for his aide and directed charges of
bossism against him. Seabury replied that he had failed
to endorse Rosenman because Democratic National headquarters had failed to endorse LaGuardia.[4] Roosevelt was
angered by this turn of events,[5] and hardly placated when
leading Fusionite C. C. Burlingham assured him that
"Rosenman would certainly have received the Fusion nomination if McKee had not come in," for "it was rumored
that Mr. Farley was behind Flynn and McKee." Under these
circumstances there had been strong opposition to all
Democratic judicial candidates. McLaughlin had finally
received a nomination because as District Attorney he had
"fought racketeers." Rosenman, however, had been associated with Jimmy Hines, and Hines was an "evil influence
here [New York City], especially with the courts." There
was, Burlingham alleged, no district leader who could
"compare with him in his activities in the District Attorney's office and with the Judges."[6]

Fusion rejection presented Rosenman with an awk-
ward problem. Not only did it promote opposition, but it
also tended to identify that opposition as dedicated to
the defeat of a Tammany dominated judiciary. In a campaign in which candidates were vying with each other to
convince the electorate of their independence from the
New York Democratic organization, this seemed an obvious

disadvantage. Rosenman's predicament, however, was eased
by the Recovery Party which subsequently endorsed the
Democratic slate for judicial office. The Recovery endorsement led to speculation that Rosenman would renounce
his Tammany nomination and support McKee,[7] but the Judge
elected to retain his Democratic support.[8] The decision
may have been influenced by the contested legality of the
Recovery Party endorsement,[9] but it was more likely dictated by his eagerness to assure a November victory. In
any event, Rosenman was now in the enviable position of
being able, when desirable, to fulminate against Tammany,
while maintaining that organization's support at the polls.

The existence of a genuine judicial contest invariably leads to the creation of nonpartisan citizen committees to promote the candidacies of each of the aspiring
judges. The more intense the political campaign, the
larger and more active these organizations become. The
great advantage of this arrangement is that through these
committees, candidates for judicial office can conduct a
vigorous campaign and at the same time retain or acquire
an appearance of remaining aloof from the squalor of partisan politics. The ability with which a candidate can
maintain this deception is regarded as a measure of his
judicial dignity.

The Non-partisan Citizens Committee to promote the
candidacy of Samuel I. Rosenman for the Supreme Court of
the State of New York was in all respects an impressive
organization. Its headquarters were located at the Wal-
dorf Astoria Hotel, and its chairman, retired Appellate
Justice Morgan J. O'Brien who was 81 years old at the
time, supplied a respected name and nominal leadership.
The actual work was conducted by younger hands, especially
Assemblyman Paul T. Kammerer who served as campaign manager. Lewis Strauss handled the very ample funds.[10]
Membership was recruited from among prominent citizens
within the judicial district. Letters were mailed to individuals under the signature of Justice O'Brien with requests that the recipients serve with him on the nonpar-

tisan committee to elect Rosenman. A self-addressed pos-
tal card was included to facilitate acceptance of Justice
O'Brien's invitation. Committee membership entailed no
burdensome participation in its affairs, and recruits appreciated their only obligation would be to lend their
names for campaign purposes. The response was gratifying,
and subsequent perusers of Rosenman campaign literature
were to discover that such stalwart citizens as John W.
Davis, Vincent Astor, Herbert Bayard Swope, and the lesser
known John Foster Dulles were serving in the candidate's
behalf.[11]

Seabury aide George Trosk, the Fusion candidate
whose name was to appear in the same column as Rosenman's
on the ballot, was, by virtue of this position on the
ballot, Rosenman's principal opposition. Also possessed
of support by a bevy of noted personalities, Trosk succeeded in having Samuel Seabury, Samuel Untermeyer, Nathan
L. Miller, and Bainbridge Colby make special pleas in his
behalf. Most forceful of Trosk's endorsements, however,
was that by the Citizens Union, which recommended the entire Fusion judicial slate. Rating Rosenman as "able and
devoted," it rated Trosk as even more so.[12]

The *New York Times* sharply dissented from the Citizens Union report and rebuked the civic group for "leaving Rosenman out in the cold." The newspaper asserted
Rosenman "deserves to be elected,"[13] and its enthusiastic
support more than compensated for the faint praise with
which the Citizens Union had damned him. Rosenman's campaign slogan, "Fit to be a Judge," an assessment neither
Seabury nor the Citizens Union ever attempted to refute,
was culled from an earlier *Times* editorial,[14] and for
those still doubting his judicial talents Rosenman reproduced an editorial from an upstate Republican daily
which predicted he would "make one of the ablest jurists
to grace the New York bench in its eventful history."[15]

The most formidable weapons in his arsenal, however,
were his judicial appointments from both President Roose-

velt and Governor Lehman.   Roosevelt had likened Rosenman
to his right arm and Lehman (another of Roosevelt's right
arms) had commended him for the "high measure of distinguished and devoted service which has marked your previous
judicial service and all your other work."[16]   Voters,
constantly reminded of these details, were encouraged to
grasp the implication that a vote against Rosenman would
be a vote of no confidence in the collective wisdom of
their President and Governor.

Rosenman's experience in state government was also
celebrated.   Acting upon the assumption that a public
record which had helped to reelect Roosevelt governor
would also prove serviceable in returning Rosenman to the
bench, the Non-partisan Committee for Rosenman resurrected
some of Roosevelt's 1930 campaign literature.   To suit
immediate purposes, however, Roosevelt's achievements
were this time associated directly with his counsel.[17]
Another tactic, and one which Rosenman had also employed
in all his previous campaigns, was to encourage personal
letters urging his election.   During the '33 campaign the
style and contents of the letters varied with the individuals who sent them, but all followed a similar pattern.
The writer would indicate his own intention to vote for
Rosenman, comment on the candidate's qualifications, and
urge support for the "Roosevelt-Lehman appointed" jurist.

Efforts by campaign headquarters to assure that
every identifiable religious, professional, and business
group possessed representatives writing in Rosenman's
behalf were eminently successful.   Attempts to minimize
duplications in mailing lists were, perhaps with some
premeditation, notably less so.   It was not unusual for
recipients of letters urging Rosenman's election to have
already dispatched similar missives of their own, and one
individual, who cited the candidate's appointment by
Lehman as the principal reason for urging support, saw
fit to include the Governor on his mailing list.   Lehman,
duly impressed with such endorsement, commended the Rosenman organization for being "really on the job."[18]

As much as the candidate wished to do so, he could
not limit his campaign to the written word, and during
the three weeks prior to election day made personal appearances in such diverse places as hotel dining rooms,
political club rooms, and church pulpits.[19] Apparently
regarding judicial restraint as essential for a campaigning judge as for a presiding one, Rosenman's speeches
were pedestrian affairs which revealed neither his talents
as a speech writer nor anything not already known to
readers of his campaign literature. Insisting that the
only important issue in a judicial campaign was the ability of the candidate to properly perform the functions of
a justice, Rosenman alleged it irrelevant to campaign on
any program of judicial reform or related political issues
which he would be powerless to effect. He might celebrate
his own experience, (Raymond Moley had opined that his
"service on the bench while short has been distinguished
by calm and independent judgments") but he could not declare himself brighter, more able, more judicious, or
even more competent than his opponents. He could, however,
expect his record and his more enthusiastic supporters to
bear this out.[20]

Judicial candidates seldom find it necessary or
possible to mount so highpowered a campaign. And even
in Rosenman's instance it was probably unnecessary. With
three major candidates vying for Mayor, it was a virtual
certainty that none would gain an absolute majority, and
the combined Democratic-Recovery endorsement virtually
assured his election. Furthermore even if LaGuardia did
triumph, Rosenman was concerned only with the returns
from the First Department, Manhattan and the Bronx. Democrats adhering to the Tammany mayoralty candidate could
be expected to vote the straight ticket and were presumably numerous enough in Manhattan to provide a plurality.
The Recovery Party had its greatest strength in the Bronx,
was thoroughly dedicated to the Roosevelt-Lehman leadership, and certain to provide Rosenman some of his most
enthusiastic support.

The Judge recognized this, but his object was not merely to win, but to win with the largest vote possible. Whatever the specific advantages of an overwhelming electoral mandate, Rosenman was most impelled by his political reflexes. The size of a victory was its own justification. He would win big for its own sake. The Fusion Party, united only in its opposition to Tammany, included potential Rosenman votes towards which the Judge directed his campaign. Like George Trosk, his opposite number among the Fusion candidates, he could claim an anti-Tammany record; yet Rosenman was the choice of Roosevelt and Lehman while Trosk was merely Seabury's man.

Appeals of this nature bore fruit. Mail received at Rosenman headquarters confirmed support from Fusionites disappointed that he had failed to gain their party's nomination.[21] The Central Trades and Labor Council of Greater New York, an A.F. of L. affiliate, endorsed LaGuardia and Rosenman,[22] and leading Fusionites A. A. Berle and Henry Moskowitz announced similar intentions to split their ticket.[23] Robert Moses lamented "that the exigencies of the campaign have put some of the judgeships into politics," and admonished that "no matter what choice a voter makes for other offices, he should vote to keep Judge Rosenman where he is, and as long as he can be persuaded to stay."[24]

While not all the electorate followed Moses' advice, Rosenman amassed the largest plurality of any judicial candidate running opposed.[25] Soon afterwards he penned an enthusiastic analysis of the voting returns for the President. Since he had been "way down at #14 on the ballot there should have been quite a falling off from the number of votes cast for Mayor." Indeed there were almost 35,000 less votes cast for the office immediately preceding the judicial contests than for Mayor. Rosenman, however, had compiled a total only 3,000 less than the combined O'Brien-McKee vote in the First Department, and he cited this as overwhelming evidence that he had run far ahead of the parties that endorsed him.

I naturally feel very gratified at this
result. Of course most of it was due to the
fact that I was appointed by you--and how I
used it in the campaign. At each meeting, at
the end of every speech, I read your statement about me at the time you appointed me,
so that after a while I felt that my audience
was repeating it with me like a litany.[26]

The President replied with a short congratulatory
note in which he asserted that he has always been confident of Rosenman's making a "grand run." He also inquired
as to how his former aide felt "making speeches yourself
instead of writing them for other people?"[27]

The Judge did not reply, but he was nonetheless
troubled by the nature of the campaign. He had "learned
at first hand what it means for a judicial candidate to
have to seek votes in political clubhouses, to ask for
support of political district leaders, [and] to receive
financial contributions from lawyers and others," and he
had not found it an ennobling experience. Nor had he delighted in making "non-political speeches about his own
qualifications to audiences who could not care less--
audiences who had little interest in any of the judicial
candidates, of whom they never heard and would never remember."[28]

As Roosevelt's Counsel, Rosenman had recommended
independent judicial candidates as a remedy for machine
dictated tickets. His direct involvement in such a campaign, however, disabused him from further such suggestions. Independent judicial candidates, he soon learned,
might be sacrificial lambs, but they also generated campaigns which were largely irrelevant for determining judicial competence and further compromised judicial dignity
and independence. Rosenman's remedy, once offered as a
harmless palliative, now appeared to aggravate the disease.
His distaste and distrust for the judicial selection pro-

cess had been heightened by the campaign, but there was
little in the way of practical reform he could hope to
effect. Having been elected to serve the next fourteen
years as a judge, he would, he assumed, have few opportunities to intrude his political views through judicial
opinions.[29]

    The New York State Supreme Court is a trial court
and seldom supreme in any literal sense. Primarily a
court of first instance, its decisions are subject to review by the Appellate Division,[30] and ultimately the
Court of Appeals; the truly supreme state court. Under
such circumstances New York Supreme Court justices are
constrained to interpret the law according to established
precepts of their more highly placed brethren rather than
according to other socio-economic or legal theories they
themselves might hold. There could be occasional instances where in the absence of controlling precedent a
Judge might successfully intrude his personal views, but
such opportunities were extremely rare. Adherence to established legal precedent (*stare decisis*) was, in Rosenman's view, no mere exercise in judicial politics, however. He regarded the ability to identify and apply the
most appropriate established precepts as the most important single measure of judicial competence at all levels.
If his own judicial record did not reflect his social
views as closely as it would had he been a judge of a
court of last resort, it was not because *stare decisis*
was a less important principle in the latter circumstances,
but because courts of last resort, by their very nature,
hear a larger proportion of cases for which precedent is
either absent or mixed. Or so Rosenman would have argued.

    Also a practicing advocate of judicial restraint,
he maintained, during infrequent opportunities to judge
constitutional issues, a scrupulous regard for legislative
opinion and almost invariably upheld the contested legislative act irrespective of its political shade. During
Rosenman's first years on the bench an activist federal
court had established precedents in striking down numer-

ous federal and state enactments, and thus adherence to
the doctrine of *stare decisis* could have logically operated against the exercise of judicial restraint. This
potential dilemma failed to materialize to any significant extent.[31]

Ironically, Justice Rosenman's first noteworthy
opinion produced outcries that he had violently rejected
the doctrine of *stare decisis*. The case *Farulla* v.
Freundlich, was heard during 1934 and the decision was
never reversed.

Ralph A. Freundlich was the proprietor of a company
located in New York City, which was engaged in the manufacture of children's dolls. Under both a regional N.R.A.
directive and a union contract, the company was obligated
to pay employees according to the prevailing union wage
scales of the area in which the factory was located.
Sometime shortly after the company had signed the contract,
it declared its intention to move its factory to Massachusetts.

Samuel Farulla, an official of the Doll and Toy
Workers Union, sought an injunction to restrain the company
from such action. He contended that the sole purpose of
the move was to provide Freundlich with a means of evad-
ing his contractual obligations. It was common practice
for factory owners who could not otherwise reduce salaries
to move their plants to areas which offered the attraction
of lower prevailing wages. These "runaway employers"
would claim that their new location absolved them from
further obligations under the original agreements and
then proceed to operate under the lower regional wage
scales.

In the particular instance of *Farulla* v. *Freundlich*,
the company argued that its contract with the union was
invalid because it contained a closed shop clause. The
principle of the closed shop, the doll maker's attorneys
maintained, had been invalidated by Section 7a of the

National Industrial Relations Act. Neither did the company regard itself as being bound by the toy industry's
regional NRA agreement, as it had been declared in effect
without ever having received the company's endorsement.
Finally, the company contended, it could not be deprived
of its right to relocate its factory even if valid wage
agreements did exist.

Justice Rosenman ruled against the contention that
the closed shop had been outlawed by the National Industrial Relations Act. "The Act," he declared "was never
intended to take away any of the rights of labor which
it had acquired after decades of struggle and conflict."
He also found that an individual company was bound by
the provisions of the NRA regional agreements adopted for
its industry whether or not the individual company was a
signatory. As for the agreement itself, Justice Rosenman
ruled that although it did not provide against the removal
of a company from an area *per se,* it did provide that such
removal did not release a party from its provisions. He
then issued a temporary injuction to restrain the company
from moving in order to determine whether or not its purpose in moving was to circumvent prior obligations.[32]
Rosenman was aware there had been contrary decisions in
other states, but no New York appeals court had yet ruled
on the matter.

The decision provoked a wide range of responses.
The New York Regional Labor Board announced it would now
be able to take a more aggressive attitude towards runaway employers, while a manufacturers group demanded that
Hugh Johnson, the NRA director, intervene to prevent "a
hasty and cursory disposition of this vital subject."
Others thought the decision only served to point up the
large wage differential between urban and rural areas and
expressed the fear that, the courts not withstanding,
larger cities would be drained of their industry. Believing that manufactories located in urban areas were
faced with unfair and insurmountable competitive advan-

tages, they argued for the modification of existing codes towards greater equalization in pay rates.[33]

The *Times* editorialized that while many businessmen sought ways to escape contractual arrangements, it seemed odd that the NRA would want to penalize those employers who moved from the larger cities into smaller towns. The newspaper viewed industrial decentralization as an outstanding feature of "the New Deal vision," and cited the Tennessee Valley Authority as one such project which aimed towards the relocation of industrial populations from large urban centers. It dismissed the paradox with the comment that it was "not the first conflict of order or aims to be observed in the New Deal."[34] The *Herald Tribune* denounced the decision as the means by which the Federal Government could anchor industries to their localities "much as serfs of old were attached to the property."[35]

New Dealer Rosenman was enthusiastic over Justice Rosenman's decision. He described it to Roosevelt as the first flat holding in N.Y. that 7a of N.R.A. does not

> invalidate or make illegal "closed shop" agreements. It is the first holding, I think in the U.S. that labor agreements cannot be torn up by the simple expedient of moving a factory. You know, I assume that in four or five other states that courts have held that 7a does make a "closed shop" unlawful.

The Judge supposed that if it had been a United States Supreme Court decision Roosevelt would say "I'm glad you decided that way, or I could not have gone along with you."[36] Rosenman's supposition was not wholly correct. The President replied that it was a "grand decision even though viewed from another angle it might keep me from decentralizing some of New York City's industries." It might be rather nice Roosevelt concluded, presumably

facetiously, to have a little fur factory transferred
from New York City to Rosenman's vacation retreat.[37]

Towards the close of the year, a Canadian journal
applauded Rosenman's decision as a reflection of "the
working of influence along reformist lines that consciously or unconsciously affect those who are called
upon to administer justice." The Montreal editor was
gratified "that even the courts are marching along with
the time."[38] His gratitude for a reforming judiciary
was premature. The courts were to emerge as a bulwark
against this "influence along reformist lines," and Justice Rosenman failed to maintain a consistent record of
decisions reflecting more advanced concepts of social
justice.

His first important decision following *Farulla* v.
Freundlich indicated more conventional judicial thinking.
A group of Negroes was picketing a Harlem shoe store in
protest against the management's refusal to employ Negro
help, and the management obtained an injunction from Justice Rosenman to prohibit such picketing. The dispute,
he ruled, was a racial rather than a labor one, and
though "present day liberal judicial attitudes towards
labor disputes...is based on judicial determination that
...all peaceful and concerted action will be permitted
as justifiable means to accomplish any purpose legitimate-
ly associated with" unionization and collective bargaining, "racial picketing" is "an inherent danger to the community" against which "the court must provide protection."[39]

On another occasion, this one occurring in 1940, a
company whose employees were members of the Teamsters
Union was being picketed because it refused to discontinue sales to a company whose employees the union was
attempting to organize. This time Justice Rosenman ordered the picketing cease because it constituted a secondary boycott; which, though not then prohibited by statutory law was not by common law doctrine a legitimate labor
dispute.[40]

Rosenman's strict view of legal precedent was by
no means limited to cases involving labor disputes. In
1935, the New York State Legislature enacted a Fair Trade
Law directed against price cutting of nationally advertised merchandise within the state.[41] Despite this law,
a large department store continued to advertise and sell
a brand of cosmetics below its nationally advertised
price. The cosmetic manufacturer, pursuant to the Fair
Trade Law, had entered into price fixing arrangements
with over 3,000 retailers throughout the state, and although the particular department store in question had
refused to enter into such an agreement, the cosmetic
manufacturer correctly maintained that advertising and
selling prices lower than those stipulated in the price-
fixing agreements, even by non-signatories, constituted
unfair competition under provisions of the Fair Trade
Act.[42]

The issue brought before Justice Rosenman was whether the law or sections of it were constitutional. Two
similar cases had already been decided in New York State
courts. In one instance the defendant had been ordered
to cease its price cutting activities. In the other the
Fair Trade Law had been declared invalid.[43] Rosenman,
who only three years previous had hailed price fixing to
be in the ultimate public interest, now asserted that
his own personal opinion, or that of others, as to the
wisdom of the enactment was of no value to the court in
reaching an opinion as to its validity. Instead, in a
decision similar to that by which the United States Supreme Court had found the NRA unconstitutional, he refused
to sustain Section 2 of the contested act. Neither the
state legislature nor any other public body he proclaimed
had determined which articles were to be regulated or at
what levels prices were to be set. These functions had
been delegated to individual producers, and this, Rosenman declared, had been established as an unconstitutional
delegation of legislative powers.[44]

In those unhappy situations which required a choice
between justice and law, Rosenman regarded himself as

obliged to opt for the latter. Nowhere is such a situation so apparent as in *Hazzard* v. *Chase National Bank*.
During 1936, stockholders in the defunct National Public
Service Corporation, a one-time Samuel Insull holding
company, sued the Chase National Bank for $10,000,000 in
damages. They charged that the bank, which had acted as
their trustee, had been negligent in permitting Insull
interests to substitute this worthless National Public
Service stock in place of more valuable securities. The
Chase National Bank had received a fee of $1,000 for its
trusteeship, a sum Rosenman regarded as small in regard
to the total amount of moneys involved, but "exorbitant"
in view of the duties performed. The Judge acknowledged
"the potentialities of fraud upon innocent investors"
which were inherent in such indentures, but they were
nonetheless "legally permissible." The bank, he wrote,
"performed in full the negligible duty imposed upon it
by the indenture. It did nothing more, but having done
that it is absolved under the law." His personal hope
was that the situation would be "changed by legislation."
Under the existing law, however, he was constrained to
conclude that the bank had successfully exempted itself
from liability in this sad picture of high finance. The
decision was based, he declared, upon overwhelming legal
precedents which absolved banks from "exercising ordinary
care" in their handling of such matters.[45]

Dictum emphasizing the primacy of legislative opinion pervade Rosenman's decisions, and except in rare instances of "overwhelming and legal precedent otherwise,"
he invariably found grounds upon which to uphold the constitutionality of contested enactments.[46] Two cases in
point were settled with a single opinion.[47]

On July 13, 1937, the New York City Council passed
the Lyons Residency law over Mayor LaGuardia's veto.
This act provided that only individuals who were citizens
and *bona fide* residents of New York City for at least
three years could be considered eligible applicants for
municipal employment.[48] The New York City Civil Service

Commission had certified Robert Mullins to be a patrolman
and Emmanuel Mongello a fireman, but withheld their final
appointments since neither qualified under the newly imposed three-year residency requirement.

The disqualified applicants then sued for their appointments on the grounds that the city could not legally
discriminate against non-city residents of the state.
The state constitution specified that "No member of the
State shall be...deprived of any rights and privileges
secured by any citizen thereof, unless by the law of the
land or by the judgment of his peers."[49] The plaintiffs
further argued that the Lyons Law was detrimental to the
public welfare as it would reduce the city's source of
prospective employees and ultimately force it to resort
to the appointment of less capable individuals.

Rosenman upheld the constitutionality of the statute. The legislative intention in enactment, he asserted,
had been to promote the economic welfare of citizens of
New York City. The State in determining what use shall
be made of its own

> moneys may legitimately consult the welfare of
> its own citizens rather than that of aliens.
> Whatever is a privilege rather than a right
> may depend upon citizenship...In view of the
> fact that the state constitution imposes citi-
> zen residence qualifications, the city under
> the home rule amendment may similarly impose
> such qualifications.

As a judge, he did not find it relevant to consider
the ultimate effect of the act upon the city's residents.
"Although the policy may be unwise, and perhaps in the
long run more expensive to the city in that it will not
always result in obtaining the best qualified employees,
the wisdom of the policy is not for the courts but for
the city's legislative body."[50]

Socio-economic predilections, as distinguished from legal philosophies, are seldom baldly stated in Rosenman's decisions. One such rare instance is the case of *Osborne* v. *Cohen*. The controversy had its inception in 1936 when the State Legislature ordered that the Board of Elections in every city with a population over one million submit a referendum on whether to adopt a three platoon system for its fire department. It was argued that this directive to the Board of Elections in New York City was in violation of the Home Rule Amendment. Rosenman denied this contention and found that the health and efficiency of the New York City Fire Department was the concern of the entire state. He further maintained that the two platoon system, then employed, compelled firemen to remain on duty for a total of 84 hours each week. In view of this, the Legislature was entirely within its rights, for this routine was not only "out of line with modern social consciousness and modern social legislation," but also impaired the efficiency of the department.[51] Rosenman's decision was reversed. The Court of Appeals found that the referendum order to the New York City Board of Elections was in violation of the Home Rule Amendment.[52]

In light of the central position of the Home Rule Amendment, it might appear that upholding both the Lyons Law and the fireman's referendum involved a legal inconsistency that could be explained by the Judge's sympathy for the objectives of the referendum. As a candidate who campaigned for office advocating repeal of the Lusk Laws, it is doubtful he would have supported those activities he condoned in *Withrow* v. *The Joint Legislative Committee*.

A few months prior to United States entry into World War II, the New York Legislature established a joint committee to investigate the state's educational system. The committee concentrated its efforts upon the detection of alleged communist activities within the schools. A number of teachers, contending that the committee had turned the investigation into an inquisition "whose purpose appears to be [the] obtaining of victims

through indictments, dismissal from positions and sus-
pensions from duties without pay," petitioned the court
to order that the committee discontinue its activities.

Rosenman was aware that "in this period of unlimited
national emergency every arm of the government must be
especially vigilant in tracking down...those in our midst
who have taken advantage of their American liberties to
destroy those liberties." A scrupulous regard for the
individual's civil liberties was necessary nonetheless,
even in the investigation of individuals who were presumed to be conspiring to destroy those same liberties.
He was compelled to assume, however, that the State Legislature and its committees were also aware of this necessity. Citing an Oliver Wendell Holmes dictum "that the
legislators are ultimate guardians of the liberties and
welfare of the people in quite as great a degree as the
courts," Justice Rosenman concluded that "the courts
therefore even if they had the power should not lay down
procedure for its coordinate branch of government--the
legislature."[53]

The most litigious hearing over which Rosenman presided, *Blaustein* v. *Pan American Petroleum*, is officially
listed as having been modified by the Appellate Division.
The modifications, however, were so substantial as to
constitute a reversal, and unofficial contemporary accounts referred to it as such.

In 1934 Louis Blaustein, a stockholder and former
President of the Pan American Petroleum and Transport
Company, had charged that the Standard Oil Company of
Indiana, as majority stockholder of the Pan American Petroleum and Transport Company, had interfered with the
proper conduct of Pan American's business, and he had
sought heavy damages against the parent organization.
The case did not receive a hearing until 1940, and by
that time Louis Blaustein had died. His heirs, however,
pursued the suit vigorously. Henry L. Stimson was retained as their attorney and John W. Davis represented

the defendants. The trial, held without jury, lasted
through almost the entire winter and spring of 1940, ultimately requiring 70 trial days, 10,361 pages of testimony, and briefs totaling 1,400 pages. Rosenman's 182
page typewritten opinion, up to that date the longest
ever filed, ordered the Standard Oil Company of Indiana
to pay the Pan American Company damages which some estimated would amount to from 50 to 75 million dollars; an
award unprecedented in New York Supreme Court history.[54]
The Appellate Division, in December of 1941, decided by
a three to two decision that damages were not awardable
as there was no tangible evidence of conspiracy. Rosenman, the court found, had drawn the court "more and more
deeply into the directorial management of the oil business" and had substituted the court's business judgment
for that of the directors.[55]

     A more unique judicial assignment resulted from a
special order from the Appellate Division that Rosenman
conduct an inquiry into bad conduct charges lodged by
Richard A. Knight against members of the state judiciary
and bar, as well as counter charges by a New York City
Grand Jury that these same charges were of an "irrespon-
sible and reckless nature."[56]

     Knight proved a difficult person with whom to re-
tain judicial propriety. A socially though not a pro-
fessionally prominent attorney, he was a highly demonstrative person who had once stood on his head at the
entrance to the Metropolitan Opera House to express his
gratitude for a performance he had just witnessed.[57] He
could be equally demonstrative in expressing his dissatisfaction. After losing a lawsuit he had brought against
his former law firm, Knight accused the Judge of complic-
ity and requested that the Manhattan District Attorney,
Thomas E. Dewey, conduct a criminal investigation of the
entire affair. Dewey refused, and Knight responded by
charging him with professional misconduct. The affair
continued in this manner until it was brought to Rosenman's official attention. By then Knight had compiled a

list of nine judges and sixteen lawyers whom he charged
with corruption. The list had been printed and distributed to approximately 3,000 bar members.

   Knight professed that he was "delighted" to have
the Rosenman hearing, but after an initial inquiry he
failed to make further appearances. The Judge offered to
schedule hearing dates at Knight's convenience, but Knight
still failed to appear. Finally concluding that he had
"defaulted in the further production of evidence," Rosenman ruled that the charges against Knight "were well
founded and sustained by the record" and recommended dis-
ciplinary action. Rosenman was commended for his "obvious judicial temperament" by the Appellate Division,[58]
and the less judicial Knight was subsequently disbarred.[59]

   Although Rosenman's judicial term would not expire
until 1947, it was apparent at the time of his inquiry
into Knight's indiscretions that he would leave the court
well before that date. The Knight assignment occupied
intermittent attention from May through December, 1941,
and coincided with the critical period in United States
pre-war mobilization efforts. Measured against the drama
and urgency of these matters, Richard Knight's disbarment
or questions relating to whether an alumnus should disqualify himself from a hearing on Townsend Harris High
School appeared insensitively banal. A judgeship had
been Rosenman's life ambition, but he now chafed under
the restraints of judicial routine. During the vast majority of cases it was probably less difficult to remain
disinterested that to keep from becoming uninterested.
The important action was in Washington, and Rosenman
thirsted for an appointment there.

   Not that his judicial office had excluded participation in executive affairs. Since 1936, Judge Rosenman
had regularly accepted assignments from the President,
and in recent years they had become so formidable to require as much attention as court business.[60] They were
doubtless more publicized.

A magazine feature on the Judge, appearing some
months before he left the court, reported that observers
of Rosenman policies in Washington and "as expressed by
his judicial opinions" place him "just a degree or two
to the right" of general Washington policy." From "such
a vantage point" he had, according to this source, "earned
the accolade of even some of the New Deal's bitterest
Tory detractors as 'the only steadying influence around
the President.'"[61] Rosenman's Washington appointment was
delayed until September, 1943. At that time he resigned
his $25,000 judgeship to become, at $10,000 per year,
Special Counsel to the President. Sixty Centre Street
had lost its luster.

Chapter Six

"SAMMY THE ROSE"

Devotees of mystery novels find exposés of presidential advisors irresistible reading matter. Through a
process of accommodation they have become the perennial
favorites of newsmagazine editors as well. Usually precipitated by an executive decision of contemporary magnitude, the articles follow an unvarying pattern. One
is first introduced to those individuals presumed to possess the greatest access to, and therefore the greatest
influence upon the President. Then the reader is offered
insights into the individual and collective strengths
and weaknesses of those men whom the author has already
identified as advisors. The climax is then reached with
the revelation of the single individual presumed most
responsible for persuading the President to make the decision which originally occasioned the article.

For those who profess to view government as a series
of conspiracies, usually unindictable, such accounts supply a satisfactory explanation of some particular event.
Few historians, however, share this view. Its principal
internal weakness is that the conspirators are superseded
with greater frequency than Presidents, who, in turn, are
generally less permanent than the policies pursued. Even
those who retain long lived membership in some particular
President's inner circle assert more or less influence at
different times in different areas. One journalistic
dividend from this phenomenon is follow-up articles trac-
ing the evolutions of new inner circles. There is also
a built-in element of suspense; the possibility that some

favorite will come to dominate the councils of power or
correspondingly some Rasputin will fall from grace. A
journalistic hazard of this inconstant circle is that an
individual overlooked in earlier articles may emerge as
the vital power behind the throne. Rather than omit any
evidence that may possibly provide clues to subsequent
presidential behavior, the most conscientious authors include mention of those individuals whose access to the
President is apparent, yet who do not avail themselves
of presumed opportunities to influence events.

During the first few years of the Roosevelt administration, Rosenman's occasional appearances in Washington coupled with the newsworthy divulgence that the President had endowed him with a pet name gained him a place
on many a who's who roster of White House personages.
His doings did not merit extensive treatment, but most
commentators knowingly categorized "Sammy the Rose" as
being highly esteemed by Roosevelt who had bestowed this
sobriquet upon him. John Franklin Carter, however, sens-
ing some deeper significance, ranked him high in an al-
literative conspiratorial hierarchy as the "Sire of the
Secret Six," a group which during the 1937 court reorganization struggle was reputed to be exercising a particularly nefarious influence upon the President. Even
Carter, however, had overlooked Rosenman in an earlier
study, authored from the perspective of 1934, and his
agonizingly sibilant effort reveals the nature of journalistic atonement more than awareness of White House
operations.[1]

In any story limited to the practical day-to-day
activities of the early New Deal, Judge Rosenman plays
no important role. Both Roosevelt and his former Counsel
accepted this as an inevitable consequence of Sammy's
choosing to remain in New York. Within a week after assuming office, the President wrote Rosenman of his expe-
riences with the first bill he was to send before Congress.
"We worked until two o'clock this morning preparing it
and it seemed queer to do this kind of work without you.

After four years of such close association it is not easy
to work with others." Rosenman had provided successors,
however, and Roosevelt assured him that his "contribution
of Ray Moley and Rex Tugwell was probably the best that
anyone made during the whole campaign."[2] Any vacuum
created by Rosenman's absence was apparently a personal
one that could be filled through their social relationship.

The Judge discovered his problems of adjustment to
be more difficult than those of Roosevelt. Along with
Mrs. Rosenman he attended formal dinners and spent frequent weekend and vacation holidays with the President.
His exclusion from high councils of state, however, produced an unanticipated restlessness. He did not observe
his eclipse from Roosevelt councils with cold detachment,
and was especially sensitive to the officious attitude
Raymond Moley displayed towards him. The Judge once commented to Henry Morgenthau that in six months Moley had
changed from a man "who used to hang outside my office...
with the hope that I would pass on some of his papers to
governor Roosevelt," to a man who "acted as if he was
running the government and that Roosevelt was carrying out
Moley's suggestions." Nor was Rosenman placated in November, 1933, when Moley undertook large efforts in behalf
of McKee's mayoralty candidacy and demonstrated apparent
disinterest in his judicial campaign.[3]

Not until May, 1935, after Moley's departure from
Washington service, did Roosevelt request Rosenman's aid
in a matter of national legislative concern. The assignment, a relatively modest one, apparently came about
through coincidence. The Rosenmans were weekend guests
aboard the presidential yacht at the time Roosevelt was
deciding upon the nature of a message to accompany his
proposed veto of a veteran's bonus bill. The bill, passed
earlier that month, would have permitted the immediate
redemption of bonus certificates scheduled to reach matu-
rity in 1945, at full value. Roosevelt so strongly opposed this bill that he determined not only to veto it,
but to personally deliver his veto message before a joint

session of Congress. The opportunely accessible Rosenman
was invited to share in the drafting of that message; an
invitation which he accepted with alacrity. After completing the task, he wrote Roosevelt to thank him "for
the opportunity to have watched the message in its making,"[4] an excessively modest appraisal of his own role in
the affair. The President replied that he had "adopted
exactly ninety-eight and one-half percent of your pencil-
led suggestions." This Roosevelt reflected, was even
better than at Albany where "I used to take only ninety-
five percent, so your batting average is improving."[5]

For someone with so high an average, Rosenman came
up to bat surprisingly few times. Exigencies of the 1936
campaign, however, soon propelled him back into the fore-
front of the Roosevelt advisors.

In large part he resumed his position through de-
fault. Louis Howe, inactive for some years, had died the
previous April. Although Moley still made occasional contributions to Roosevelt speeches, both he and Hugh Johnson,
who had been recruited into the brain trust at the time
of Roosevelt's nomination in '32, and left government
service to become increasingly vehement critics of administration policies. Rexford Tugwell, still a member of
the President's official family, had become the whipping
boy for many of the New Deal's alleged inadequacies and
it was politically inexpedient to use him prominently in
the presidential campaign. Rosenman, who had cautioned
against the brain trust's hegira to Washington, was the
only member of the 1932 speechwriting corps who remained
available.

Roosevelt, mindful of the need for a new literary
coalition, chose the Rosenmans and the Stanley Highs as
his guests during the 1936 Decoration Day weekend. High,
a professional journalist whose services had been retained
the previous year to help organize the Good Neighbor
League, was introduced to Rosenman as someone who had
helped Roosevelt "on several speeches in 1935 and 1936,

and as one of the people whom he had asked to help in the
coming campaign." During this first meeting Rosenman was
encouraged to elaborate for High memorabilia from the
speechwriting experience he had accumulated in earlier
campaigns. Roosevelt gave no indication that he expected
the Judge to work with High, and Rosenman assumed that
these reminiscences were all that would be solicited of
him.[6]

He was mistaken. A few days before the convening
of the Democratic National Convention, Marguerite LeHand,
Roosevelt's private secretary, telephoned Rosenman. She
announced that the President had requested his presence
at the White House during the convention period. In
reply to the Judge's remonstrances that his lack of day-
to-day knowledge of the administration made him a questionable asset, Missy LeHand answered that he was needed
because he could work with the President without making
him nervous. To Rosenman, and Marguerite LeHand, as well,
such an explanation was compelling. They had long recognized that Roosevelt regarded his ability to work comfortably with certain individuals an even larger consideration than whether the individuals were experts in any
special field.[7] Furthermore, the Rosenmans maintained a
warm personal association with Missy LeHand, and in times
of exceptional stress she welcomed the Judge's presence
at least as much as the President.

Rosenman spent the first night at the White House
with Stanley High working out a draft of the Democratic
convention platform. They themselves devised some of
the planks, others were incorporated into the body of the
platform after being suggested by interested parties.
Donald Richberg contributed a plank on recent Supreme
Court decisions, and William Bullitt authored a section
dealing with foreign affairs. Roosevelt had originally
intended to utilize a peroration submitted by Harry Hopkins, but Senator Robert LaFollette phoned Rosenman to
inform him that the peroration was almost a duplicate of
one his father had used during the 1924 campaign. There-

upon Rosenman and High composed a new one. The final
result was approved by the President and sent along with
Senator Robert Wagner to the Philadelphia convention.[8]

Their next task was the composition of Roosevelt's
acceptance speech. Moley and Thomas Corcoran were simi-
larly occupied. Although both groups had been assigned
the task by the President, neither was at first aware of
the other's activities. Duplication of assignments was
a notorious Roosevelt practice, but it was rare in speechwriting. Never certain as to how much of this was pre-
meditated and how much a consequence of temperament,
Rosenman attributed this particular duplication to Roosevelt's reluctance to advise Moley that his effectiveness
as a presidential speechwriter had been destroyed by his
intrusion of political and economic views out of harmony
with those of the President.[9]

It was inevitable that both groups would learn of
the other's existence. The presidential solution to this
dilemma was to have Rosenman combine the moderate Moley-
Corcoran draft with the more militant Rosenman-High product. The final draft included far more of the Rosenman
than the Moley effort. Even before it was delivered,
however, Roosevelt precipitated a final break with Moley.
At a dinner party to which all four speechwriters were
invited, the President chose to bait Moley about his "new
conservatism." Moley responded with what Rosenman has
termed "justifiable heat." The resulting accusations and
recriminations made any reconciliation impossible.[10]
Moley had written his last speech for Roosevelt, but as
advisor he had yet to play his final scene.

Rosenman, High, and Corcoran, who were now working
as a team, were subsequently invited to Hyde Park to help
prepare an address to the New York State Democratic Convention. The speech was regarded as especially important
in that it would mark the formal inception of Roosevelt's
1936 campaign. When they arrived at Hyde Park, however,
they discovered their presence to be a cause of great

embarrassment to the President. Raymond Moley was also
expected as a guest, and Roosevelt dreaded having to confront him in the presence of his new speechwriting team.
To prevent this the President had arranged to have his
speechwriters, along with Mrs. Rosenman and Thomas Corcoran's secretary, hidden away in an apartment above a
Hyde Park tearoom during Moley's entire stay.

     The former presidential intimate had been invited
to Hyde Park at the insistence of Frank Walker and had
ostensibly come to discuss "what line" Roosevelt ought
to take in the campaign. The President, however, was
unwilling to readmit Moley to his confidence and did not
even refer to the speech in preparation. Instead they
discussed campaign strategy in very general terms, and a
reconciliation having failed, the disenchanted New Dealer
left Hyde Park never again to see the President.[11]

     With Moley's final departure, the conspirators
emerged from the tearoom and Rosenman openly assumed the
chairmanship of the President's speechwriting corps.
The first major assignment after completing the state convention effort was to prepare a speech for delivery in
Forbes Field, Pittsburgh. There in 1932, Roosevelt had
promised that if elected he would balance the national
budget. Not having done this, he directed Rosenman to
the task of explaining the promise away. Unsuccessful
in efforts to develop an argument that Roosevelt had not
really meant a truly balanced budget, Rosenman instead
argued that the deficit spending had produced substan-
tially better government than would otherwise have been
possible. "To balance our budget in 1933 or 1934 or
1935 would have been a crime against the American people."
Sensitive to charges that the Roosevelt administration
had operated under deficits larger than Hoover's, Rosenman maintained that these deficits were necessary to provide the proportionally greater benefits required by the
American people. These benefits were most apparent in
the rising national income, and if the national income

continued to rise at its then present rate, the nation,
Roosevelt promised, would have a balanced budget in two
years.[12]

The Pittsburgh address was well received by the
usually hostile local press and the Judge passed on some
articles and editorials to Stephen Early along with the
suggestion that the Press Secretary send notes of appreciation to the responsible journalists.[13] The Judge frequently sacrificed literary artfulness to gain oral effect, but he was nonetheless aware of the power of written argument. Because of this, a scrupulous regard for
the sensitivities of newsmen emerged as an added dimension in Rosenman's speechwriting chores. He had become
increasingly conscious of the speech reading public. The
opposition of an overwhelming percentage of the nation's
press to Roosevelt's candidacy had imposed added significance to the President's speeches, and they were regarded
now as his only reliable weapon in the battle of words
which are inextricable from political campaigns. As comments from the press became increasingly hostile toward
administrative policies, publication of Roosevelt speeches
was encouraged to publicize the Roosevelt point of view.
To facilitate the printing of presidential addresses,
Rosenman made special efforts to get mimeographed copies
to the press prior to 7 PM East Coast time. This enabled
newspapers, such as *The New York Times*, to include the
texts of Roosevelt addresses in their first, which was
also usually the out-of-town, edition. Rosenman was
pleased when an opposition newspaper devoted wide coverage to some presidential address but was elated at the
printing of a speech in its entirety.

During the week following the Forbes Field speech,
Roosevelt's eleven-car campaign train left Washington for
a tour of the Mid-West. Much of the material to be incorporated into the speeches had been prepared previously
and members of the speechwriting corps maintained contact
with the campaign train. The Judge, accompanied by Mrs.
Rosenman, was the only speechwriter actually included in

the campaign entourage. The Rosenman compartment served
more as a storage depot for his voluminous red manila
folders than as a sleeping accomodation, but the Judge
flourished under the pressure of working around the clock
throughout the nine-day tour.

> The excitement and exhaltation are too absorb-
> ing for you to notice that you are not getting
> enough sleep, or that you never get your food at
> the right time, or that you do not get a chance
> to take a bath, or do not even have time to read
> the newspapers thoroughly. It is impossible to
> describe to one who has not been on a trip of
> this kind the thrill of crowds of cheering people
> station after station, city after city, the ap-
> plause of ten thousand enthusiastic rooters in-
> side an auditorium or the shouts of a hundred
> thousand people in a ball park, the mounted po-
> lice holding back the crowds as the cars parade
> through the streets, the excitement and rush of
> getting out one speech and starting immediately
> on the next one.[14]

Most of the reporters assigned to the campaign train duly
noted Rosenman's presence. The McCormick press, however,
ignored his speechwriting activities and instead reported
that the Judge's presence had "occasioned speculation
that the President was perhaps seeking advice on what
steps to take concerning the Soviet airplane deal involving his son Eliot."[15] Nowhere, not even in the most violently anti-Roosevelt press was there speculation as to
whether Justice Rosenman's activities during the campaign
constituted the slightest violation of judicial ethics.

The Mid-Western tour was the only extended one of
the campaign. Roosevelt's other trips were one or two
day affairs for which his more important addresses were
prepared prior to departure. Rosenman considered the final major speech, delivered in Madison Square Garden, the
best of the campaign.[16] He, High, Corcoran, Corcoran's

constant collaborator Benjamin Cohen, and Roosevelt himself worked harder and spent more time on it than any
other address. According to one political commentator,
the collaborators were so divided as to how deeply they
should dip "their pens in vitriol," that "there was almost an outburst before Sam Rosenman could get agreement
on a completed draft."[17] Despite some apprehension that
the militant tone of the final draft might alienate uncommitted conservative voters, Roosevelt, three days after its delivery, achieved the most overwhelming electoral college triumph ever posted in a contested presidential election.

     In addition to whatever personal satisfaction
Rosenman received from his efforts during the campaign,
he was also rewarded with a prized Christmas gift from
the President; a set of cuff links, one link engraved
with the initials S.I.R., the other F.D.R. Heretofore,
only Roosevelt associates during his unsuccessful 1920
vice-presidential race had ever received such a gift.
The President, who looked upon the recipients as members
of some sort of special club, had instituted the custom
of having them gather at the White House for the President's birthday dinner at which they celebrated both
Roosevelt and their mutual friendship. The choice of
this particular gift was formal acknowledgment that the
Judge was not only an intimate political associate but
also an old and valued friend. Rosenman acknowledged the
cuff-links as the "nicest Xmas present I ever received."
Using the pretext that continuous attendance at court
made him feel "too strongly virtuous," he assured the
President that "if you think I can be helpful on any occasion in the coming weeks, months or years, I wish you
would call on me."[18]

     On January 29, 1937, Missy LeHand phoned Rosenman.
The Judge planned to be in Washington the following evening for a cuff-links dinner, and she requested that he
arrive a few hours earlier to attend a presidential conference whose nature she did not disclose. The Judge

complied with his instructions and shortly after reaching
the White House learned that the conferees would include
Donald Richberg, Attorney General Homer Cummings, and
Solicitor General Stanley Reed.[19]

Once the proceedings began it became apparent that
Roosevelt had seized upon a specific plan to reorganize
the United States Supreme Court. Rosenman had, of course,
been aware of Presidential dissatisfaction with recent
decisions restricting state and national regulation of
economic activities. As an advocate of both the New Deal
and judicial restraint Rosenman shared the President's
disappointment with the court and had indicated so in
private discussions. It was not until that conference,
however, that Rosenman was made privy to the precise plan.
His assignment was to draft a message presenting it to
Congress.

Although Judge Rosenman supported the President's
view that the number of Justices on the Court be enlarged,
the purpose for the reorganization plan, he resisted efforts to justify such action on the basis of an overworked
federal judiciary. Along with Donald Richberg and Stanley Reed, he believed it more advisable to emphasize
"that because of the age of the present justices, the
Court needed and could be given a more resilient outlook
by the addition of young men."[20] The argument of an
overworked federal judiciary had, however, a fatal appeal
to Roosevelt, and he insisted that Rosenman work out the
message giving an overcrowded docket as the prime reason
for the requested legislation.

Another problem was to designate the proper time
to release the message. The annual White House Judiciary
Dinner was scheduled for February 2, 1937. Since all the
conferees would be present, it was agreed that if the
plan could be kept secret until after that event, much
social embarrassment would be avoided. It was also believed important to release the plan prior to February 9,
when the constitutionality of the National Labor Relations

Act (Wagner Act) would be argued before the court. February 5, was the date chosen.[21]

Rosenman was holding court in New York City when the message was thrust upon the public. He was, he informed the President, praying even while listening to testimony.[22] His prayers not withstanding, immediate congressional, press, and public sentiment were against the plan. When it was learned that the Judge has assisted in the preparation of the message, some of the sentiment was directed against him. One syndicated columnist reported that "Sammy the Rose" had devised the entire court packing scheme,[23] while another attributed only the reasons advanced for the plan as the invention of his fertile brain.[24] The *Christian Free Press* proclaimed that the Supreme Court had been "destroyed by Jewry." According to this account, which was distributed to all Congressmen, Rosenman had taken his court plan from the Protocols of the Elders of Zion. The Protocols were purported to maintain that no one should "hold judicial office after fifty-five because old men hold more obstinately prejudiced opinions."[25] Some, who recognized the Protocols as disingenuous, thought the "real purpose" of the scheme might nonetheless be revealed if Rosenman were forced to give testimony before the Senate Judiciary Committee.[26] Close observers, sympathetic and otherwise, agreed that if the court plan passed, the forty-one year old Rosenman would stand an excellent chance of receiving one of the first appointments to the expanded bench.[27]

Criticism of the plan, the President, and the Judge himself did not alter Rosenman's conviction that passage was both desirable and possible. Insisting that newspaper reaction was not always synonymous with public opinion, he believed that there was an "overwhelming sentiment" that considered the proposed plan to be "the only way to break through the wall and get a real working democracy." He likened press response to the plan to press response to Roosevelt during the recent election campaign. "It is the grand opportunity of third and

fourth raters to make the first page by yelling at the
President. The louder they yell the bigger the space in
the newspapers." In this instance he underestimated the
degree to which editorial policy represented, if it did
not mold, public opinion. Disturbed that some New Deal
supporters remained uncommitted to the plan, Rosenman reported they doubted the method rather than the objectives
of court reorganization. Because Rosenman believed this
group to be composed in large part of "lawyers who instinctively, it appears, rebel at reliance on anything
but death to change a court," he advised the President to
emphasize that the method of reorganization proposed was
the only practical one and "that if the present plan
fails, everything really liberal is completely sunk for
decades."[28]

The number of New Dealers included among the opponents of the plan proved far greater than either Roosevelt or Rosenman estimated, and on March 9, Roosevelt delivered an address geared to win this group to his cause.
During the preparation of this address Rosenman included
much of what he had previously suggested. Discarding
the argument of an overworked judiciary, the President
now admitted his real reason for proposing reorganization
was his belief that the court had assumed the power to
pass on the wisdom as well as the constitutionality of
congressional acts, and he cited dissenting opinions registered by the Supreme Court to substantiate this charge.
Reorganization, he argued, would allow him to appoint
younger men--men who were more willing to move with the
times and would act as justices and allow the determination of policy, wise and otherwise, to the appropriate
legislatures. He then attempted to persuade his listen-
ers that the proposed plan was the only practical method
of reorganization.

The March speech was an effective argument, but it
was too little and too late to overcome the unfavorable
impression created by the February effort. The Senate
Judiciary Committee held extensive hearings on the bill,

during which Senator Burton J. Wheeler released a letter
from Chief Justice Hughes, concurred in by Justices
VanDevanter and Brandeis, which served to demolish Roosevelt's original argument that the court was unable to
keep pace with its calendar.[29] Finally, in mid-June the
committee voted unfavorably upon the plan, and the next
month the Senate voted overwhelmingly to return it to
committee. Although the bill was now dead, circumstances
had so altered since its original proposal that court reorganization could be rationalized as no longer essential.
On March 29, 1937, the Supreme Court had announced the
first in a series of decisions upholding New Deal legislation,[30] and in May, Justice Willis Van Devanter, a
staunch conservative, announced his retirement from the
court.[31] Roosevelt insured a continued pro-New Deal majority by appointing Alabama Senator Hugo Black in Van
Devanter's stead.

Despite assurances of the constitutionality of New
Deal legislation without recourse to the reorganization
plan,[32] rejection was a bitter personal defeat for Roosevelt. Control over Congress was not readily restored,
as evidenced by the rejection of two of the President's
major legislative programs later in the year.[33] Rosenman, who in retrospect would privately acknowledge Roosevelt had been "thoroughly beaten" and "completely humil-
iated,"[34] did not advance so dismal an interpretation to
the President. Certainly he was disappointed in defeat,
and of course he knew Roosevelt would try again, but:

> if nothing else comes of your message to Con-
> gress on the judiciary, than the...recent lib-
> eral decisions of the court which have done
> so much to repair the damage done by its for-
> mer decisions, the message will have earned
> its place among the historical documents of
> America which have done the most to shape
> its destiny and promote its progress.[35]

Chapter Seven

FOR THE RECORD

Thucydides, in Book I of *The Peloponnesian War*, compares certain speeches included in his history to those actually delivered. On some occasions Thucydides had been present; on other occasions he had had to rely upon reports. In all instances it had been quite impossible to "carry them [the speeches] word for word in one's memory," and Thucydides adopted the scheme of having his "speakers say what was in my opinion demanded of them by the various occasions, of course adhering as closely as possible to the general sense of what was really said."[1] Pericles' funeral oration and less familiar speeches designed for Brasidas, Nicias, Gylippus, and others--many of whom are remembered only through the words Thucydides would have them say--have provided source material for historians for almost 2,400 years. Subsequent historians held Thucydides' judgment in respect. No other available sources seemed so authoritative and complete. During the twentieth century, despite the availability of recording devices and the *New York Times*, Samuel I. Rosenman emerged as a Thucydides for the New Deal. Although Franklin Roosevelt deliberately set in motion the machinery which brought this about, it is highly improbable that he ever anticipated the full impact that Rosenman was to assert upon New Deal historiography.

The 1936 presidential campaign had reestablished the Judge's eminence among Roosevelt aides, and this time he had no intention of relinquishing his status. Preparations for the 1937 State of the Union Message, the in-

augural address, and court reorganization plan details
kept Rosenman in constant contact with the White House.
During increasingly frequent visits to Washington he
lodged there.   When in New York he relied upon telephone
conversations for direct access to the President.   During
a March call to discuss the impact of a court reorganization speech, Roosevelt suggested they publish a collection
of his speeches and other papers.   Ernest Lindley, the
President revealed, wanted to undertake the project, but
Rosenman already had the speeches through the 1932 campaign, and "we have the rest down here."   Why, the President asked, "should Lindley get the Royalties" when you
and I can do it 50-50?"   Despite some subsequent joshing
over whether this motivation was due to Roosevelt's
"*Dutch* blood," or as Rosenman suggested, an infusion of
his "Jewish blood,"[2] Lindley's scheme inadvertently suggested far grander opportunities.

The President conceived of the publication as only
part of a larger project--to establish a library at Hyde
Park which would ultimately serve as a repository for
all his papers and a center for the study of his administration and personal career.   After 1940, he suggested,
he would be returning to Hyde Park, where, with Rosenman's
aid, he could author his autobiography.[3]   In the meantime,
proceeds from the sale of the published papers would provide revenue to help underwrite the costs of the library.

Greeting the idea with enthusiasm, Rosenman immediately set to work preparing a multi-volume edition of
the President's speeches and other public papers.   Private letters, papers, and memoranda, they decided, would
not be included in the collection.   After drafting some
sample explanatory notes to supplement the public messages, Rosenman submitted his materials to Random House,
a contract was negotiated, and the plans to publish the
Roosevelt papers were made public.[4]   The plans for a
presidential library were not disclosed; they were, in
fact, masked in elaborate secrecy.

The decision to publish Roosevelt's official utterances was consistent with established New York precedents FDR had followed as Governor. Two volumes of his gubernatorial papers had been published prior to his election to the presidency, a third was made available in April, 1937, and a fourth was to appear in 1939.[5] Students of New York State history were thus accustomed to recent state papers readily available in published form. Franklin Roosevelt was, however, the first President to provide for the publication of his papers while he was still in office. The practice has since been formalized into law, but, editors subsequent to Rosenman have not been intimates of succeeding presidents.

The first volume of the Rosenman edition of the *Public Papers* consists largely of papers also included in the four volume gubernatorial series supplemented by some extemporaneous remarks made during the Hoover-Roosevelt interregnum. Each subsequent volume was devoted to a succeeding year. Portions of press conferences were also included and sometimes contained material which had originally been "off the record." In such instances Rosenman gave prior notification to the press so that he would not be in the position of having scooped the reporters on their own press conferences. The five volume set was only an installment, and the Judge disclosed plans to issue an additional volume "after each year of his [Roosevelt's] second administration."[6]

All modern Presidents expect that their papers will be subjected to intensive study. Roosevelt, however, was so historically conscious as to engage his principal speechwriter as the editor of his papers. Performing both these functions *simultaneously* provided Rosenman with an outlook and authority he would not have possessed had he been limited to either one of these tasks. His roles, intellectually and emotionally inextricable from each other, further confirmed his conviction that oral presentation was only the most obvious dimension to the task of bringing Roosevelt speeches to their intended audience.

Rosenman increasingly came to regard these speeches as
directed not only to the largest possible contemporary
public, but to future generations as well. Arguments as
to how some particular message might appear in the light
of history possessed a special potency on those infrequent occasions when Rosenman would insist either for or
against some particular course of action. In such instances, he insisted that Roosevelt must speak for the
record "irrespective" of what anyone else might do. The
President who once thought to tease a reporter with the
threat that his rather ill considered question would be
"going in Sam's book," was himself susceptible to such
tactics; and on at least one occasion the Judge succeeded
in gaining his way by applying them.[7]

     That Roosevelt should have selected Rosenman for
the job of editing his papers was regarded as a matter of
course. Among the most scholarly of Roosevelt intimates,
the Judge further qualified because he lacked any official
connection with the presidential administration. He insisted he had been "virtually conscripted" for the assignment.[8] Roosevelt, in a short general introduction to the
first volume, wrote that he knew "of no one better equipped for this task by training or by experience."[9] The
President's passion to have posterity view him in the
best possible light led him quite naturally to delegate
to his counsel the job of amassing the evidence. Not
only was Rosenman among those individuals most familiar
with his gubernatorial and presidential papers, but also,
despite the Judge's intense personal partisanship, he could
be relied upon to avoid the pitfalls of a campaign biographer. Moreover Rosenman was firm in the belief that
"more than any other President--perhaps more than any
other political figure in history--Franklin D. Roosevelt
used the spoken and written word to exercise leadership
and to carry out policies."[10] So profound a commitment
was ample insurance that Rosenman would regard his mission as an important one.

The Judge alleged that the idea of publication had
come to the President "after he had received thousands
of letters and inquiries asking if he had made particular statements on certain dates." Hereafter when people
wrote to the White House for such information or for
copies of speeches that were out of print, Rosenman explained, there would be a standard work to which they
might be referred.

Another avowed objective, one that has had an immense influence upon subsequent students of the New Deal,
was to "demonstrate the continuity and development of Mr.
Roosevelt's social and economic philosophy in the recent
years of his life and to show that the major outlines of
the New Deal should have been fully expected by those who
followed his career at Albany."[11] Central to this premise was the "Message Recommending a Relief Administration," which Roosevelt had delivered to an extraordinary
session of the New York Legislature in August, 1931. The
recommendation was, by and large, enacted into law. It
resulted in the establishment of a temporary agency to
expend state monies on public works for the employment of
residents of the State. Rosenman, who regarded the "Message" as a landmark in the history of governmental social
thinking in the United States, credited it with establishing the principle "that it is the duty of government to
use the combined resources of the nation to prevent dis-
tress and promote the general welfare of all the people."
In Rosenman's subsequent writings, he has cited this more
than any other single attribute as justification for his
labeling Roosevelt's gubernatorial administrations as the
Genesis of the New Deal.[12] Not noted, but also of more
than passing interest is that Harry Hopkins eventually
directed the New York agency's activities and was brought
to Washington to adapt its program to national purposes.

The only impassioned controversy sparked by the
volumes flamed prior to their publication. It blazed
briefly, but with an intensity usually associated with
works of an erotic nature. Elements of the press, ap-

palled that Roosevelt and Rosenman might realize personal
earnings from the publishing venture, vehemently denounced the scheme. Roosevelt was particularly sensitive to
this criticism, and directed Press Secretary Early to
announce that "not a penny from the net proceeds from the
newspaper syndication and the magazine publication will
go into the pockets either of the President or Judge
Rosenman." Unwilling to disclose the library project,
Early revealed that all such proceeds would be devoted
to a "useful public service" under government direction.[13]
The statement only stimulated the controversy. It was interpreted to mean that while the income from newspaper
and magazine sources would be contributed to Roosevelt's
"useful public service," book royalties were to be divided between Roosevelt and the Judge.[14] Rosenman's
share was alleged to be 35 percent.[15]

Only after he had deposited his royalty advance
from Random House in a special account earmarked for
Roosevelt's still undisclosed "useful public purpose" was
the controversy stilled.[16] A few weeks later, after the
volumes had been released, Roosevelt expressed his pleasure over the "exceptionally good" reviews and hoped that
his collaborator would feel them "some slight compensation for the months of drudgery which the editing entailed."[17]

An appraisal by Elmer Davis, published in the *Saturday Review of Literature*, was representative of the reviews to which Roosevelt referred. Davis, with only a
single casual reference to the Judge, described the work
as a "source book indispensable to any student of history
of the recent past or of the near future."[18] Commercial
success, however, did not follow the critical acclaim,
and when the *Public Papers* of Roosevelt's second presidential administration appeared in December, 1941, they necessarily bore the imprint of a different publisher:
Macmillan Company. These volumes were also well received.
Henry Steele Commager, ebullient over the "second installment of the great collection of public papers and address-

es which President Roosevelt and Samuel Rosenman have
prepared for us," thought, "from the point of view of
usefulness," the volumes constituted "the best job of
editing in the whole of our political literature."[19]
Again reviews were more impressive than sales records,
and when, in 1948, Rosenman produced the concluding volumes of the Roosevelt administrations, they appeared under
still another aegis: Harper and Brothers.

The publication of these final volumes, after Roosevelt's death revealed much about Rosenman's editorial responsibilities, which historians had not previously known.
Roosevelt, speaking in 1937, described the task of ready-
ing his papers for publication as involving glue and
shears but no writing[20]--rather disingenuous phrases by
which to describe any sizable editorial undertaking; particularly this one. The volumes contain forewords, pre-
faces, and extensive notes; and although some of these
were signed by Rosenman, most were either signed by or
otherwise ascribed to the President. Davis thought "the
notes made on many of the documents by the President himself" to be "possibly the most valuable part of the whole
publication."[21] The explanatory notes for the four volumes issued after Roosevelt's death were attributed to
Rosenman. It is now apparent that, notwithstanding their
appearance over the President's signature, the bulk of the
notes in the first nine volumes were also prepared by the
Judge. At least one historian has speculated as to "whether the Presidential contribution to the Notes in the *Public Papers* amounted to any more than the wielding of an
editorial pen over Rosenman drafts." He concluded that
even if "*that* was, in fact, the case, the Notes to the
first nine volumes have special interest because of the
presumption that every one of them had a close reading
by Franklin Roosevelt previous to publication, and especially because of the time of their appearance."[22] The
obvious and reasonable assumption, is that Roosevelt would
not have accepted responsibility for them had he not inspired or at the very least concurred in, the sentiments
expressed in the notes.

It would be of no particular value to calculate just how much of the material Roosevelt himself wrote. Moreover, all of the notes which Roosevelt did not write cannot be directly attributed to Rosenman. Other than Kenneth Hechler and Richard Salant who at different times formally assisted the Judge in preparation of the thirteen volumes,[23] account must also be taken of the research and literary efforts of numerous governmental agencies. In preparation for the first five volumes, letters were dispatched over the signature of the President's secretary to selected Washington bureaus requesting memoranda relating to their general activities for the years 1933 through 1936 as well as for specific background material for messages ultimately selected for inclusion in the *Public Papers*. From these Rosenman eventually compiled the notes for the first set. Now on deposit at the Roosevelt Library, these memoranda provide evidence of departmental contributions to the *Public Papers*, and also, in Rosenman's estimation, the best available materials on the activities of the early New Deal.[24] Although the typescripts and galleys indicate that on occasion Roosevelt altered Rosenman's quotations and revisions of the detailed departmental memoranda, there is no evidence that Roosevelt ever directly consulted the memoranda.

There was less departmental assistance in preparation of the papers of the second administration; and for the third and final set, Rosenman and personal aides relied almost exclusively upon their own research.[25] Rosenman's memoir of the seventeen years spanned by the *Public Papers*, *Working With Roosevelt*, originally conceived as an introduction to the last four volumes--serves as an important supplement to the entire series. Although not designed as a substitute for Roosevelt's abortive autobiography, it did contain some materials not quite categorized as public papers which political prudence as well as editorial format precluded from inclusion in the *Public Papers*. In most instances these were materials which serve to enhance the "liberal image" of the late President, and would doubtless have been revealed through the

autobiography. Roosevelt had intended to omit details of
his life story prior to his becoming Assistant Secretary
of the Navy as largely irrelevant to his latter career.
This was a judgment in which Rosenman largely concurred.[26]

Rosenman's own career since 1940 compensates somewhat for the death of Roosevelt and the lack of assistance
from the executive department in the editing of later
Public Papers. From 1940 through 1945, the Judge was
centrally involved in White House activities. Consequent-
ly, he not only possessed a more extensive personal file
but also a greater first hand knowledge of the President's
public expressions: many of which he had originally drafted with the aid of departmental memoranda. Furthermore,
since Rosenman articulated his public views of national
politics in a manner similar to *his* President, the selections of messages and *substance* of the notes pertaining
to the final volumes probably bear a distinct resemblance
to what would have appeared had Roosevelt been available
for "editorial duties." Thus carefully used, the final
four volumes provide autobiographical clues inherent in
the volumes published during Roosevelt's lifetime.[27]
Certainly, if a larger and more inclusive edition of
Roosevelt papers is ever attempted, the notes to the
first nine volumes would appropriately be included.

The ultimate value of the *Public Papers* depends
largely upon the reliability of the published documents
themselves, and a first consideration for any evaluation
is how closely the published documents correspond to what
was really said or issued by the President at the time.
Rosenman did not regard the reproduction of verbatim
transcripts--for their own sake--as his primary editorial
duty. Some of the documents he selected for publication
were, in his judgment, either too long or possessed of
too ephemeral interest to merit reprinting in their entirety. Where there are extensive omissions from speeches
and press conferences, Rosenman labeled the selection an
excerpt and indicated the point of omission with three
dots.[28] There is, however, no indication as to how ex-

tensive any deletion is. In Roosevelt's gubernatorial
papers, published by New York State;, there is no indication of deletions; and thus, despite their wealth of material on his gubernatorial years, the reader is never
certain whether he is reading a complete text.[29]

The President's propensity to deviate from his prepared text, coupled with Rosenman's failure to discern
such deviations in every instance, has received some critical attention. Charles A. Beard, the first historian
to report a textual discrepancy, pointed out that in the
Public Papers, the first sentence of Roosevelt's 1933 inaugural address differed from some other published accounts.[30] After some checking, Rosenman discovered his
Public Papers version to be incorrect. The Judge had
relied upon the official copy of the address, which had
been issued by the Government Printing Office, and he
concluded that "the President added the sentence after
he [Roosevelt] had sent the mimeographed speech to the
printing office." Rosenman assured Beard that errors of
this sort were not likely to recur.

> In subsequent speeches a stenographer took
> down each speech as delivered and I was, there-
> fore, able to correct the mimeographed releases
> of speeches with the stenographic notes so as
> to include any substantial alteration in the
> mimeographed copy. However, there was no of-
> ficial stenographer who took down the First
> Inaugural with that in mind.[31]

Possessing stenographic notes of subsequent speeches
did not, however, prompt Rosenman into reproducing those
speeches verbatim. In addition to indicated deletions
from the texts the Judge also omitted certain *ad-libs*
without indicating that he had made changes. He reasoned
that since readers couldn't realize today "the context in
which it [the *ad-lib*] was delivered twenty years ago,"
they would find such passages "almost silly." He assumed
that to reprint them under such circumstances would pro-

duce an even greater distortion of the speech than to delete them entirely, and often chose the latter alternative. Occasionally he included the material after adjusting the grammar.[32]

This editorial procedure has prompted comment. The most extreme, which premises that "the imprint of Sam Rosenman [is] probably to be found on more of the Roosevelt utterances than any individual besides F.D.R. himself,"[33] concludes that since Rosenman appears to have redrafted Roosevelt's speeches after, as well as before delivery, the Roosevelt which emerges from the *Public Papers* is a composite of Roosevelt and Rosenman rather than a reflection of the President himself. While not commenting directly upon this point, which he regarded as approaching an indictment of his integrity, the Judge has disclaimed any expectation that his work should serve as a definitive collection. "To really do a complete job," he once explained, "no one has the right to do what I did."[34] It would be an impossible task to apply any quantitative measure to any distortions which Rosenman's emendations may have corrected or produced. The omission at the opening of Roosevelt's 1933 inaugural remains the most spectacular deviation noted.[35]

The further question remains whether Rosenman's selectivity in the choice of documents favored the Roosevelt administrations. The Judge has accepted the responsibility for the content of the volumes. "Once we had gotten up the idea," he has since recalled, "it was all practically done by me." *All* included the selection of materials, the idea of the explanatory notes, the topical tables, and all the other mechanical aids. Although it was the Judge who usually determined for the President what they would include and exclude, he did not have *carte blanche* in the matter. No commercial publisher, Rosenman reasoned, would ever "include thousands of executive orders or proclamations which had no general policy effect."[36] To exclude the least consequential of Roosevelt's public papers hardly served to diminish the

President's stature as a far-sighted and articulate
spokesman for pertinent liberal principles. Moreover,
those messages which were most illustrative of Roosevelt's
thinking and informative as to his programs were usually,
at least in Rosenman's opinion, the messages which the
President and his speechwriters most carefully prepared
and from which Roosevelt was least likely to deviate.

The extensive use of the *Public Papers* has had a
profound effect upon subsequent scholarship. Since the
initial installment in 1938, it has constituted the most
complete and authoritative collection of New Deal materials readily available. The Roosevelt Library was officially dedicated in November, 1939, but it was not until 1947 that it acquired actual physical possession of
the Roosevelt papers. By then, nine volumes of the *Public Papers* and numerous studies of the New Deal had already been published. A review of Basil Rauch's *History
of the New Deal*, the most important of these latter works,
is critical of Professor Rauch for relying too heavily on
the *Public Papers*, while authors of less significant publications have been rebuked for not using them enough.
A number of government printings as well as commercially
published Roosevelt collections have been compiled from
the Roosevelt volumes; and in some instances, the editors
have borrowed from the notes as well.[37]

Scholars who must go beyond Rosenman's collection
have, for some time, had such materials available to
them at the Roosevelt Library. Holdings relevant to a
more complete study of F.D.R.'s papers are, however, so
immense, that the Rosenman volumes, when not used as a
source, serve as an indispensable guide. The task of
compiling a definitive edition of Roosevelt's papers
staggers the imagination. Beyond the power of any single
scholar in any single lifetime, it will require a committee effort, involve many years, and necessitate the
publication of the largest single set of papers yet attempted. The sheer bulk of such a collection, if not
prohibitive in scope, would impose an inherent restric-

tion on its usefulness. Given such prospects, the Rosenman volumes seem destined to retain their eminence as the
principal point of departure for studies of the New Deal
for some time to come.

Despite the subsequent appearance of various memoirs
and greater accessibility to source materials which
Rosenman excluded from the *Public Papers*, either unwit-
tingly or by design, the sense of order which his selection imposes upon the New Deal has not been rejected by
more recent research. Davis believed the "tremendous
historical drama" as depicted in the *Public Papers* was
determined "not by any deliberate arrangement but by the
logic of events."[38] Even those historians who hold that
any logic in history is imposed by the person who selects
and describes events have not repudiated Rosenman's original overview. There have been modifications, qualifications, and refinements, but the intellectual framework
which the Rosenman volumes provided has remained sufficient to support subsequent interpretations of the New
Deal. In retrospect it has become apparent that the most
ambitious of the historian's tasks--to provide a working
synthesis for any major political occurrence--had been
achieved even before the Roosevelt Library opened its
holdings to interested scholars.[39]

Rosenman's most important efforts toward the actual
operation of the Library[40] were conducted jointly with
Grace Tully, Roosevelt's Private Secretary. Named by
Roosevelt as executors of his papers, the duty devolved
upon them, after the President's death, to select those
materials to be made immediately available and those
papers which would be temporarily closed. Eventually
eight categories of papers were sealed. Probably most
important were those documents "prejudicial to the maintenance of friendly relations with foreign states," and
"papers dealing with...personal affairs of named individuals."[41] The importance of the first category is self-
evident. The second category may contain interesting
sidelights on Gubernatorial, New Deal, and World War II

personalities. Whether it contains material significant
enough to alter existing impressions is a question yet
to be answered.

However, the questions that were answered by the
appearance of the *Public Papers* in 1938 established Rosenman as the earliest and foremost scholar of the New Deal.
Roosevelt's assertion that the Judge knew "more about my
papers than anyone else," can hardly bear challenge.[42]
Other students, both inside and outside the administration, turned increasingly to him for encouragment and aid:
and Roosevelt at times even used the Judge as an *alter
ego* to grant biographical interviews and to provide other
source data.[43] Rosenman retained some of this role for
over a quarter century after Roosevelt's death. Yet even
those who regard history written by survivors as inher-
ently conspiratorial seldom predicate that the "Roosevelt-
Rosenman conspiracy" was motivated by a conscious will to
deceive.

By 1939 it had become of paramount significance to
the President that Rosenman's continuous research on the
Public Papers combined with his speechwriting activities
provided the Judge with a uniquely comprehensive perspective of administrative operations. Determined to utilize
this perspective in war mobilization efforts, Roosevelt
increasingly employed the Judge to assist in the creation
and reorganization of defense agencies. Rosenman relished
these opportunities and regarded his special task as one
of helping to mold a bureaucracy capable of coping with
wartime problems with a minimum curtailment of that New
Deal legislation and philosophy he was detailing with
such dedication in the *Public Papers*.

Chapter Eight

FORTUITOUS PHRASES

On January 21, 1940 Henry L. Stimson wrote United
States Justice Felix Frankfurter of a New York case in
which Stimson was counsel. His client was seeking multi-
million dollar damages against a major oil company, and
the proceedings were long and agonizingly complex. Frankfurter knew the presiding judge, so Stimson appended an
appraisal of the trial. "Rosenman," he wrote, "is one
of the best judges I have ever been before; very patient
and courteous and quick and accurate with his ruling."[1]

Justice Rosenman also took note of Henry Stimson.
Stimson was already 73 years old and left most of the
trial work to a younger associate.[2] He was, nonetheless,
an awesome personality. Secretary of War under William
Howard Taft when Rosenman was still a school boy, he had
last held high public office as Secretary of State under
Herbert Hoover. The often cited Stimson Doctrine, providing for non-recognition of territories obtained by
acts of aggression, had been announced by Stimson in consequence of Japan's 1931 invasion of Manchuria, and non-
recognition of Manchuria was still popular in the United
States. True, it had not inhibited subsequent Japanese
territorial expansion, but it had put the United States
on record as opposing it. It was assumed there was little
more the United States could do, especially since it was
generally supposed that the principal foreign threat to
American security emanated not from Asia but from Europe.

In September, 1939, European hostilities had been
formally declared and during 1940 Hitler succeeded in
subjecting almost the entire continent to German power.
Despite the belief of a vast majority of Americans that
this German power was hostile to United States' interests,
the biggest political issue of 1940 was whether "that man
in the White House" would run for a third term. Some
observers conjured important clues to Roosevelt's political intentions from Rosenman's personal activities.

The Judge's reticence to disclose information he
obviously possessed had earned him such sobriquets as
"the mystery man of the New Deal", "the New Deal enigma",
and the "Number one Anonym." It had also led reporters
to assume he knew a great deal more than he actually did.
Early in 1939, Dorothy Kilgallen, a widely syndicated
columnist, predicted the Judge would soon resign from
the bench to reenter private practice. Walter Winchell,
a columnist with an even wider audience, revealed that
the resignation would occur only if the President decided
not to run for reelection. In that event, Winchell disclosed, Roosevelt would at some later date, join the law
firm Rosenman was to establish.[3]

The Judge was himself uncertain as to Roosevelt's
intentions, and as late as Fall 1939, the President acted
out preparations for an imminent return to private life.
One such exercise was to arrange for the Rosenmans to
view property he hoped they might purchase near his Hyde
Park estate. If they were neighbors, he explained, it
would simplify matters "when I come up here next year,
[and] we can work on the papers together." Although the
Rosenmans never purchased the property, the Judge was
nonetheless convinced that prior to the German invasion
of Norway (April 1940), Roosevelt expected to retire after his second term, and that subsequent events led the
President to reconsider.[4]

Only after he learned that Roosevelt intended to
appoint prominent Republicans to head the War and Navy

Departments was Rosenman *certain* the President would seek a
third term. Announcing the cabinet appointments on the eve
of the Republican nominating convention, as Roosevelt intended to do, had obvious political advantages. The very
fact that respected Republicans accepted such responsibilities under Roosevelt would blunt partisan criticism
of military preparedness in the forthcoming campaign, and
might even elevate support for an extensive mobilization
program to bipartisan status. Doubtless, this was one of
the major attractions of the plan, and since the reelection of Roosevelt and national mobilization were, by
Rosenman's standards, the nation's first priorities, he
was enthusiastic with the overall plan.

Felix Frankfurter not only shared Rosenman's views
of the primacy of mobilization needs, but, in addition,
had promoted the candidacy of Henry Stimson as Secretary
of War. Hearing rumors that F.D.R. intended to appoint
Fiorello LaGuardia, he phoned Rosenman, and as he anticipated, Rosenman was distressed by the news. Unlike
Frankfurter the New York Judge did not have his own candidate, but questioned LaGuardia's competence. "While
the duties of Mayor [of New York City] demanded qualities
LaGuardia may have possessed in profusion," Rosenman
doubted these were the same qualities essential to a good
Secretary of War.[5]

As a general rule Rosenman never went to Washington
unless invited and never offered his opinion unless asked.
In this instance he made an exception and visited with
the President for the sole purpose of expressing his unsolicited disapproval of the prospective appointment.
Others, including Governor Lehman, also opposed naming
LaGuardia as Secretary of War, and Roosevelt's ultimate
selection of Henry Stimson was a more satisfactory choice
to the President's New York State advisors and Felix
Frankfurter as well.[6]

Roosevelt, appreciating that LaGuardia would be
sorely disappointed by his rejection, felt obliged to

reveal his change of plans at a personal meeting. The
President was seldom forceful in such circumstances and
in a characteristic though ludicrous attempt to absolve
himself from culpability told the Mayor he had been forced
into the decision by Rosenman's veto, an explanation that
served to publicize and magnify Rosenman's efforts.[7]
Moreover, while White House correspondents might not know
of Frankfurter's precise role in the affair, his public
support for Stimson lent credence to reports of a sometimes formidable personal alliance between the two jurists.
Specific illustrations collaged by the press to attempt
to document their collaboration were often either exaggerations or made from whole cloth. But, especially after the Spring of 1940, Rosenman did frequently consult
Frankfurter on speechwriting and related policy matters.[8]
Hostile interpreters termed it a conspiracy.

Although Rosenman was young enough to have been a
student of Frankfurter's, they met as peers. During
Roosevelt's first gubernatorial administration the then
Harvard Law professor had singled out a commutation order
in which the Governor had set aside a death penalty as
meriting "an honored place in the history of the pardoning
power," and Roosevelt soon after introduced Rosenman to
Frankfurter as the commutation author.[9] From then on they
corresponded directly and met socially. Roosevelt, however, continued to serve as the linchpin of their association.

Collaborations between Rosenman and Frankfurter were
often depicted as sententious affairs, but they were not
without their lighter moments. One such occasion was
Roosevelt's second presidential inaugural. They attended
with their wives and the Rosenman children and viewed the
proceedings huddled beneath umbrellas with rain and sleet
pelting their faces. Cold and wet by the end of the
ceremony they had set up a temporary refuge in the Senate
Office Building, when one of the Rosenman children com-
plained of a pungent odor. An investigation revealed the
source to be Professor Frankfurter's wet shoes which he

had set to dry atop a radiator. The shoes not only stank,
but also had curled in at the toes. After a provident
custodian miraculously restored them to serviceable condition, the party prepared to depart while Rosenman sought
to leave a few dollars for the help. Frankfurter impor-
tuned Rosenman to do no such thing. He feared the custodian would be offended by a money offering and recommended a copy of the professor's latest book as a more
appropriate reward. In this particular instance of divided counsel, Rosenman's view prevailed.[10]

Upon politically weightier matters their views were
usually quite close, and Rosenman welcomed Frankfurter's
recommendations, solicited and otherwise, which he continued to receive over a wide range of matters after
Frankfurter ascended to the United States Supreme Court.
It was incidentally, in preparation for Senate hearings
on this judicial confirmation in January, 1939, that
Rosenman's friendship proved most comforting. During the
weekend after his nomination, Frankfurter called from Cam-
bridge, and, in a tone more desperate than the situation
seemed to warrant, elaborated upon a potential stumbling
block to his Senate confirmation. Shortly after his
twelfth birthday he had emigrated with his parents from
Austria. As a minor he had automatically attained citizenship when his parents were naturalized some few years
later. In such circumstances the law maintained that if
questions of citizenship were to arise the burden fell
upon the alleged minor to provide he was indeed a minor
at the time his parents were naturalized. Frankfurter
possessed no documentation of his age and therefore no
legal proof of his citizenship. Moreover, he was convinced that Senator Kenneth McKeller knew this and would
grasp upon the "technicality" to block his confirmation.
Frankfurter had resided in New York City through his college years, and Rosenman was confident finding some proof
of age would not be especially difficult. He began by
checking upon Frankfurter's elementary and high school
records. In both instances the records had been transferred to a central warehouse, and the warehouse had since

burned down. The City College of New York, Frankfurter's
alma mater, still had his records, but there was nothing
in them that could provide legal proof of age. The initial Senate hearings were scheduled for Tuesday and it
was already Saturday; Rosenman was beginning to sense
something of his friend's desperation.

The Immigration service was the logical next step,
but Rosenman knew the service neither issued certificates
of arrival nor was required to keep extensive records until 1906. Hoping there might nonetheless be some record
of Frankfurter's entry into the United States, Rosenman
phoned Secretary of the Treasury Morgenthau for assistance. After some checking of his own, Morgenthau located
a warehouse in which the customs manifests for the period
in question were stored. Since the next day was a Sunday,
Morgenthau would, he assured Rosenman, initiate a thorough
search the first thing Monday morning. Rosenman demurred.
A subcommittee hearing was scheduled for Tuesday morning
and no one really knew how long it would take to locate
the manifest or even whether it would contain the information they wanted. The Secretary agreed that under the
circumstances it would be prudent to begin the search
Sunday. The manifest was uncovered early that morning
and itemized, among other things the luggage of Felix
Frankfurter, "age 12." For Rosenman the eventual unanimous Senate confirmation was anti-climactic. The high
drama was in the favor he had been able to do for Felix.

In January, 1939, when Roosevelt had submitted
Frankfurter's name to the Senate, he believed he was embarking upon his final two years in office. By the eve
of the Democratic National Convention (June 1940), his
political expectations had altered radically. He had
decided upon a third term and was virtually certain of
nomination. Now the key concerns were how to announce
his candidacy and who his running mate would be. When on
July 10, Rosenman dutifully arrived at the White House
for a working vacation, neither of these questions had
been resolved. Since Roosevelt had made no formal decla-

ration of his intentions, Rosenman's appearance was itself interpreted as further evidence Roosevelt had decided to make the race since his "political counsellor of
former times" could be expected to assist in the preparation of an acceptance speech.[12]

Roosevelt had planned to formally reveal his candidacy through House Speaker William Bankhead. As convention keynoter, it would be appropriate for Bankhead to
read the assembled delegates a message from the President
asserting that he had no "wish or purpose to remain in
the office of President, or indeed in any public office
after next January."[13] By not declaring that he would
refuse the nomination if tendered, he would in effect be
announcing his candidacy. The delegates could either recognize this fact or be apprised of it. The President,
who had earlier neglected to withdraw his name from some
important primaries, had no illusions that there was any
such thing as a *bona fide* draft at a national convention.
He was, nonetheless, unwilling to create the appearance
of actively soliciting the nomination. When it became apparent that James Farley would stage a fight against the
nomination, albeit an ineffective one, Roosevelt determined it would enhance his stature as a draft candidate
if he formally released all delegates pledged to him.
Rosenman, who had anticipated this strategy, happened to
be carrying such a letter in his brief case, and the letter to Bankhead was amended to contain the release.[14]

Roosevelt's aides at the Chicago convention feared
Farley's strength and advised against the President sending any message. Rosenman never shared this view, and
apparently neither did Roosevelt. The President insisted
upon the message for the "purposes of History." He wanted
it as part of the written record that he was not an active
candidate for office, and to make it "clear that all
delegates to this convention are free to vote for any
candidate." In view of Bankhead's evident coolness to
Roosevelt's candidacy, however, the President was persuaded to entrust the message to Senator Alben Barkley.
Barkley, in his capacity as Permanent Chairman, read it

before the convention during the proceedings of the second day. Phrased so as to appear as a statement prepared
by the Senator and released with the President's approval,
nothing so attests to the significance which Roosevelt
and Rosenman attributed to it than that it was the only
indirect utterance of F.D.R. to be included in the *Public Papers.*[15]

Despite the expected opposition, Roosevelt was
easily renominated on the first ballot with a total large
enough to dispel any illusion of a party split and adequate enough to enable him to maintain the pose of a reluctant but acquiescent public servant. To secure the
nomination of his Vice Presidential designee was a more
difficult matter.

Harry Hopkins had alerted Rosenman to the President's
preference for Henry Wallace the day after the Judge arrived in Washington. It was not a choice with which the
Judge initially found fault. "Wallace," he has written,
"was then an out-and-out New Dealer, in whose hands the
program of the New Deal--domestic and international--would
be safe." His own role in the Wallace selection was, however, a passive one. The President, confronted with evidence that the convention delegates might rebel against
Wallace and instead nominate a running mate who was unsympathetic to much of his program, presumably Bankhead, prepared to decline his own nomination. Drafting a note to
that effect, he handed it on to Rosenman to prepare for
possible release. The Judge opposed the idea, but nonetheless worked over the declination statement while its
substance was "leaked" to the convention leadership. The
subsequent nomination of Wallace after the first roll
call rendered its formal transmission superfluous. Wallace,
however, who had hoped to deliver an acceptance speech,
was persuaded by Harry Hopkins "not to show himself."[16]

During the greater part of Rosenman's stay at the
White House he had been occupied in the preparation of
Roosevelt's acceptance address and a party platform. Just

what additional activities might be required of him during the course of the campaign were not made specific. Roosevelt had announced in his acceptance address that although he expected to make his "usual periodic reports to the country through the medium of press conferences and radio talks," he did not "have the time or inclination to engage in purely political debate." He would, however, "never be loath to call the attention of the nation to deliberate or unwitting falsification of fact which are sometimes made by political candidates."[17]

Accepting the spirit of Roosevelt's apolitical pose and uncertain whether his services would be further required, Rosenman left Washington to join his family on an extended vacation trip. He remained with them until the first week in September when Missy LeHand and Harry Hopkins phoned him in Portland, Oregon, to request his return to Washington to work on a campaign speech; a speech scheduled for delivery on September 11, to the annual convention of the Teamsters' Union. The Judge arrived back in New York within two days. Learning that the President was in Hyde Park, he went directly to the Roosevelt home to begin work.[18]

The Teamster Address was classified by the Roosevelt camp as nonpolitical and the President withheld formal acknowledgment that he would actively campaign until October 18. On that date, the White House issued a formal statement that owing to "a systematic program of falsification of fact by the opposition," Roosevelt had decided to make five political speeches. That the candidate had reserved such a "right" in his acceptance address was carefully underscored.[19] While it was on the basis of this reservation that Roosevelt justified his avowedly political activities, it was quite obviously the growing popularity of Wendell Wilkie, the Republican presidential candidate, that provided the motivation. Rosenman never doubted that Roosevelt would not "have made the campaign he did in 1940 if Wilkie had not been making such great headway."[20]

In light of the President's newly ambitious speaking schedule, Rosenman disclosed that his own campaign
duties would necessitate Herculean labors he was quite
frankly incapable of completing. Court had been resumed
after its summer recess, and Rosenman's judicial responsibilities, theoretically requiring his full attention,
would certainly require much of his time. To complicate
matters further, the Judge had come to constitute the entire presidential speechwriting team. Stanley High, his
collaborator during the 1936 camapign, had been exiled
from the White House soon after the elections as a result of articles he had written for national magazines.
In his capacity as a professional journalist, High had
prognosticated that the President's discontent with conservatives holding office under the Democratic banner
might lead him into efforts to remold his party.[21] Vice
President Garner, a prototype for the conservative Democrats to which High was referring, found the articles
particularly offensive, and along with like-minded Congressman, demanded High's dismissal. Roosevelt complied,
and Rosenman thought the dismissal appropriate. He had
always maintainted it was "a mistake" for a speechwriter
to make "public utterances about current political affairs." One could not do this and expect "to remain part
of the intimate White House group."[22] He preferred,
therefore, that High's successor not be a professional
journalist.

The services of Thomas Corcoran were also no longer
available. Through his aggressive tactics Corcoran had
gained the animosity of party leaders such as Farley and
Flynn, and, despite his fanatical adherence to Roosevelt's
policies, he fell an election-year victim to party harmony.
Simultaneously, and as a direct result of Corcoran's decline, Benjamin Cohen, his intimate associate, also experienced a temporary exclusion from presidential circles.

Harry Hopkins could be expected to lend occasional
assistance, but his other assignments precluded a large
scale personal involvement in writing speeches, and, after

conferring with Rosenman, Hopkins agreed to locate a new literary collaborator for the Judge. His search culminated in the recruitment of Robert Sherwood, a successful politically oriented playwright, whom he introduced to Rosenman while the latter was at home working upon a presidential Columbus Day address. The three men then engaged in easy conversation until Rosenman broke it off with the dramatic announcement, "Well gentlemen--there comes a time in the life of every speech when it's got to be written." The speech marked Sherwood's debut as a ghostwriter. Combining a facile pen and an easy going personality, the Judge enjoyed working with him more than any other speechwriter.[23] They remained collaborators until after Roosevelt's death.

In 1940 their major assignment was to prepare the five "campaign" speeches for the President to deliver in the two weeks before election. Of these, the address given in Cleveland on November 2, Rosenman designated the best of all Roosevelt orations. "The contents expressed the President's hopes, philosophy, and aspirations; it laid out a blueprint for the America of the future as he would wish it." Furthermore Roosevelt's "delivery in this speech," the Judge has written, "was better than in any other I heard him make." Other Roosevelt aficionados have echoed this assessment.[24]

Even more effective as a partisan political effort, however, was a Madison Square Garden speech for October 28. Rosenman and Sherwood had hoped to saddle Republican leadership with charges of opposition to Roosevelt's mobilization and military aid programs. To emphasize this charge they selected Joe Martin, Hamilton Fish, and Bruce Barton as three Republican legislators whose voting records were consistently at odds with the President's proposals. The Embargo Act had been repealed despite Republican opposition, and among the opponents of repeal were, they enounced, "now wait, a perfectly beautiful rhythm. Congressmen Martin, Barton and Fish." They further insisted that "Great Britain would never have received an

ounce of help from us--if the decision had been left to
Martin, Barton, and Fish."[25] The "fortuitous catch phrase"
was so well received that it was repeated throughout the
rest of the campaign, often with the audience anticipating its carefully staged intonation and participating as
in a choral reading. Willkie was reported to have said
that when he "heard the President hang the isolationist
votes of Martin, Barton, and Fish on me, and get away
with it, I knew I was licked." Barton, then a candidate
for the Senate from New York likewise credited the catch
phrase with being an important factor in his defeat. Joe
Martin, Willkies's campaign manager who escaped personal
defeat, nevertheless also regarded it as a political liability.[26]

        For a time Rosenman feared the President might, in
the person of Henry Wallace, also be saddled with a significant political liability. Never doubting the Vice-
presidential candidate's committment to Roosevelt, both
Rosenman and Hopkins concluded that certain of Wallace's
non-ideological indiscretions jeopardized the success of
the Democratic ticket.

        Soon after the Democratic Nominating convention, it
was rumored that an officer of the Republican National
Committee had come into possession of letters Wallace had
written to a Dr. Nicholas Roerich. Roerich, who at some
time had exercised influence over Wallace, was a White
Russian mystic who styled himself as the exclusive representative of the White Brotherhood of the East. The
letters which Wallace had written to Roerich, whom he
often addressed as Dear Guru, were replete with cabalist-
ic references and other mystical allusions, and Rosenman
feared that "the contents of some of them might well have
been used to expose Wallace to ridicule if published."
The situation was complicated by the fact that Wallace,
who was apparently familiar with the committeeman's holdings, admitted that some but by no means all of the Guru
letters were authentic. The most damaging carried a typewritten rather than an autographed signature, and the can-

didate insisted that most of those with typewritten signatures were forgeries. Despite Wallace's disclaimers,
Rosenman and Hopkins maintained that the existence of
any such letters constituted a heavy liability to the
Roosevelt campaign. Sometime late in September they
brought the matter to the attention of the President--
along with the extraordinary recommendation to discard
Wallace as his running mate. Roosevelt was no where near
as disturbed by the possible publication of the Guru letters as his aides and summarily dismissed any suggestion
to dump Wallace.[27] In the context of the political situation there was little else he could have done, even had
he desired to do otherwise, which is doubtful.

Fortunately for both Roosevelt and Rosenman, the
Judge's other recommendations were without exception less
precipitous, and his judgments were often imposed *because*
of his forebearance under stress. Accompanying Roosevelt
through most of the campaign, his judicial probity was a
force in dissuading the President from impulsive actions
which at any time other than the stimulus of a campaign
might seem inappropriate. One such instance involved
Steve Early, who became a center of controversy after a
fracas involving a Black New York City patrolman. Roosevelt's annoyance over the original incident was compounded
by subsequent Republican efforts to convert it to political advantage as an indication of the President's anti-
Negro bias. Tempted to dismiss the incident itself and
to concentrate on what he regarded as the larger hypo-
critical charges, he instead permitted Rosenman to chart
a different course. Except for publicly requesting the
Judge to conduct an investigation, the President personally remained aloof.

Rosenman's report exonerated everyone. The incident
had occurred shortly after Roosevelt's Madison Square Garden address when three patrolmen, acting under orders as
they understood them, blocked Early, other White House
staff, and newsmen from the Presidential train. Early
protested, and in some jostling and shoving, a policeman,

James Sloan, was seriously injured. That Early had kicked
the patrolman was established beyond any doubt. Since the
"accident" was "void of malice," however, Rosenman suggested an apology from Early as the most appropriate remedy. Patrolman Sloan not only accepted the verdict graciously, but had earlier cooperated with Rosenman in
turning the investigation to Roosevelt's advantage. In a
well publicized written release, Sloan castigated Republican efforts to turn him "against our great President
who has done so much for my race," and announced his intention "to vote for Mr. Roosevelt regardless of what his
secretary may have done."[28]

While there was doubtless some disingenuousness on
all sides, the affair itself was hardly all sound and
fury empty of significance. The fact that a President of
the United States would entertain charges by a Black
against a member of his personal staff--especially a south-
erner--was news in 1940. Furthermore, while the attacks
arising from the incident ceased on Election Day, the issue itself was not dropped until December when Patrolman
Sloan publicly accepted Early's apology and "cast all
thoughts of the affair into the sea of forgetfulness in
the midst of the joy that has come to me [Sloan] and my
family over the reelection of President Roosevelt."[29]

Other similar Rosenman contributions must be determined indirectly; yet statements Roosevelt did not make
or provocations that did not grow into ugly incidents lend
themselves to documentation. Furthermore, Roosevelt was
never solely dependent upon Rosenman for such advice although he did value and appreciate it. Shortly after the
election he commended the Judge for "how very much of a
help" he had been, "not only in the aiding of the draftsmanship, but also in helping me to keep both feet on the
ground."[30]

Post-election exchanges of letters had by now acquired an element of ritual, but Rosenman never regarded
his own note to Roosevelt as a perfunctory gesture or 1940

as just another election year. He had tried "to be objective" and to "forget personal relationships," yet he
was nonetheless convinced that "it was this election
alone which has saved, for a time at least, the kind of
America I want my children to live in--perhaps the only
kind in which they would be permitted to live at all."[31]

Despite the extravagant rhetoric, there is no reason to doubt Rosenman's sincerity or passion. It had
been a long time since he had held a detached and indifferent view of Roosevelt's candidacies, and his personal
commitment to the President had grown and intensified
over the years. Nonetheless he did believe there was
something special about the 1940 elections; a something
illustrated by the fact he assumed his concern over whether his children "would be permitted to live at all" would
be accepted literally. Such an interpretation, unthink-
able in 1928, had become increasingly credible with the
rise of Hitler who combined in his person a worldwide
threat both to political liberty and the very existence
of a Jewish people. There were also virulent forms of
domestic anti-Semitism with which to contend. Some hoped
to blunt its effectiveness through Jewish self-denial. A
practical application of this formula was represented by
a Jewish delegation requesting that Roosevelt not appoint
Felix Frankfurter to the Supreme Court for fear the appointment might further stimulate anti-Semitic outbursts.[32]
Rosenman rejected such tactics as unwarranted appeasement
and instead affirmed Judaism as traditionally American.
Education in a specific religion was so thoroughly American, he avowed, that it was "the duty of an American Jew
to give his child a religious education." The first duty
of every American--Christian or Jew was to America."[33]
There was, he insisted at every opportunity, no inherent
social, political, or economic distinction in interests
between American Jews and other Americans; nor should
there ever be.

Such a doctrine made special pleadings for particular minorities suspect, and especially suspect were

special pleadings for co-religionist nationals of other
countries. Yet even apart from any specific identity
with particular persecuted minorities, humanitarian in-
stincts impelled some form of government action. The appropriate American response would require no discrimination; either against or in behalf of Jews. On this point
Rosenman's views exemplified the American Jewish Committee
of which he was a director.

During December, 1938, he outlined his position to
the President through an unsolicited memorandum on the
"refugee problem." Any increase in immigration quotas,
he opined, was "highly inadvisable." To begin with,
larger quotas would hardly "scratch even the surface of
the problem," and the then high level of unemployment
"makes it impossible even if guarantee is given against
refugees becoming a public charge." Further the "opposition and debate" such a proposal would engender "will delay any other comprehensive solution." If quotas were
somehow raised, "it would merely produce a 'Jewish problem' in the countries increasing the quota." Rosenman's
recommendation was to create a "new and undeveloped land
in Africa and South America...a new haven of refuge for
all victims of persecution similar to America in the
17th century." It was stressed that such a program should
not be restricted to any race or nation, but must ultimately involve all central Europe. "Private funds in huge
quantities can be raised," but the program required government assistance.[34] The memo was followed by further
discussions. Within a year the outbreak of World War II
intensified the refugee problem while simultaneously re-
legating it to even less immediate consideration.

Rosenman's solution would have required years, more
properly decades, to implement, and it is now apparent
there was no surfeit of time. Yet this spectacular mis-
calculation was widely shared, not only in the United
States,[35] but among European Jewry as well; with tragic
consequences even for those capable of influencing their
ultimate destiny. In addition to efforts toward a massive

government sponsored resettlement program, numerous United
States citizens worked through existing immigration laws
to assist the flight of prominent European emigres and
more obscure personal relatives. Among those assisted
by the Rosenmans was a first cousin, an ambitious and
well educated nephew of Sam's mother. He had emigrated
from Poland to the United States in April 1939, and
planned to have his wife and three children join him after
he had become acclimated to the new world. Classical pat-
terns of resettlement, however, had become singularly ill-
adapted to political realities. Within six months Germany
and Russian invaded Poland clogging ordinary channels of
immigration. Rosenman, at first disposed to resort to
extraordinary efforts, was discouraged by the State Department which advised that because of Rosenman's prominence
it would be disadvantageous both in Poland and the United
States to draw special attention to his relatives. The
Judge, much to his later regret, complied with the State
Department recommendations and desisted from further efforts.[36] Variations of this experience were widely shared,
and in few instances did the Europeans survive the inaction.

In retrospect it has become apparent that to assist
the survival of greater numbers of central and eastern
European Jews would have required wholesale modifications
of traditional diplomacy as well as other cherished values.
Indeed, the very issue to which Rosenman addressed him-
self--where and under what circumstances these people might
be resettled without creating a "Jewish Problem"--is now
assumed peripheral to how many could have been saved under
any circumstances. The urgent question now appears to
have been how many should be permitted to live at all. Yet
in 1940, Hitler had not yet embarked upon his "final solution" to the "Jewish Problem" and even his intense and
ruthless anti-Semitism could somehow be perceived as ap-
proximating the classical mold. Ironically, it would
have required a ruthless toughmindedness to act upon fore-
knowledge of Hitler's ultimate plan. For given the context of domestic political realities, of which Rosenman
was an astute student, it would have *at best* required

willful abandonment of hope for the vast majority to secure survival for a numerically small group. It has since
required irrefutable evidence of an act no less egregious
than the physical destruction of European Jewry to make
such an unattractive alternative appear the least illu-
sory alternative.

        It would, moreover, be misleading to single out
Hitler's anti-Semitism as the factor exclusively condition-
ing Rosenman's views toward Nazism. He conceived the Nazis
as a personal threat because he was a Jew but also because
he was an American. His "own personal stake in the [1940]
election," he had written to the President, was "multiplied
by 130,000,000, [for] that is the stake of the people of
the United States whether they realize it or not."[37]
Roosevelt concurred in this evaluation. To deny Hitler
ultimate victory was the first order of government business, and to that end the most immediate task was to marshal public opinion in support of a heavily increased production of war material coupled with a willingness to
transfer some of these materials to nations already at war
with the Axis. At a mid-December press conference, Roosevelt initiated a campaign to sell the concept of Lend-
Lease. The Judge assisted in his two most important public efforts in that direction; a fireside chat in late
December and the annual message to Congress the following
January. Called to Washington the day after Christmas, he
stayed at the White House along with Hopkins and Sherwood
and worked for long periods with the President. Many of
the problems they discussed that December persisted long
after the country formally became involved in war and some
were never completely resolved. The most pressing was to
persuade a large majority of both Congress and the general
public that the utilization of American equipment and munitions by non-American forces, even at a time when war materials were in short supply, was in the best national interest. In his fireside chat the President maintained
that the fall of Great Britain would so jeopardize national interests as to constitute an American defeat of the
first magnitude. In the State of the Union message he
made a formal request to Congress for a Lend-Lease Bill.

Although not directly involved in the actual drafting process, Rosenman was reluctant to remain away from
Washington during its legal inception. No sooner had he
returned to New York after the State of the Union address
than he indicated his "willingness to assist" in the composition of the inaugural speech.[38] An invitation to do
so was promptly forthcoming.

The inauguration ceremony took place ten days after
the Lend-Lease Bill had been introduced in the House of
Representatives. In his address the President affirmed
that in contrast to his first inaugural, his third was
occurring at a time when the greatest threat to American
democracy came from external forces. The speech also
contained an argument against those who acknowledged this
threat, but opposed aid to the Allies because their cause
appeared doomed. Although the speech reads as one of
Roosevelt's greatest efforts, it failed to provoke wide
popular response.[39] The Lend-Lease Bill engendered three
months of bitter public and congressional debate. Wendell
Willkie's support was a pleasant surprise to Rosenman.
The Judge had feared Willkie an isolationist, and attributed the Republican leader's militant internationalism
to what he termed the lesson Willkie had learned in defeat. In Rosenman's judgment, he developed into a "truly
great statesman" during the post-election period.[40]

Lend-Lease became law on March 11, 1941, but it
proved no panacea to the problem of successfully combat-
ting the Axis. There was even grave doubt whether sufficient safe deliveries of material could be made to meet
British needs. German submarines were sinking merchant
vessels at a rate twice as rapid as the combined United
States and British replacement output. If sinkings continued at that rate it seemed obvious Lend-Lease could
not succeed, and thus its effective implementation required additional United States commitments not called
for in the law itself. The administration was preoccupied
with this concern when in May, Rosenman was called to
Washington to work on an address in observance of Pan
American Day. The speech, originally scheduled for May

14, and postponed to May 27, developed into a prime object
for speculation. The arrival of Judge Rosenman on May 23,
seemed an even greater indication that it would contain
"bigger things" than the usual assurances of hemispheric
solidarity.[41] Press Secretary Early confirmed suspicions
in a release some days prior to the speech itself. Admitting that Rosenman and Sherwood were working on the address, Early claimed that until a few days before he
would have "cautioned reporters against saying the speech
would be dynamic and momentous," but since it was then
being redrafted "in the light of rapidly changing conditions abroad," he was no longer advising journalistic restraint. Exercising little restraint himself, the press
secretary predicted that after its delivery "there will
no longer be any doubt as to what the national policy of
this Government is."[42]

During the drafting of the speech, it had become
apparent without explicit presidential verbalization, that
Roosevelt was inclined toward concluding his address with
an emergency proclamation.[43] Rosenman, Sherwood, and
Hopkins, veteran advocates of an enlarged United States
war effort, believed it would help accelerate such a
course, and without direct consultation with the President
designed an address to announce a declaration of Unlimited
National Emergency. At the same time they requested Attorney General Robert Jackson prepare a formal proclamation to that effect. When the speech draft was given to
Roosevelt for his initial review, Hopkins, who was quite
ill at the time, absented himself and Rosenman and Sherwood "were appalled at being left to face it out alone."
Alleging to have been unaware of their activities, the
President began reading and then looked up to ask "Hasn't
someone been taking some liberties?" There was no further
discussion of the declaration and it remained in the
speech.[44]

Its impact was lessened at a post-speech conference
when Roosevelt qualified away much of what he had seemed
to say. Ickes reported Rosenman as "furious" with the

President's action,[45] but the Judge nevertheless persisted in the belief that the declaration "would at least create a better atmosphere for drastic action if he [Roosevelt] should decide to take it." It was, in any event, now part of the record.[46]

The following weekend Rosenman accompanied the President by train to New York. The *Times* reported that during the trip they worked over some volumes of the *Public Papers* scheduled for publication that October.[47]

Chapter Nine

POLITICS OF REORGANIZATION

In 1941 the United States strode towards the expansion of its administrative as well as industrial and military complex. Before the end of 1942, the proliferation of wartime agencies became so great that a mere listing would consume almost fifteen printed pages.[1] Many of these were *ad hoc* organizations that continued to exist long after they had outgrown their need, or, as was also often the case, the need had outgrown the organization. Constant reorganization and consolidation of existing agencies, along with the creation of new super agencies with extended powers, was Roosevelt's favorite method of dealing with changing needs and unresolved problems. Arbitrating the details of interagency feuds and administrative reshufflings were frequently delegated to Judge Rosenman.

From 1941 until 1943 Rosenman's vacations and weekends were spent in Washington studying the minutia of these entanglements and negotiating new designs in the bureaucratic maze. Conceiving his "role to act for the President in such a way that [Roosevelt] would not be burdened by many conferences or the working out of compromise,"[2] he also constituted himself a guardian of the New Deal ethos. His goal was to *maintain* as much of its program as he considered feasible throughout the national emergency.

The prestige accrued to Rosenman as a presidential intimate often served to assure all but top level administrators that in assigning their interests to the Judge, the President had not relegated them to perfunctory treatment. Simultaneously, the Judge's facility in achieving compromises, and the President's implicit confidence that such compromises were consistent with his own personal interests, permitted Rosenman a leeway which could promote further accord without requiring Roosevelt's personal intervention.

One such instance was a squabble that broke out in May 1941, involving interagency disagreements over tax amortization procedures for new plants and tools. The dispute raged intermittently until September when the Judge, together with representatives of the War, Navy, and Treasury Departments, negotiated an accomodation that was subsequently enacted into law. Rather than consult the President as to terms, Rosenman simply informed him that the issue had been settled. "If you are interested in hearing the details of the fight itself or the settlement," he wrote, "I can give them to you either orally or in writing."[3] There is no indication that the President ever requested such information, but James Forrestal and Robert Patterson, Under Secretaries of the Navy and Army respectively, labeled Rosenman's aid "of the greatest service to the War and Navy Departments," and sent their "thanks."[4]

Achieving compromises in disputes over matters such as amortization was a relatively simple procedure when compared with reorganization matters. Not because reorganization necessarily involved larger matters of policy or national interest--although at times they did--but because they were also more public affairs directly involving the careers and status of individuals. Under such circumstances appeals to the President directly were more frequent. The Judge still asserted powerful influence, but in the form of recommendations to the President rather than agreements in his name.

One of his earliest reorganization ventures resulted
in the establishment of the Supply Priorities Allocation
Board to supersede the Office of Production Management.
In January 1941, the Office of Production Management (OPM)
had been established to simplify and concentrate the responsibility for the production of defense materials.[5]
In April, the Office of Price Administration and Civilian
Supply (OPACS) was created to prevent price spiraling and
to "stimulate provision" for the supply of materials and
commodities required for civilian use which did not conflict with the needs of national defense.[6] The two agencies were expected to work in tandem, with the OPACS dependent upon OPM priority power; power to allocate materials towards the manufacture of consumer goods deemed
most essential. Ironically, but arguing from a sound
administrative rationale, the civilian supply agency
agitated for more complete conversion to war production
than the OPM. Leon Henderson, the OPACS Director, was
particularly unhappy with OPM Director William Knudsen's
unwillingness to demand heavier cuts in the production of
automobile and other durable consumer goods. This well
publicized interagency feud reflected the fact that increasing pressures upon the nation's resources were ex-
acerbating the difficulties of priority allocation, and
in August 1941, Roosevelt directed Rosenman to study the
problem.

He had been at work only a few days when news of
his assignment reached the Press, where his sudden emergence as a defense organization expert occasioned some
surprise. Hugh Johnson, who thought him "one of the sweet-
est characters in public life," wondered "what the hell
does he know about industry, organization and especially
the bedlam of present-day Washington confusion."[7] As to
industry and organization, Rosenman proved an apt student,
but in dealing with the bedlam of Washington confusion
his talents became immediately discernible. Within the
defense organization structure there was a multiplicity
of contending interests which made outright concessions

to any single group unpolitic. What might logically appear as the most efficient reorganization plan could in
actual operation become unworkable. Another undesirable
alternative was a workable scheme that would undermine
existing socio-economic legislation. To mitigate against
the latter, Rosenman's plans were invariably designed to
retain or strengthen F.D.R.'s personal control over policy.

Among the contending forces were industrialists reluctant to curtail consumer goods production and invest
additional capital in expanding their facilities for war
production. Fearful of existing non-converted sources of
competition and a future replete with surplus plant capa-
cities, they were unwilling to convert or expand without
assurances from the government. Government assurances
usually took the form of generous tax write-offs for new
plants[8] and the appointment of prominent industrialists
to important government positions. Only partially satisfied by these gestures, members of the business community
and like-minded congressional and military supporters further pressed for the appointment of a single economic
czar to whom the President would delegate powers previously reserved for his own person. This proposed czar would
presumably be one of their own number, or, short of that,
someone less sympathetic to the cause of organized labor
than the President.

Organized labor, on the other hand, was gaining an
enviable position due to increasing demands for manpower,
and it was feared that once the unemployment slack had
been taken up, unions would exert pressures upon industry likely to initiate an inflationary spiral. Attempts
by the administration to retain the cooperation of labor
included providing it with representation on important
councils. However, the retention of such legislation as
the Wages and Hours Act and the adoption of maintenance-
of-membership agreements afforded more tangible short
and long term advantages.[9]

Striving to devise a priorities system that would gain the approbation if not the enthusiasm of both industry and labor, Rosenman, prepared, with assistance from the Bureau of the Budget, three separate but similar plans. These were readied on August 18, and then studied and altered until a single compromise plan gained acceptance. Comment was also invited from other interested persons. The general consensus of solicited opinion was that the revision was a good plan, "but not the final form of the defense reorganization."[10] Well before its public announcement, Rosenman described it to Secretary of Interior Harold Ickes as similar to but simpler than a reorganization plan upon which Bernard Baruch had been working, and one which would "eventually lead to the Baruch plan."[11]

The heart of the Baruch Plan was its proposal for a single economic czar. Rosenman, however, had rejected such urgings and instead established a seven man Supply Priorities and Allocation Board which would have, subject to the President's reversal, final word on all priority allocation. The general administrative rationale was that the chief officials of principal agencies with a primary interest in the allocation process would collectively determine which of their demands merited fulfillment and in what order. So as to be operative, the board would be limited in size and yet representative of the competing military and civilian requirements.

To be named to membership of such a board would presumably enhance the nominee's personal effectiveness and official status. Not to be named would almost certainly have a contrary effect. Under these circumstances some aggressive jockeying for nomination was inevitable and, for those who failed to gain the prize, disappointment especially bitter. Harold Ickes had presented the case for his own appointment directly to Rosenman,[12] but it hadn't helped. The President, he now came to reason, had rejected the Baruch plan because he "apparently could not go along with Bernie and at the same time, keep cer-

tain people, including myself, in their places." Ickes
concluded with uncharacteristic understatement that the
President had "called upon Rosenman to do the kind of
job he [Roosevelt] and Harry [Hopkins] wanted."[13]

The kind of job Roosevelt wanted was precisely the
kind of job Rosenman had set out to do. While from purely an administrative view SPAB left much to be desired,
it did accomplish a number of Roosevelt's more immediate
aims. Most important it provided for a temporarily workable system while permitting Roosevelt to retain, without
sharing, all of his presidential powers. The most obvious
effect of the reorganization was to replace William Knudsen with Donald Nelson as the key figure in the production
program. Furthermore, the composition of SPAB, which
Vice President Wallace chaired, seemed to promise closer
coordination with the White House and incidentally provide
a more sympathetic reception for the President's impending implementation of Lend-Lease aid to Russia.[14]

The President kept Rosenman's plan on his desk for
over a week before putting it into effect. During the
interim *Time Magazine* explained that the plan was "merely
a reshuffling" and the President was searching for a more
positive scheme.[15] After the plan was officially announced,
however, *Time* described it as "the greatest single step
forward yet in the defense program and honestly represented the most possible reorganization short of an earth-
quake."[16] Others were less enthusiastic. Bernard Baruch
described SPAB as a "faltering step forward,"[17] and the
New York Times lamented editorially that the board contained "several men not ideally fitted for their post.[19]
Father Coughlin protested against Rosenman's having taken
over the job of regimenting America and predicted "further drastic orders to regiment and coerce the American
people to be issued by Sammy the Rose."[20] I. F. Stone,
noting that Judge Rosenman had "labored and brought forth
a Rube Goldberg gadget," cautioned his readers against
confusing SPAB with Spam.[21]

The Supply Priorities Allocation Board functioned only until January, 1942. Although "no causal relation can be inferred between the order [creating SPAB] and the upward production trend,"[22] during its short existence defense production increased significantly. After Pearl Harbor the inefficient and agonizingly slow process of board action was no longer feasible, and the President responded by bestowing most of SPAB's authority directly upon Donald Nelson as Director of a newly designed War Production Board.[23] Nelson possessed great power, but power hardly commensurate with those of an economic czar.

Rosenman had hardly started upon the SPAB realignment when the machinery was set in motion for his next major reorganization assignment. In mid-July, 1941, Eleanor Roosevelt had requested that Harold Smith, Director of the Bureau of the Budget, discuss the unhappy predicament of the United States Housing Authority with the President. Smith promised he would do so and added that he was "painfully aware of the disintegration that has taken place, not only in the relationship of the United States Housing Authority with Congress, but in the Authority staff itself." He suggested that if Mrs. Roosevelt were interested in "taking over the housing situation *generally*," he would "be pleased to be of service."[24]

At the time there were, including the War and Navy Departments, sixteen federal agencies handling the various aspects of public construction and aid to private housing construction.[25] The pressures accompanying mobilization called for a more coordinated housing program. The industrial expansion which marked even the earliest stages of mobilization had brought about a sizable increase in employment throughout the United States. Not only were there pressures for increased housing facilities in previously heavily populated area, but new industries were also being located in regions where living accomodations for workers had not previously existed. Some of the need was for housing of a permanent nature, and some,

such as living quarters for personnel engaged in the construction and servicing of military posts, was expected
to be for a more limited duration.

The multitudinous agencies involved in housing programs competed for priority items, duplicated efforts,
and engaged in numerous jurisdictional disputes. In 1940
President Roosevelt had appointed Charles F. Palmer as
Defense Housing Coordinator to superintend the activities
of the various agencies and bring some order out of the
chaos. Palmer was at best only partially successful, and
the specter of diminishing material resources increased Palmer's problems. Possessing few powers other than persuasion,
cooperation among the housing agencies remained most noticeable by its absence.[26] The situation was so thoroughly confused that the President, alert for any constructive
suggestions, encouraged Mrs. Roosevelt to accept the Budget Director's invitation to discuss housing issues with
her.[27] The meeting was held in late August, and Mrs.
Roosevelt prepared a memorandum of it for her husband.
She reported that the Budget Director felt it "really
necessary...to let him talk to you about this whole housing situation. He would like to do it alone, and then he
thinks you will have to have two or three people together
and do some reorganization."[28] Two days after the establishment of SPAB, Roosevelt presented all the correspondence and memoranda on the matter to Rosenman, together
with the curt note, "to take up with Smith."[29]

Rosenman concurred with Smith that a general housing
reorganization was advisable and took on the job.[30] The
Judge had maintained an active interest in the subject
since his days as an Assemblyman, and in more recent years
Mrs. Rosenman had become Chairman of the National Committee on the Housing Emergency. In this position she served
in an advisory capacity to Housing Coordinator Charles F.
Palmer and had already made known her own views favoring
a complete reorganization of the hydra-headed federal
housing program.[31]

With the Cabinet Room of the White House as his base
of operations, Judge Rosenman began work in October. The
administrative problems were not difficult and "a consolidation of the scattered agencies involved in housing was
the logical solution right from the start."[32] The political factors were, however, as complex as any with which
the Judge had had to deal. Housing reorganization developed into a long drawn out process requiring more time
and necessitating more interviews than any other single
reorganization problem upon which the Judge worked. On
a single weekend he scheduled appointments with sixteen
different interested persons and received written memoranda, many of them unsolicited and exceedingly lengthy,
from an even greater number.[33]

On November 12, 1941, Rosenman proposed a tentative
plan to the President.[34] Contrary to previous experience,
details were not revealed to the press prior to presidential action and the *New York Times* attributed this to "the
President's confidant...having discussed the matter infor-
mally instead of submitting a written report." The Judge
was believed to favor a huge new agency which was not to
be established immediately. He reportedly advised the
President that "to make such a change would delay the
housing program for months rather than advance it."[35]
Actually Rosenman's position was somewhat more equivocal.
Although favoring the immediate establishment of a central housing agency, he believed the President lacked the
authority to put the plan into effect through executive
order and doubted Congress would agree to provide him with
the necessary powers.

The United States Housing Authority was the crux of
this matter. Established by the Wagner-Steagall Act of
1937 to stimulate slum clearance and the construction of
low rent housing projects, it thereafter encountered opposition from Congress. Suspected of radical objectives
it consistently suffered from what its supporters considered insufficient appropriations, and the National Defense

Housing Act of 1940 (Lanham Act) had bypassed the agency
completely in its appropriation of funds for the construction of accommodations for defense workers. It was this
circumvention which had occasioned the creation of many
of the new housing agencies.

Powerful opponents of the USHA such as Fritz G.
Lanham, chairman of the House Committee on Public Buildings and Grounds,[36] and his fellow Texan and Commerce
Secretary Jesse Jones, were reluctant to support any reorganization plan which might allow for prominent use of
the agency, as they feared it would enhance USHA opportunities to conduct an expanded program after the war.
On the other hand, such New Dealers as Mrs. Roosevelt, the
Rosenmans, and Senator Robert Wagner believed the USHA
should be given expanded jurisdiction so as to enable it
to share in that portion of the defense housing program
construction which appeared to fill a permanent housing
need.

Senator Wagner, the original sponsor of USHA, was
especially alarmed by the manner in which it was being
squeezed out of defense housing programs. He insisted
that of all the existing housing agencies it "has the
most experience and has done the best job," and it was on
such non-ideological grounds that he urged it be given a
role in wartime housing construction. He was willing to
avoid, "at this time," problems of regular slum clearance,
and he was also prepared to sacrifice the then existing
USHA leadership. The USHA administrator, Nathan Straus,
Rosenman's former New York Legislative colleague, had
combined a militant advocacy of public housing with a
disdain for the sensitivities of important opponents. He
had, for instance, been one of the very few federal directors requiring non-discriminatory hiring practices by
contractors. Wagner suspected that "if the personality
problem is first cleared up," the chances for acceptance
of Rosenman's reorganization scheme would be enhanced
considerably, and Wagner agreed to support it on those
terms.[37]

The reorganization was ultimately resolved without direct congressional action. After Pearl Harbor, the President acquired additional powers sufficient to effect reorganization through executive order. He did not act immediately, however, for if Congress remained unsympathetic to the plan it might presumably retaliate by blocking a $300,000,000 housing appropriation then before it. During the next few weeks the appropriation bill was approved, Nathan Straus resigned, and Rosenman made some alterations in his plan to counter persisting criticisms. He also determined upon an individual who would be acceptable to all elements involved to administer the super housing agency.[38] On February 24, 1942 Roosevelt issued an executive order implementing the Rosenman proposals. The keystone to the plan was the creation of the National Housing Agency (NHA) into which the sixteen established agencies were consolidated. The Administrator of the NHA was to be John B. Blandford Jr., Assistant Director of the Bureau of the Budget.[39] Rosenman, apprehensive as to how the Blandford appointment would be received by Congress, was relieved when no protests ensued.[40]

Charles Palmer, displaced as Coordinator of Housing, congratulated Rosenman on the establishment of the NHA,[41] and wrote the President that by its establishment "you did more for housing than anything which has been done since you started housing in the country back during the NIRA PWA days of 1933." He added that "it has been an inspiration to work with Sam Rosenman."[42] The Judge himself was "very confident that the new housing setup will work out particularly well, not only for the present, but for the future post-war days." Rosenman had "every confidence in Blandford; although the reorganization had been a long tough job," he was "quite content with the result."[43] Some observers commenting on its political implications pointed out that it had resulted in the transfer of some housing agencies previously under the control of Jesse Jones to the NHA.[44] The transfer was regarded as an inevitable consequence of consolidation, and the NHA was accepted as "war project and not a socio-economic experiment."[45] The NHA also provided for a truce between private and public housing advocates; presumably one which would not prove disastrous to the ambitions of post-war public housing enthusiasts.

As could be expected, the formal entry of the United States into World War II intensified Rosenman's personal efforts towards administrative mobilization. His activities in Washington had centered upon the cause of preparedness. Once war was declared the need for even greater effort had presumably become self-evident and mobilization would be effected more readily. At least political bickerings could be expected to give way to the best possible solution irrespective of socio-economic views, or so Rosenman hoped. Yet although overshadowed by the issue of national survival, domestic political issues retained their potency and could never really be ignored. A decision affecting production and pricing inevitably affected labor-management relations, and the Judge, whose commitment to his wartime assignments included a spirit of urgency not universally shared, was increasingly prepared to yield his own socio-economic predispositions, if to do so seemed likely to promote otherwise unobtainable compromises favorable to more effective conduct of the war. Establishing a pattern analogous to his record on the court, he attempted to restrict partisan political predilections from his reorganization work. The task was facilitated by a personal commitment to Roosevelt, and the Judge seldom asserted views, even New Dealish ones, which might have diminished, if not destroyed, his usefulness to the President. In other instances, acting directly as an instrument of the President, he was unable to express them at all. In December 1943, Roosevelt defended administration policies inconsistent with the New Deal by expounding upon how the problems created by the war had made it necessary to turn from the ministerings of "Dr. New Deal" to those of "Dr. Win the War."[46] Shortly afterward he reassigned Rosenman to post-war planning, presumably in consultation with Dr. New Deal. During 1942 and 1943, however, Rosenman relied almost exclusively upon the diagnoses of Dr. Win the War.

The early months of 1942 marked the high point of the nation's war reorganization activities. The results of Rosenman's housing efforts had hardly been announced before he was set to work assisting in the creation of a War Manpower Commission. Although through most of 1942 manpower remained one of the nation's most abundant resources, in anticipation of an extended war with its expectant increased military and industrial demands for personnel, attempts were made to prepare against predictable labor shortages. It was inevitable that someone should suggest, as the first step in any concerted national program of this sort, a consolidation of the twenty-odd federal agencies active in the labor supply field, and a series of plans were drafted to effect this. In February 1942, the President approved, in principle, a Bureau of the Budget plan establishing a centralized independent organization. Before implementing it, however, he exposed it to the criticism of the government agencies and private groups most directly affected.[47]

The War and Navy Departments along with Federal Security Administratior Paul McNutt supported the plan. Some prominent labor leaders agreed to consolidation, but rather than establish an independent agency, preferred that it be placed under the aegis of the Department of Labor. Secretary of Labor Perkins and Sidney Hillman denied even the desirability of a commission.[48]

Roosevelt attempted to sidestep the labor criticism by appointing a special committee consisting of Rosenman, Harold Smith, Supreme Court Justice William O. Douglas, and Anna Rosenberg, who had headed the New York Office of the Federal Security Agency, "to recommend a plan of manpower organization and nominate a candidate for manpower administrator." As might be anticipated from their instructions, their final recommendations closely followed the lines of the Budget Bureau's February proposals, with Paul McNutt as their candidate for War Manpower director. The President accepted the findings he had hoped for, and on April 18, issued an Executive Order enacting them into law.[49]

    Justice Rosenman was by then established as the per-
sonification of executive reorganization. A popular magazine reported that Rosenman's arrival in Washington was
"usually the tipoff that a super-duper shakeup is due in
some top government agency."[50] *Times* columnist Arthur
Krock examined the situation in greater detail. "If you
want to alarm any member of the Administration from the
Cabinet level on down," he wrote, "just whisper in his
ear one of two dread sentences: 'Sam Rosenman is in town'
or 'the chief has an executive order on his desk that
affects you!'" The political commentator went on to explain that since all executive orders pass through the
Bureau of the Budget, its Director, Harold Smith, was a
"human battleground between the power-seeking groups which
afflict all administrations." Judge Rosenman's "connection with these dread documents," he continued, "is unofficial, but his influence is accepted as greater than
that wielded officially by Director Smith."[51]

    Even these two titans of the executive order suf-
fered their reverses, however, and at no time was it so
evident than when Krock was writing of their strengths.
Early in March 1942, the President "turned his concentrated attention" toward efforts to consolidate the activities
of all government agencies engaged in the dissemination of
information. Criticisms of confusion, contradiction, and
duplication were rampant, but probably of greater influence upon Roosevelt, were allegations by Rosenman, Ickes,
Hopkins, Sherwood, and others that the "facts of the war"
were being insufficiently impressed upon the American
people. Shortly after Pearl Harbor Milton Eisenhower,
then with the Agriculture Department, was assigned to prepare plans for an inclusive information agency. He submitted the plans to Roosevelt in March. The President,
after viewing the plan and submitting it to a preliminary
study by the Bureau of the Budget, passed it along to
Rosenman with the charge of "coordinating the various
agencies and consolidating them into one overall information agency."[52] Ultimately these efforts were to cul-
minate in the Office of War Information (OWI), but during

the three months in which Rosenman worked on the consolidation, a disproportionate share of his time was spent
in efforts to include within the OWI the information activities of Nelson Rockefeller's Office of the Coordinator
of Inter American Affairs (CIAA), and the foreign infor-
mational functions of General William Donovan's Office
of the Coordinator of Information.

The Judge, Harold Smith, and the Eisenhower plan
had all recommended that Rockefeller and Donovan relinquish such activities, but both men fought hard to retain
them, with Rockefeller succeeding in bringing his own
case directly to the President. Roosevelt was not easily
persuaded by the arguments, and Rockefeller persuaded
Cordell Hull and Sumner Welles to intercede further in
his behalf. They "argued convincingly that the close relationship between information and other activities in
Latin America made it more advisable to retain all activities in relation to Latin America in one office," but
Rosenman was unmoved. A mid-May high level White House
conference partially overruled the Judge. There it was
agreed to omit Rockefeller's but include Donovan's infor-
mational activities within the OWI. Once this had been
decided reorganization proceeded at a rapid pace with the
final obstacle being the selection of a Director. Ever
the compromiser, Rosenman had regarded General William
Donovan as the likely choice, but Roosevelt vetoed his
appointment. At the suggestion of Rex Stout, a popular
mystery writer then heading the War Writers Board, Rosenman carried the recommendation of Elmer Davis to the President. Roosevelt, "liked the idea" and prevailed upon
Davis to accept the appointment. Executive Order 9132
establishing the Office of War Information was announced
on June 12.[53]

Rosenman's well publicized but unofficial influence
over administrative reorganization did not preclude activity in other areas, and he routinely dispatched assignments of the less spectacular variety. While simultaneously working on the information problem, he negotiated a

truce between the Justice Department on one side and the
War and Navy Departments on the other. The War and Navy
Secretaries contended that Assistant Attorney General
Thurman Arnold's vigorous prosecution of anti-trust suits
was hampering the war effort and requested a suspension
of such activities. The President was unwilling to grant
industry blanket immunity from the anti-trust laws, but
at the same time, he feared that the vigorous prosecution
of these laws would retard war production. Rosenman was
called in to study the problem, and, along with Arnold
and the three cabinet heads, worked out a *modus vivendi*.
The Justice Department agreed to suspend those anti-trust
proceedings which either the War or Navy Department deemed
prejudicial to the war effort. At the same time all three
departments agreed to call upon Congress to extend the
statute of limitations so that no violator might escape
eventual anti-trust prosecution by reason of the wartime
moratorium. Congress complied, and the agreement remained
in effect until after the war. During the life of the
legislation twenty-five anti-trust prosecutions were postponed.[54]

Throughout the war, the administration was involved
in devising and implementing plans calculated to control
inflation. Regarded as the greatest non-military threat
facing the United States, almost every administrative activity touched upon it in some way. As a reorganization
expert, Rosenman did not get to deal directly with the
problem until the Fall of 1942, as a speechwriter, however,
he began such work six months earlier. In April the President decided to send a special message to Congress outlining an integrated anti-inflation program. In order to
secure agreement on specific recommendations, he instructed Rosenman to parley with agency heads possessing official
interest in the development of any such program.

The conference was held on April 10, in the Cabinet
Room of the White House, and a confidential memorandum
prepared by the Bureau of the Budget provided the basis
for the discussion. Various points led to vehement con-

troversy and there were some issues upon which no agreement could be reached. In these instances the Judge prepared a special memorandum for the President in which he
presented the arguments of the officials in dispute "as
fully and as fairly as I could."[55] The conference stimulated rather than concluded discussion of the anti-inflation proposals. The number of interdepartmental conferences multiplied and many officials sent Rosenman formal
memoranda stating their views. The Judge usually presented these with summaries, either written or oral, to
the President. Officials who had more ready access to
Roosevelt insisted upon submitting their proposals directly.

The President decided to present a seven-point stabilization program to Congress on April 27, and to follow
it up with a fireside chat the next day. Rosenman, along
with Robert Sherwood, began preparing the messages on the
evening of Wednesday, April 22. Working continuously until late Friday, they paused only to send copies of their
draft to the Secretary of the Treasury, the Director of
the Budget, and the Administrator of the OPA. OPA administrator Leon Henderson, dissatisfied with the message,
arranged a meeting with Rosenman and Sherwood for Sunday
morning. Henderson insisted that adherence to that part
of the message which dealt with farm prices would result
in a drastic rise in the cost of living. In particular
he protested against the provision, consistent with federal law, which permitted the prices of some farm products
to rise above parity before they would be frozen. Rosenman and Sherwood, whose personal conviction had been that
prices should be frozen at existing levels even when below parity, now became advocates of Henderson's plan for
parity ceilings. They invited Harry Hopkins and Harold
Smith to hear the OPA administrator's reasoning, and then
Hopkins, Rosenman, and Sherwood, fortified by Henderson's
arguments, marched off for lunch with the President.[56]

As the President then envisioned his seven-point
stabilization program[57] only the section dealing with in-

creased taxes would require congressional action. By not
insisting on a parity ceiling Roosevelt hoped to avoid a
second congressional confrontation. In January 1942,
Congress had passed the Emergency Price Control Act which
allowed the freezing of farm prices only after they had
risen significantly above parity levels. Roosevelt feared
that Congress might prove unwilling to repeal this act to
allow him to fix prices at parity. If Congress did refuse,
he reasoned, then labor leaders might refuse to agree to
the stabilization of wages.

Roosevelt's luncheon companions countered with the
argument that:

> the President in his recommendations to the
> Congress ought to be right in his economics,
> irrespective of what Congress did with them
> afterwards. We [Rosenman, Sherwood, and Hop-
> kins] argued that if Congress refused to ac-
> cept the perfectly fair and traditional New
> Deal policy toward farm prices, the burden
> of the blame would be on Congress, and not
> on him.[58]

The President acquiesced, and the following afternoon in his message to Congress he declared that "As a
national policy, the ceiling on farm prices...should be
set at parity.[59]

Congress took no action on either the tax or the
farm pricing recommendations and instead embarked upon an
informal summer recess. In July, Leon Henderson announced
that he had presented Judge Rosenman with a new proposal
calculated to strengthen farm prices and wage controls,
and the press interpreted this as an indication that the
Judge was preparing some special report. The President,
however, pointedly denied this and insisted that the Judge
was merely collecting and boiling down information.[60]
The Henderson proposal had suggested the establishment of
a director and advisory board to coordinate all the ele-

ments of the anti-inflation program and the use of sub-
sidies to maintain OPA ceiling prices. The Justice Department declared itself in substantial agreement with the
scheme. The public members of the National War Labor
Board suggested to Rosenman that the Little Steel formula,
"if applied efficiently and courageously would cover the
needs of the wage program," and Paul McNutt, Chairman of
the War Manpower Commission, supported this contention.[61]
The Treasury Department submitted a plan of stabilization
through credit control, and the principal labor unions
opposing all "proposals which set up an all-powerful administrator or super board" as "inconsistent with the
basic democratic principles of our nation," brought forth
separate schemes of their own.[62]

Mid-August rumors contended that Rosenman's inflation study was nearing completion, and that he had prepared an executive order establishing an Economic Stabilization Authority with power to coordinate all phases of
the anti-inflation program.[63] The President, when asked
to confirm this, avoided a direct answer by again discount-
ing Rosenman's role in the inflation study. Describing
the Judge as just another among 40 or 50 people with whom
he had discussed the problem, he denied that Rosenman
could even be called a "fact-finder."[64] Despite the President's denial, which the press remarked upon as disingenuous,[65] Rosenman's study and subsequent discussions
culminated in plans to appoint a stabilization director
to coordinate the seven phases of Roosevelt's still pend-
ing anti-inflation program.[66] Before establishing any
such office, however, it was necessary to provide the
director reasonable opportunity to coordinate the program,
and it would be next to impossible to control wages while
the administration could not prevent the rise of farm
prices.[67]

Secretary of Agriculture Wickard had abandoned his
earlier January Price Control Act stand and now supported
a policy of parity or present prices, whichever was higher.[68] A number of Roosevelt's aides contended that his

presidential war powers provided him with sufficient authority to fix farm prices at levels less than the minimum
directives of Congress in the Price Control Act, and they
urged the President to cease waiting for congressional
concurrence and put his stabilization program into effect
through executive order. Rosenman who was an ardent advocate of this course of action, drafted and brought such
an order to the President.[69]

The President was reluctant to sign it, and the
scheme was debated among his aides for several days.
Harry Hopkins who had supported issuing the Rosenman order during a staff conference, later advised Roosevelt
to offer Congress another opportunity to pass legislation
on the matter.[70] Supreme Court Justice James F. Byrnes
and Harold Ickes also advised the President to resubmit
the matter to Congress.[71] Roosevelt decided upon a compromise plan. On September 7, 1942, in both a message
to Congress and a fireside chat, he announced that although his war powers were broad enough to enable him to
act unilaterally, he preferred to give Congress until
October 1, to act on his stabilization program. If there
was no definite action by that date he proposed to effect
the parity ceiling through executive order.[72] On October
2, Congress acquiesced by amending the Emergency Price
Control Act of 1942 to enable the President to fix prices
at parity, and the next day the President established the
Office of Economic Stabilization.[73] James F. Byrnes resigned from the Supreme Court to become Director. The
Press, overstating Byrnes' powers, hailed him as the long-
awaited economic czar.

The endowment of the OES with powers greater than
those previously exercised by its component agencies led
to hopes that similar arrangements could be made to reconcile competing civilian and military requirements for
manpower. Not unexpectedly, Rosenman was reported to be
working on such a plan.[74] Speculation that a massive
cabinet reorganization calculated to replace Frances
Perkins with Harold Ickes who would then exercise leader-

ship over an "enlarged and remodeled manpower organization,"[75] came to naught. There were, however, attempts
to increase the War Manpower Commission's scope from that
of coordinating to an operating authority, and on December
5, the Selective Service System was put under its jurisdiction.[76] On February 9, 1943, in an effort "to solve
serious manpower shortages in critical areas," the President proclaimed a minimum 48 hour, as opposed to the
generally prevailing 40 hour work week.[77]

    This apparently worsening labor crisis led Rosenman
to suggest that the President set up a special clearance
committee to deal with bottlenecks in production and mobilization and interagency feuds. The President acted
upon the suggestion and the resulting committee included
Byrnes as chairman with Rosenman, Hopkins, Baruch and
Admiral William Leahy as members. Commonly referred to
as the Little War Cabinet, the committee possessed no
special authority and during its short existence dealt
mainly with manpower problems. Paul McNutt had earlier
suggested compulsory methods of allocating civilian labor and a compulsory labor service bill was then before
the Congress.[78] Whether the committee should advise administrative support for the measure was the most politically potent issue it faced. On March 14, after a series
of "secret" hearings at which the committee elicited testimony from labor leaders and government officials, it
reported that "the people at that time were not ready to
accept a national service act."[79] Newspaper accounts,
later proven accurate, revealed that the committee had
stood four to one in favor of the measure with only Baruch
dissenting.[80] Roosevelt, who unofficially supported the
measure, was as yet unwilling to insist upon it without
Baruch's support, and the best the committee could do was
to predict that if the war did not end shortly, "a draft
of manpower and capital through national enactment of a
national service act was inevitable."[81] Disappointed
with the report, Roosevelt dismissed it as possessing
neither conclusions nor findings.[82]

In retrospect the fact that the report would indulge in implicit speculation as to the war's early end,
itself merits comment. By March 1943, it had become evident that the military tide had turned. Axis drives had
been stopped and its armies were giving way to Allied advances. In the face of combined British-United States
operations the Afrika Corps, once a threat to Suez, was
being driven out from Africa, and the significance of the
Russian defense of Stalingrad had become apparent from
subsequent Soviet victories. In the Pacific the Battle
of Midway had halted Japanese advances and the American
conquest of Guadalcanal pointed the way towards the course
of future operations. The United States was immune from
direct attack. The critical period had passed. Defense
might have justified continued recourse to increased government controls, but the security of military advantage
served to assure the public of the adequacy of existing
arrangements. Roosevelt could call for more drastic actions, but the mood of the nation had altered measurably
since Pearl Harbor, and by March 1943 the sense of urgency had so diminished that the need for additional civilian mobilization hardly seemed apparent. The administrative machinery then in operation was destined to
carry the nation through the war, and despite Rosenman's
own continuing efforts to modify that machinery, his impact upon its design had been second to no man save the
President himself.

His plan of operation had been quite simple. The
war, he reasoned, had necessitated a reorganization to
enable the government to better direct the nation's military and industrial activities. This required more government planning and the authority to implement such plans.
It also required the creation of a new intermediate level
bureaucracy to exercise powers hitherto eschewed by the
federal government. Almost but never quite balancing
these defense needs was Rosenman's hope to maintain the
substance of the socio-economic reforms of the New Deal.
Paradoxically, men exercising those powers Rosenman re-

garded as essential to achieve national mobilization could
also subvert the New Deal program in the course of their
mission. The Judge had attempted to resolve this dilemma
through increasing the President's personal control over
the economic and propaganda processes while simultaneously
selecting agency directors and subordinate staff personnel
with New Deal convictions.

These efforts combined with his judiciary functions
physically exhausted him. Two weeks after submitting the
inconclusive manpower report to the President he entered
Johns Hopkins Hospital.[83] As a consequence of overwork
and nervous strain he had temporarily lost his sight in
one eye.

Chapter Ten

THE PALACE GUARD

A story, doubtless apocryphal, alleges that the Judge had labored upon a reorganization assignment for twenty consecutive hours, exhausting two different teams of administrators in the process. Still desiring additional information, yet appreciating the impropriety of scheduling a conference during the last remaining hours before dawn, Rosenman reluctantly set aside his materials on reorganization to study briefs and other matters relating to his judicial assignments. He might have continued indefinitely, but after two hours found it necessary to verify a point of law. A volume containing the information was shelved on the opposite side of the room and the Judge would have to get out of his chair to reach it. The thought of this physical exertion so exhausted him that he capitulated to sleep.

Circulated as a commentary on the Judge's disinclination towards physical exercise, the story also underscored his prodigious capacity for other activities. Rosenman's eye disorder was, however, to curtail simultaneous involvement in two careers, the previous pattern of his adult life. Discharged from the Johns Hopkins Hospital after four weeks, he remained in Baltimore an additional two weeks for continued observation. In mid-May when he returned to New York City for further rest, he still had blurred vision. His physician, Dr. Alan Woods, suggested that as "it was overwork and nervous strain that had affected the nerve and temporarily destroyed the sight; that continued work at the same rate

might cause a recurrence in both eyes." The prescribed
treatment was to either relinquish his judicial post or
cease working for Roosevelt. Rosenman, who had for some
time wanted to resign the Judgeship, found it "nothing
short of torture" to be away from Washington,[1] and under
the circumstances Roosevelt concluded that the time had
come for him to leave the court.[2] The precise office
Rosenman would hold was as yet undetermined; it was, however, arranged that the Judge would resign from the bench
sometime after the summer recess.

In 1933, Rosenman had recognized that there was
"something about administrative power along the Potomac
that excludes the concept of anonymous helpfulness." It
was just as true in 1943, but this time it appeared as
the alternative to providing no help at all. Already a
prominent Washington figure, it could have been argued
that official appointment would effect little real change
in his status. Such was not the case. In the three weeks
between Roosevelt's announcement of Rosenman's full-time
service in Washington and the actual appointment, charges
directed against the Roosevelt administration increasingly
involved the Judge.

The war had so enhanced Roosevelt's reputation for
leadership that many of even the most vehement presidential critics showed a reluctance to oppose him with the
malevolent directness applied in earlier years. Perhaps
regarding it as unpatriotic to accuse a wartime president
of treason in a non-election year, they instead concentrated their verbal pyrotechnics against his principal aides.
The President himself was cast as a familiar historical
prototype--a weak but well meaning ruler constantly being
misled by his most intimate advisors. The most nefarious
plotters of this White House Palace Guard were Harry Hopkins, Supreme Court Justice Frankfurter, and now, Samuel
Rosenman. On occasion Presidential Assistant David Niles
was numbered among the collaborators. Usually depicted
as conspiring to alter the economic and social order,
Rosenman was also, on less frequent occasions, coupled

with Admiral Leahy as "rightist pipelines into the White House."[3]

The most sensational charges were aired by the *Chicago Tribune*, a veritable cornucopia of accounts of "leftist plots." A week prior to Rosenman's assuming his Washington office, the newspaper revealed that he, along with other members of the palace guard, were involved in the formulation of a "nothing less than treasonous plan." According to Michigan Congressman Paul W. Shafer, the source of this particular story, Rosenman, Hopkins, Frankfurter, and Niles were attempting to "create a global WPA program through the war department for the purpose of capturing a fourth term." *The New York Daily News*, through the columns of John O'Donnell, revealed that the conspirators hoped to "kick General Marshall upstairs" and replace him as Chief of Staff with General Brehon Sommerville. Sommerville was also reported as scheduled to receive the 1944 Democratic Vice-presidential nomination.[4] O'Donnell's exposure of the plot presumably disarmed the plotters.

The Roosevelt announcement which had signaled Rosenman's prominent status in the revolutionary junta, had been made at a September 14 press conference in which it was stated that Rosenman was coming to Washington as Special Counsel to the President at, stressed the President, a salary less than half of that which he had earned on the bench. The position had been especially created for the Judge and the title was apparently selected in deference to their Albany affiliation. In anticipation of questions as to the Special Counsel's precise duties, Roosevelt explained that he would handle "quasi-legal stuff" such as draft deferments and courts-martial upon which the President functioned as the final court of appeal. The President wanted these "reviewed just like the --normal cases--criminal cases that came to me as Governor when I was down at Albany, which Sam Rosenman handled."[5]

The press reported Roosevelt's explanation, and proceeded to speculate as to what deeper meanings the appointment might hold. The *Times* analyzed it "as an administrative measure as distinguished from a policy move." Although it served to throw the "spotlight on the presently dominant advisory group around the President...of which Judge Rosenman is decidedly a member," it was simply a "further step toward putting the 'upstairs' of the war administration on what might be called a more routine operational footing."[6] The *Times* anticipated Rosenman would continue the very same activities he had engaged in prior to his appointment. The principal opposition to the appointment had come from Attorney General Francis Biddle.

Biddle, regarded Rosenman as a "first rate man... needed for the particular jobs for which the President wanted him", but had strenuously objected to establishing an office of Special Counsel. If Rosenman "had been made Special Assistant or Executive Assistant I would have made no objection," Biddle has reminisced, "but Special Counsel connotes legal advice to the President and this I thought reflected upon me and the office of Attorney General." Since the Attorney General acted by statute and tradition as legal adviser to the President, Biddle had argued that the appointment of a Special Counsel was not only unnecessary, but would further serve to diminish the stature of his own office.

Roosevelt, "who was apt to disregard correct administrative procedures when he wanted to do something" made the appointment anyway. Selecting as the date for Rosenman's actual appointment a time when Attorney General and Mrs. Biddle were in Mexico, Roosevelt summoned the Judge from New York on October 1, for a swearing-in ceremony. Biddle, who learned of the appointment through a cable from Rosenman, accommodated himself to the *fait accompli*, regarding it as a minor matter not meriting additional comment.[7]

Despite persistent press reports that the Special Counsel and his family actually resided in the White House, their Washington residence was an apartment in the Wardman Park Hotel.[8] The Judge, whose unofficial office had always been located in the White House, was provided a desk in the West Wing which, though separated from the President's office by a wall was located--and this was regarded as significant--only a few feet from it. His personal staff consisted of two secretaries, but he also called on members of the regular White House staff for occasional clerical assistance.[9] For non-secretarial aid he relied upon a small group of Washington attorneys attached to various government departments whom he had come to know from previous assignments. Oscar Cox and Morton Handler were among the most frequently consulted.[10]

By October, 1943, the more hectic days of government reorganization had passed. The administrative machinery designed to carry the United States through the war was already in operation, and although Rosenman's activities in the preparation of presidential messages continued to involve him in current administrative policy, the special projects handled by the Counsel were increasingly involved with post-war concerns.[11] As in their gubernatorial collaboration, the true measure of Rosenman's assistance to Roosevelt is in the wealth of detail and the diversity of assignments to which he attended rather than the special significance of any single task. In contrast to Albany, however, even routine White House activities were suspected as newsworthy. Any scrap of information was scrutinized and speculated upon by the massive Washington press corps. Rosenman himself acquired and retained high celebrity status, but his precise activities remained unpublicized and presumably obscure to the press.

Apart from the drafting of presidential addresses and messages, which were recognized and accepted as part of the Counsel's routine, Rosenman now concerned himself more frequently with the substance of presidential reports.

During 1943, the most ambitious of these undertakings
were a 10,000 word message to Congress outlining a program to alleviate world food shortages,[12] and a not un-
related Lend-Lease report.[13] Less literary efforts included an assignment as unofficial arbiter for negotiations leading towards the acceptance of a Phillipine independence program,[14] and activities leading to the repeal
of the Chinese Exclusion Acts.[15] Important efforts were
also directed towards a legislative program for veterans.
The most pertinent aspects of this program related to
educational opportunities.

In August 1943, a committee of educators appointed
to devise a comprehensive program for the education and
training of returning veterans submitted a report to the
President. Roosevelt, pleased with the recommendations,
instructed Rosenman to prepare a message for Congress
urging their enactment. Congress readily complied, and
the proposals provided the core of legislation hailed as
the GI Bill of Rights. Rosenman has since insisted that
the proposals were discerned by both the President and
himself to have a potential value in fields far broader
than veterans' legislation. Aspiring to raise the educational level in the poorer states, they envisioned federal aid to education as a means to such an end. Heretofore effectively resisted by individuals arguing that
federal aid would lead to federal controls over local
school systems, it was apparent that "even the most rabid
opponent of federal aid to education would not dare to
raise his voice against federal financial aid for educat-
ing GIs." The administration, Rosenman has written,
viewed the programs as a "kind of entering wedge," believing that once accepted it would become easier to get "more
and more federal aid for all children in states that could
not provide decent educational facilities out of their
own resources."[16]

Most congressmen, eager to associate themselves
with veterans' legislation, were more than willing to
support such bills, and the administration's greatest

difficulties were in restraining congressional enthusiasm
for benefits significantly more generous than those the
President had proposed. Whenever a proposal, presidential
or otherwise, however, did receive congressional approval,
Rosenman would prepare an ebullient statement for the
President to release upon signing the bill into law. In
such statements the President, "as modestly as possible,"
assumed credit for initiating the legislation.[17]

Rosenman's personal relationship with individual
members of Washington officialdom was profoundly influenced by his reputation as principal presidential draftsman. Serving to enhance his official prestige by marking
him as a conduit to Roosevelt, it could also provide a
source of serious embarrassment. More than most Presidents,
Roosevelt used his speeches and messages to develop and
carry out policy, and responsible government officials
were understandably incensed when, as was his occasional
wont, he surprised them with a speech which proposed a
course of action they either opposed or to which they
had not been made privy. Often these officials suspected,
especially when such proposals coincided with Rosenman's
known views, that the Judge had urged the policy upon the
President and kept the information from them so that they
would be unable to offer effective opposition. The most
extreme instance of this occurred after the presentation
of the 1944 State of the Union Address.

The advisability of requesting national service
legislation which would authorize the government to draft
civilian workers into high priority industries had been
debated since the start of the war. Rosenman, long an
advocate of such action, believed it would serve both
to increase war production and to impede inflation. During March 1943, the Little War Cabinet had rejected offering such a recommendation largely because of the opposition of Bernard Baruch. It had, however, predicted
that unless the war ended shortly "a draft of manpower
and capital...was inevitable." Roosevelt, who had hoped
for a more affirmative announcement, reluctantly decided

against including the national service act as part of his
administrative program until it had acquired more definite
support.[18]

       During preparation of the 1944 State of the Union
message, there had been no noticeable increase in enthusiasm for a civilian draft.   The President, nonetheless,
responding to military counsel, believed it desperately
needed.   Dictating a paragraph requesting such national
service legislation, he gave it to Rosenman and Sherwood
with instructions they work it into the annual message
in the event he decided upon using it.   The President
wanted no further discussion on the matter, and to insure
against continued debate instructed his collaborators to
keep the proposed insert "a complete and absolute secret."
Rosenman, who advocated the policy and was painfully aware
of difficulties involved in keeping secrets in Washington,
instituted elaborate security precautions.   The insert
was kept separate from the rest of the message, and typed
through various drafts by the President's personal secretary.   Mimeographing of the message was delayed until
the last possible moment, and only then was the insert
incorporated into the main text.[19]

       While working on the message, and in pursuit of
other duties, the Judge discussed manpower issues with
diverse administrative personnel including Jimmy Byrnes
and Bernard Baruch.   Although both these men possessed an
important official interest in the manpower situation,
Rosenman did not inform them of the President's intention
to request a national service act, and it was not until
after the presentation of the annual message that they
learned of it.   Their reactions were almost violent.

       Byrnes reasoned that if anyone was to have known
of the request in advance, he, in his capacity of Director
of War Mobilization--and acknowledged Assistant President
--was certainly entitled to that privilege, and stormed
into the President's office with his resignation.   Although persuaded to remain as director, he was never re-
conciled to not having been alerted to the contents of the

message.[20] His relationship with Rosenman, never cordial, worsened further.[21]

Baruch was also incensed, but his association with Rosenman, of longer standing and more cordial than Byrnes' had ever been, was only momentarily disrupted by the incident. The Judge, in Baruch's view was "filled up with Roosevelt." He might argue with the President, and he might not always agree with the President, but once "FDR says so, that's it." In the light of Rosenman's strong personal devotion, Baruch concluded he had "acted as a man ought to do."[22]

The tumult over the State of the Union message proved a harbinger of subsequent events. Harry Hopkins entered the Mayo Clinic early in 1944 and on February 21, the *Chicago Tribune* proclaimed that "Sammy the Rose" had superseded him and was now "current Field Marshall" of the Palace Guard.[23] It seemed as if the *Tribune* had flashed a signal.

On February 22, the President, openly feuding with Congress, vetoed a revenue bill with an accompanying message that declared it "not a tax bill but a tax relief bill providing relief not for the needy but for the greedy."[24] The veto message touched off a spectacular political display. Senate Majority Leader Alben Barkley, a supporter of the bill, angrily resigned his post insisting that the message denoted a lack of confidence in him by the administration. Roosevelt moved to placate rising congressional dissension by disclaiming any such intention, and endorsing the Kentucky Senator for reelection as Majority Leader. Barkley was unanimously reelected and the tax veto was overriden. The derogation of congressional integrity remained a public issue, however, and Rosenman was widely censured as the alleged author of the veto message's most contumely phrase.

Republican Congressmen hoped to make political capital of the incident and struck at Rosenman not only for having allegedly written the veto message, but also for the prominent role he played in the formation of the President's legislative program. "I do not believe," Senator

Arthur Capper of Kansas proclaimed, "that any intelligent American will maintain that the people of the United States elected Judge Rosenman of New York to write our laws."[25] A number of southern Democratic Congressmen also indicated an open hostility to the Judge's legislative efforts. Steve Early came to Rosenman's defense with a categorical denial that he had written any portion of the veto message. "As a matter of fact," the presidential press secretary insisted, "he didn't even see the message."[26] Despite his extraordinary attempt to absolve Rosenman from culpability--it was later verified that Early was accurate in his denial--the attacks upon the Judge continued. Commenting upon congressional Democratic intransigency in the matter, columnist Marquis Childs observed that "consciously or unconsciously these loyal Democrats have been influenced by the Hitlerian propaganda against Rosenman carried in the McCormick-Patterson press in recent weeks."[27] This was perhaps part of the explanation, but the southern Congressional attacks upon Rosenman were far more significant as manifestations of their instinctive opposition to Roosevelt's domestic legislative program.

More overt indication of southern disaffection with Roosevelt leadership was provided that May, over the selection of presidential electors for 1944. Faced with the near certainty of Roosevelt's renomination by the Democratic National Convention, several state Democratic conventions, led by Texas, nominated electors and then adopted resolutions which absolved the electors, except under certain conditions, from any obligation to support the nominees of the national convention. The conditions under which they would support the national candidate included restoration of the two-thirds rule for presidential nominations and the rejection of an anti-poll tax plank and any references to racial equality from the national platform.[28]

Pro-Roosevelt Texas forces labored to undo the convention arrangements, and Representative Lyndon Johnson, through Rosenman, kept the White House informed of their

progress. After the national convention, 15 of the 23
Texas electors declared their intention to vote against
Roosevelt, and a special state convention withdrew their
nominations and substituted a pro-Roosevelt slate of electors. The Roosevelt slate, after some litigation, replaced the original electors on the ballot, and Johnson
jubilantly concluded his progress reports to Rosenman with
the observation "we are all set now."[29]

The Judge, though gratified by the results, was
plagued by apprehensions that ultimately southern electoral votes would be less consequential than southern
congressional support. Despite the basic opposition of
this contingent to the President's domestic program, it
consistently voted in support of his foreign policy program. The President believed United States participation
in an international organization to be the single most
important object of his postwar administration, and the
need for continued southern support of this project seemed
underscored by the results of the 1944 Republican National
Convention. On June 28, 1944, the Republicans nominated
Thomas E. Dewey as their presidential candidate. Many
observers interpreted the rejection of Willkie, now regarded as the foremost Republican internationalist, as
an indication that the party was assuming an isolationist
posture and could not be counted upon to support United
States membership in an international organization.[30]

The President was disposed to believe such speculation and proposed to resolve the dilemma which tied him
ever more closely to southern congressmen through a plan
to have himself and Willkie lead like-minded elements of
their respective parties into a new political coalition.
Willkie had already expressed interest in such a plan, and
Roosevelt arranged for Rosenman to make definite overtures. The Judge conferred with Willkie on July 5, 1944
at the St. Regis Hotel in New York City. At the meeting,
which was not disclosed until almost eight years later,
Willkie indicated that he was receptive to the idea of

forming a new party, but was unwilling to further discuss
the matter until after the 1944 elections.[31]

    While the assignation seemed to bode prospects for
a sensational political realignment at some future date,
it accomplished nothing in the way of lessening Roosevelt's
immediate reliance upon southern congressional support.
Vice President Henry Wallace had long been a *bête noir*
to conservative leadership, and this alone may have dictated against Roosevelt's insistence upon renomination of
his 1940 running mate. Wallace, however, had also aroused
formidable opposition elsewhere. Democratic National
Chairman Robert Hannegan reported that political leaders
throughout the country regarded him as a liability to
the ticket. Other advisors concurred, and the President
agreed to the political wisdom of Wallace withdrawing his
candidacy. Reluctant to tell him so directly, he instead,
assigned the task to Rosenman. Had Wallace known of the
Rosenman-Hopkins 1940 recommendation that he be dropped
from the ticket, the Judge would have been a singularly
inappropriate choice as envoy. As it was, however, the
Vice President was ignorant of the affair, and Rosenman
approached his assignment with his accustomed equanimity.
During the most recent vice-presidential jockeying, he
had been informed rather than consulted on Wallace's status. His own views on the Vice President's renomination,
he has insisted, were determined by Democratic leadership
reports.[32]

    Wallace was then on his way back from a mission to
China and expected to arrive in Seattle within a few days.
Rosenman hoped to meet him there and to confer with him
during the flight back to Washington. Apparently alerted
to the purpose of the proposed conference, neither Wallace
nor his staff made any particular effort to schedule such
a meeting. After considerable delay the Judge was informed that the Vice President was to return home by way
of Chicago rather than Seattle. Rosenman replied that
he would meet Wallace in Chicago or any other place that
he desired. To add to the confusion one of the plane's

pilots became ill with scarlet fever, and the plane was
forced to land in Canada. There was some speculation
whether it would be necessary to quarantine the crew and
passengers. Rosenman, fearing that any additional delay
would prevent him from seeing Wallace until after it was
too late to forestall a convention struggle, notified the
Vice President's staff that the President wanted Wallace
in Washington as soon as possible.

     In the interim between Rosenman's initial attempts
to arrange a meeting with the Vice President and its
eventual scheduling for July 13, Harold Ickes convinced
Roosevelt that he too should be a party to the conference.
Had Rosenman known this in advance, he would have resisted
the arrangement. "Ickes and Wallace had been bitter enemies for a long time," Rosenman had written, "and I knew
that any chance of persuading Wallace to do anything voluntarily would be wiped out if Ickes joined the conference."[33] Rosenman's expectations that the conference
would prove a failure were fully realized. The Vice President sat silently, his face "immobile as stone," while
both Rosenman and Ickes presented the case against his
candidacy. Only after they had exhausted their arguments
did Wallace speak. The display of human suffering which
he had encountered in China, he contended, had so distressed him that he possessed no interest in discussing
politics at that time. He assured them, however, he would
discuss the matter during a luncheon he had arranged with
the President for later that afternoon.[34]

     Rosenman's failure to persuade Wallace to withdraw
his candidacy precluded any resolution to the vice-presidential dilemma prior to the convention. Roosevelt had
detailed the Judge to perform a task he knew he himself
was incapable of executing. At the luncheon Wallace made
a direct appeal to the President, and Roosevelt in his
"most extreme instance" of temporizing, agreed that Wallace might remain in the race.

     That evening, with the convention only six days
off, Roosevelt left Washington on an extended trip to the

Pacific. Rosenman was among the staff accompanying him
aboard the presidential train. The Counsel's responsibilities during this period had become almost routine.
He helped draft the party platform; he assisted in the
preparation of an acceptance address; and during appre-
hensive moments which the conventions inevitably produced,
he supplied Roosevelt with companionship. On July 15,
the train paused in Chicago where Robert Hannegan came
aboard and made final arrangements for Harry Truman's
nomination.[35] The Presidential Special then proceeded to
San Diego where, after the Roosevelt-Truman ticket had
received official Democratic endorsement, Roosevelt delivered his acceptance address. Soon afterwards the presidential party sailed for Pearl Harbor aboard the cruiser
Baltimore.

        Rosenman used some of the time in Hawaii to inves-
tigate conditions relating to the continued governing of
the Islands under martial law. During much of his stay,
however, he relaxed beneath the palms along Waikiki Beach,
while Roosevelt, closeted with a specially assembled collection of generals and admirals, discussed the military
situation in the Pacific.[36] The military conferences were
concluded on July 29, and Roosevelt sailed from Pearl Harbor for an inspection tour of Alaska. That same day Rosenman left the presidential party and flew back to Washington. His sudden return was motivated by political considerations relating to his own rather that the President's
future.

        Rosenman had been giving thought to resigning his
post in Washington. He had assumed the counselship as
a war assignment and the salary he received was neither
commensurate with his earning power nor adequate to provide for his family in a fashion to which they had grown
accustomed during his years as a Judge. By July 1944,
with allied victory apparently assured, he began to reflect upon opportunities for a postwar career. One such
opportunity was that of Democratic nominee for the New
York State Court of Appeals, and Rosenman was ready to

seize upon it. According to published reports, the Democratic state machine could be expected to endorse Rosenman as a sop to the CIO for its continuing support of
Roosevelt, after Wallace, its avowed favorite, had been
discarded as the Democratic vice-presidential nominee.
The President was, of course, supporting his Counsel's
candidacy.[37]

Rosenman conferred with Ed Flynn as to the prob-
abilities of his nomination and election, and the conference results were disappointing. The Bronx Leader agreed
that should Rosenman insist upon the nomination it could
be obtained for him. He pointed out, however, that the
nominee for the vacant seat was traditionally selected
from an upstate county and that this particular nomination was tacitly recognized as the property of Monroe
County. Insistance upon Rosenman's candidacy, Flynn
warned, might so antagonize upstate Democrats as to cause
temporary disaffection with the party.[38] Since there was
then some doubt that Roosevelt would be able to carry New
York in November, Rosenman, as Flynn expected he would,
withdrew his candidacy.

The 1944 campaign was in many respects similar to
that of 1940. Roosevelt did not begin formal campaigning
until after he was convinced that his opponent was making
substantial progress among the electorate. He delivered
a total of seven major campaign speeches and Rosenman
worked on all of them. Sherwood returned from an OWI
assignment in Europe in time to assist in the last drafts
of the first of these, but Hopkins was still too ill to
be of much assistance. Incidental to his speech writing
activities, Rosenman kept careful watch over the campaign
orations of the leading Republican candidates, and culled
from their speeches material which he labeled "misstate-
ments of fact" and "distortions of truth."[39] Since the
President, as a matter of policy, usually refused to refer
directly to opposition charges, his Counsel prepared several pages listing the specific "distortions" accompanied
by documentation of such charges. Steve Early distributed

copies to reporters, "not as a White House release but as a memorandum for their guidance to help them in writing their stories." That many of the reporters utilized the material was a source of pride to Rosenman.[40]

Election results revealed a Roosevelt victory by over 3,500,000 votes, and the comfortable majority by which the President carried New York State indicated to Rosenman that he had erred in agreeing to Flynn's argument against his own race for the Court of Appeals. The Judge had incorrectly gauged his own state. He was, however, most accurate in his estimate of Roosevelt strength throughout the nation. His pre-election estimate was only one vote short of the President's electoral total.[41]

A few days after the campaign Roosevelt wrote that although Rosenman understood "the extent" of his "appreciation and affection," he nonetheless wanted "to put on paper" his "gratitude" for the "good sense, wise loyalty, and hard work which I have so long been able to count upon from you."[42] The Judge had received similar notes in the past; they never ceased to provide a source of exhiliration.

Chapter Eleven

THE END OF AN EPOCH

   Reflecting an austerity appropriate to a nation at
war, Roosevelt's fourth inaugural was a simple observance.
The principals gathering onto the White House south porch
for a morning ceremony were met by raw wintry temperatures
and the remnants of an overnight snowstorm. It was as if
the ceremonies' committee had arranged bleak weather especially for the abbreviated rites. Outgoing Vice President Wallace duly swore his successor into office and
Chief Justice Stone administered the oath to Roosevelt.
In rapid succession the President delivered his address,
Monsignor John A. Ryan offered a benediction, and a band
played the Star Spangled Banner. Then, as the band struck
up Hail to the Chief, Roosevelt waved to the crowd, step-
ped back, and retired into the White House. The entire
ceremony was completed in under twenty minutes.

   Post inaugural festivities were also abbreviated
and it was 8:30 in the evening when the Rosenmans returned home. Too early to retire, they instead called upon
the Wallaces who maintained an apartment in the same hotel.
The former Vice President had been passing the inauguration evening attempting Russian language study from pho-
nograph records, and the Rosenman visit took on aspects
of a condolence call. The Judge voiced his admiration
and gratitude for the loyalty Wallace had maintained towards Roosevelt during the recent campaign, and left after exchanging some further pleasantries.[1] Wallace presumably returned to his language records.

        Secretary of Commerce Jesse Jones, Wallace's most
persistent foe in government circles, passed the evening
in a far less serene manner. At 5 o'clock he received a
phone message from the White House requesting his appearance at noon the following day. Moments later a letter
was hand delivered from the President requesting his
immediate resignation so that Roosevelt might appoint
Wallace in his stead.[2] The dismissal had been rumored
for some days,[3] but the President had not consulted with
his staff or Jones on the matter. Despite the suggestion
of his personal secretary, he conferred with neither his
Counsel nor his Press Secretary on the contents of the
letter.[4]

        Although Rosenman might have suggested a less
brusque dismissal letter, he was not unhappy with Jones'
ouster. Apart from divergent ideologies, Rosenman was
influenced by evidence that Jones had lent his tacit pre-
convention support to the Texas anti-Roosevelt movement.[5]
Wallace, on the other hand, had demonstrated his continued
loyalty, and Rosenman considered his appointment as fulfillment of a bargain the President had struck with his
ex-Vice President.[6] Although not causal to subsequent
events, the political atmosphere was charged with liberal
discontent which had been heightened by Roosevelt's appointment of six assistant secretaries of state whose
domestic political philosophies were at apparent variance
with the New Deal. Rosenman, who had himself expressed
disappointment over the assignments, was among those charged with culpability.[7] The replacement of Jones with
Wallace would, incidental to other considerations, serve
to placate liberal fears. Senate confirmation of Wallace
proved, however, difficult to secure, and at times Rosenman seemed more anxious for it than the President.

        Jones launched a well publicized campaign to pre-
vent Wallace's appointment, and as the former Commerce
Secretary had long been a favorite of Congress the circumstances of his dismissal served to generate an even
greater sympathy for his cause. Wallace, never popular

with the legislative branch, now appeared even less acceptable to it. His nomination was bitterly opposed both within and without the Congress, and it soon became obvious that it would not be confirmed without direct White House intervention. Roosevelt and most of his staff, however, had left Washington January 22,--two days after the inauguration--for the Yalta conference.[8]

The remaining White House staff agreed that if the federal loan agencies then being administered by the Secretary of Commerce were removed from Commerce Department control, the Senate would agree to Wallace's appointment to the emasculated post. Accordingly, Rosenman and Mrs. Roosevelt sent a joint telegram to the President urging an executive order to effect transfer of the loan agencies from the Department of Commerce. Roosevelt was not receptive to the plan and left the telegram unanswered.[9]

In the interim a House approved measure to effect such a transfer had been introduced in the Senate by Walter George, but appeared unlikely to secure passage without some indication of the President's approval. Mrs. Roosevelt and Rosenman thereupon dispatched a second telegram requesting the President to indicate whether he would sustain the bill. It was essential, they asserted, that he reply immediately in the affirmative to assure Wallace's confirmation. The President, after conferring with Byrnes, who was accompanying him to Yalta, agreed to the proposed measure. An appropriate message was accordingly rushed off to the White House[10] and relayed by Rosenman to Senate Leader Barkley.[11] It arrived only minutes prior to a vote on the transfer bill and contributed materially to its passage. In due time the Wallace appointment received the Senate's unenthusiastic confirmation.

During the afternoon of inauguration day, Rosenman, like Jones, had also received a personal letter from the President. Unlike Jones, however, the Counsel had been privy to its contents and eagerly awaited its receipt. Roosevelt had written that "In addition to your position

as Special Counsel...I want you to undertake a mission to
the United Kingdom, France, Belgium, and the Netherlands
as my personal representative with the rank of Minister."
He was to report upon what measures might best be taken
by the United States and its allies towards the winning
of the war "with respect to the flow of vital supplies
other than finished munitions to these countries." Not
disclosed at the time, but also included in his letter
of appointment, were instructions to ascertain these nations' postwar reconstruction needs "in terms of possible
credits or other financial assistance, which may be made
available by this country by means already at hand or
through recommendations for appropriate legislation."[12]
Independent of his mission responsibilities, Rosenman was
to discuss plans for trials of captured Nazi leaders with
appropriate British officials.[13]

The assignment fulfilled a longtime personal ambition and Rosenman was "deeply honored and thankful." The
Judge had remained occupied with domestic matters long after his associates had assumed roles as world statesmen,
and he could not help but be envious of their opportunities. The task of placating a Congress hostile to the
appointment of Henry Wallace seemed indeed trivial when
compared to those issues being discussed at Yalta. Operating in a narrower and more technical sphere, the significance of Rosenman's efforts had usually been dwarfed
by some simultaneous event of international diplomacy.
His work on SPAB had coincided with the Atlantic Conference, and his discussions with Roosevelt over housing reorganization had taken place during moments the President
was able to spare from the Arcadia Conference. Even before becoming Counsel he had expressed, according to one
1942 magazine article, regrets at not being given assignments with international or military implications. The
"appreciation and gratitude" which he professed to the
President "for sending me abroad on this mission" was
heartfelt.[14]

Some observers concluded otherwise. Public announcement of the Rosenman mission sparked rumors that he would not return to Washington as Counsel. President Roosevelt, it was alleged, was already inquiring among Senators as to whether they would be willing to confirm the Judge as either Solicitor General or Labor Secretary,[15] and when, a few days prior to leaving on his mission he was admitted to practice before the United States Supreme Court, it was regarded as a prelude to his appointment as Solicitor General.[16] The rumors were not without substance. Jimmy Byrnes had persuaded Roosevelt of the wisdom of transfering Rosenman from the White House staff, and as the post of Solicitor General was soon to be vacant the President offered it to his long-time aide. Rosenman protested against any such appointment and reminded the President that he had resigned a $25,000 a year judgeship to come to Washington so that he might assist in the war effort. He would, he contended, have little such opportunity as Solicitor General. Rosenman expected to leave Washington shortly, and when he left he hoped it would be from the Counselship.[17] Roosevelt, who possessed a notorious weakness for arguments placed on a personal basis, made no further plans to transfer Rosenman from his White House staff. *The Chicago Tribune* consoled by a report that Byrnes and Biddle had forced the mission on Rosenman, assured its readers that the Judge was to remain away from Washington for an "indefinite period of exile."[18]

Whatever the motivation for assigning Rosenman to head the mission, the mission's potential significance was tremendous. Conceived by Oscar Cox,[19] it was anticipated that the investigation would provide the data from which Roosevelt might formulate the basis of United States reconstruction policy. Even before the war's end the need for some workable program had become obvious. To meet the requirements of the Allied military forces advancing through Germany, a constant flow of supplies had to be channeled through Belgium and France. People of these nations, as well as other liberated areas, were suffering

from the most severe shortage of food, clothing, and
transportation facilities they had yet been forced to en-
dure, and the military hazards of discontented civilians
behind military lines were well advertised. Humanitarian
considerations also impelled immediate action. As a result of a severe winter and material deprivations the
western European death rate from tuberculosis had risen
to nearly half again as high as before the war. Rickets
among children had increased five fold. The infant mor-
tality rate had spiralled to appalling heights and paper
was commonly resorted to for swaddling clothes.[20] It
seemed folly to have liberated the populations of Europe
from Nazi tyranny in order that they might freeze or starve
to death under political democracy, or equally appalling
to American postwar sensitivities, fall prey to Communist
inducements.

It was hoped that the Rosenman mission would supply
"the factual dynamite for President Roosevelt to blow the
lid off Europe's muddled relief and rehabilitation situation." This was expected to require "enough evidence to
blast open the issue, force legislative action to revise
the Johnson act, and provide new measures for foreign
cash credits."[21] Such credits were required for raw material, fuel, and machinery essential to permit the reconstruction of European productive capability. A first
step, however, was to put the population on subsistence
levels, a task obstructed by limited shipping and port
facilities.[22]

From the receipt of his instructions until February
5, Rosenman selected the personnel and detailed the operations for his mission. Although officially sponsored
by the Foreign Economic Administration, the Judge consulted and staffed his mission with officials of the State,
War, and Treasury Departments as well as the FEA. Con-
stituting "the largest number of economic and other spe-
cialists ever sent abroad on a single mission since the
United States entered the war,"[23] they left Washington
February 9, and arrived in Great Britain the following

day. Upon arrival Rosenman was greeted with instructions
to join the President who was journeying back from Yalta
aboard the battlecruiser *Quincy*. Roosevelt desired his
Counsel's assistance in the preparation of a report to
Congress on the results of the Yalta negotiations, and
had arranged to have Rosenman meet the *Quincy* at Algiers.

As Rosenman left London, his mission commenced to
survey the stockpile of civilian supplies stored in Eng-
land to determine how large a share might be transferred
to continental Europe. Members of the mission also conferred with representatives of occupied nations in London
to evolve preliminary indications of their needs.

The Judge had hoped to return after a few days and
expected that if he and the President began work immediately and prepared a good first draft, he would be able to
leave the *Quincy* at Gibralter and fly back to London. In
this he was disappointed. The *Quincy* did not reach Algiers
until February 18, and Roosevelt, who appeared "all burnt
out," was unable to settle down to the routine of speechwriting. Furthermore General Edwin "Pa" Watson had suffered a stroke and lay dying in one of the cabins. Hopkins had declared himself too ill to continue the trip
home and prepared to rest for a few days at Marrakech.
It was Hopkins' scheduled departure that had made Rosenman's attendance aboard ship so imperative.

At Admiral Leahy's suggestion, Hopkins, Early, and
Charles Bohlen, who had acted as interpreter at the conferences, had a two hour meeting with Rosenman in Hopkins'
cabin where Bohlen gave the Judge all of the signed agreements and initialed memoranda of the Big Three and Foreign
Minister conferences at Yalta. He also provided a six-page
memorandum which he had dictated to assist in the preparation of the President's address. Then all of the conferees
except Rosenman and Leahy departed the ship.[24]

Possessing the complete records of the conference,
the Judge was nonetheless handicapped by not having been

present. By the time the President began work on the
speech the *Quincy* was far out on the Atlantic, and Rosenman had given up hope for an early return to London. Not
completed until after the presidential party had returned
to Washington, the speech was too long and revealed far
too little. Furthermore, at the time of its delivery
Roosevelt was far from his oratorical best. Rosenman "was
dismayed at the [President's] halting ineffective manner
of delivery." Frequent ad-libs, some of which the Judge
considered bordering on the ridiculous, further detracted
from the speech. The following morning the Judge attended
the usual 9:30 staff meeting in the President's bedroom.
After it was concluded he remained behind to inform Roosevelt that he intended to leave Washington immediately to
rejoin his mission. They exchanged a short farewell, and
the President jocularly warned his aide that as London
was very wet in March to be sure to remember his rubbers.
Rosenman hurriedly departed the White House and flew to
Great Britain.[25]

Reaching London on March 6, his arrival coincided
with an announcement from Washington that twenty tons of
clothing and thirty tons of food were to be diverted from
British stockpiles to help supply liberated France.[26]
These stockpiles had originally been amassed as insurance
against the disruption of communications by air and sea
attacks, and Rosenman assumed the improved military situation had so enhanced British security as to make them
partially expendable. Prime Minister Churchill, however,
announced his opposition to any such redistribution plan,[27]
and Judge Rosenman was rumored ready to "insist that they
[Great Britain] at least cut back their import requirements for three or four months so that current supplies
can be channeled to the continent."[28]

Rosenman refused to confirm such reports and repeatedly asserted that his mission had "no authority to
make promises or commitments to the governments of liberated areas but is exclusively on a factfinding task to
report to the President."[29] Churchill feared, however,

that he would probably suggest the diversion of supplies
and "had a good talk with Rosenman about our daily
bread."[30] The Prime Minister emphasized that although
the British diet was adequate in terms of calories, it
was limited in variety. Rosenman was quick to acknowledge that the British diet was indeed dull and monoto-
nous,[31] but insisted that the problem was hardly as desperate as that posed by the calorie-deficient western
European diet. He assured the Prime Minister that he
would make no final recommendations, however, until after
he had concluded a scheduled inspection tour of the continent and agreed to another conference upon his return.

The Rosenman mission began its continental tour
with Paris, where for about a week it held extensive conferences with SHAEF and French government officials.[32]
The Judge also managed such activities as a field trip
through northern France and an informal tour of the Paris
slums and food shops.[33] After inspection of French port
facilities the mission visited Belgium, Luxemburg, and
Allied occupied Germany, conferring with civilian officials
as well as General Dwight D. Eisenhower and his staff. On
April 1, the mission toured Holland where it encountered
the "gravest problems and starkest scenes of desolation"
of the entire trip and the following day, after twenty
days on the continent, returned to Brussels and departed
that city by air to arrive in London later in the evening.[34]

Once back in the British capital the mission proceeded to correlate and interpret its data in preparation
for a final report. Rosenman so engrossed himself in the
task that even a memo from Sherwood advising him of "some
talk of a speech coming up for Jefferson Day, April 13,"
hardly seemed relevant. "Not a delivered speech but a
message," Sherwood would handle it himself. He did not
know as yet "whether a draft has already been made by
anyone, but I guess it will be just one of those things."
The forthcoming United Nations Organization meeting was
a different matter, and undoubtedly, Sherwood warned
Rosenman, "there will have to be something more momentous

for the San Francisco Conference."[35] The Judge was less
troubled with speechwriting assignments than his stateside
collaborator. His immediate concern was a confrontation
with Churchill. Prepared to discuss his mission report
and the proposals to provide trials for captured Nazi
leaders, he arrived at Chequers, the Prime Minister's
retreat, early in the evening. It was not, however, until
after 2 a.m., that Churchill first inquired as to Rosenman's food report. He especially wanted to know whether
the Judge anticipated taking food away from the British.
Armed with the statistics of Lord Charwell, his personal
economist, he proceeded to bombard the Judge with calcu-
lations to prove the folly of diverting substantial
amounts of food from the British Isles to the continent.

Rosenman countered with his own statistics as well
as a "firsthand knowledge of the tragic suffering of the
people in the cities of" the continent. He would report
that while there was an adequate supply of foodstuffs in
many western European rural areas, the lack of internal
transportation facilities, fuel, and a stable currency
had made it impossible to bring those supplies into the
cities. The problem was further complicated by a shortage
of Allied shipping facilities. Military operations continued to monopolize almost all available trans-Atlantic
shipping. Rosenman insisted that the immediate assumption
of cross channel relief operations was the most expedient
and painless method of compensating for Allied inability
to transfer relief supplies directly to the continent
from the United States. Although Rosenman did not acquit
himself as well as he had hoped--he attributed his fail-
ings more to the late hour than the potency of the Prime
Minister's arguments--Churchill "seemed fairly well satisfied with the report."[36]

Before returning to London later that morning, he
stopped at Churchill's bedroom to say good-bye. The Prime
Minister, who was breakfasting in bed, immediately engaged his guest in a discussion of the proposed war trials,
and repeated the same arguments Rosenman had recently heard

from other British officials. The Prime Minister supported some war crime trials, but had come to conclude
it best if the six or seven top Nazis were disposed of
simply and summarily. His most compelling reason was that
any open and prolonged trial of Hitler would be denounced
by public opinion as a farce.[37] Roosevelt had held a
similar view but the previous January his thinking shifted
somewhat and he assigned the Judge to study the question.[38]
Rosenman conferred with the State, Justice, and War Departments and they reported unanimously in favor of trials for
all captured war criminals.[39] Roosevelt had accepted these
conclusions, and Rosenman told the Prime Minister that
"he was sure" the President would never agree to summary
executions. Churchill was not persuaded, but agreed to
the suggestion that "the matter might properly be made a
subject for discussion at the United Nations Conference"
scheduled for later that month in San Francisco.[40]

     The Judge then returned to London where his staff
was at work on the report. Scheduled for completion sometime after mid-April, Rosenman hoped to accompany his mission home at that time. Bernard Baruch, also in London
and quartered in the same hotel, was planning to return
to Washington on April 13, aboard the President's personal
plane, the *Sacred Cow*. On the evening of April 12, he invited Rosenman to accompany him on the return trip, but
the Judge preferring to remain with his mission, declined
the offer.

     Later that same evening Rosenman received a call
asking if he would come to see Baruch immediately. Fearing that the elder statesman had become ill, he was assured this was not the case and donning a bathrobe crossed
to Baruch's suite. "Now Sam, steady in the boat!" Baruch
cautioned as the Judge entered the bedroom, "...the radio
has announced that the President is dead."

     Rosenman would be returning with Baruch after all.
The mission--its assignment now so seemingly unimportant--
would follow later. Elliot Roosevelt and Ed Flynn were

also in London, and the next day at noon all four left
aboard the *Sacred Cow*. They arrived in Washington before
midnight.[41]

On the morning of April 14, as the train carrying
Roosevelt's body from Warm Springs, Georgia, arrived,
Judge and Mrs. Rosenman were among those waiting at Union
Station. When the funeral procession formed, Mrs. Rosenman and the Judge, "his face dulled and shoulders sagging"
entered one of the limosines for the strange silent ride
to the White House.[43] Services were conducted that afternoon in the East Room. The coffin was then returned to
the waiting train and transported to a simple grave within
a Hyde Park rose garden.

Train rides from Washington to Hyde Park were a
familiar experience for the Judge. He had made the trip
with Roosevelt many times before. This time, however, it
marked the end of an epoch in his life. During the seventeen years since their first meeting, Rosenman's initial
skepticism of the Hudson Valley squire's "liberalism" had
been transformed into unabashed adulation of the world
leader's vision. Throughout those years his own staunch
loyalty had been reciprocated; a priceless favor only few
could claim. Forever awed by the crippled Roosevelt's
majestic figure, the man and the presidency had long since
blended into a single integrated form. Roosevelt had become the President and the presidency was Roosevelt. When
Roosevelt died the Vice President had succeeded to his
office, but the President was dead. There could be no
doubt the trip back to Hyde Park ended an era in Rosenman's
life. He believed it would mark "the end of an epoch for
the United States too--and for the entire world."[43] That
just another Jefferson Day Address, scheduled for delivery
the day after the President died had become his valedic-
tory. "Let us move forward with strong and active faith."
So Roosevelt spoke--had he lived.[44]

Chapter Twelve

WORKING WITH TRUMAN

On April 16, 1945, the editorial writer for the *Chattanooga News-Free Press* exclaimed that "if any news in the world could leave a person breathless in these days of 'big news' it is the dispatch from Washington which says that President Harry S. Truman has kicked out the Felix Frankfurter-Samuel Rosenman-Harry Hopkins advisory council." He concluded that the "ending of the era of the Frankfurter-Hopkins-Rosenman triumvirate is about as much joy as the country can take at one juncture."[1]

Rosenman, along with other members of Roosevelt's Cabinet and staff, submitted his resignation. Restaffing required time, however, and at Truman's first news conference he announced that he had "asked Mr. Early and Mr. Hassett, Mr. Daniels and Judge Rosenman...to stay and help me get things organized...My staff," he had decided. "will stand the training with these gentlemen."[2] The Judge's interpretation of the situation was that he would remain only another month or so. Since he had contemplated resigning even before Roosevelt's death, this would require no alteration of his personal calendar.

Even had Rosenman hoped to stay on, it seemed unlikely he would be invited to so do. The post of Special Counsel to the President had been specifically created as an appropriate position from which the Judge might continue to serve Roosevelt, and political pundits often described the Counsel as disinterested in all things pol-

itical except Roosevelt. Rosenman, Stanley High once
wrote, had "nothing to prove and no plan to put across.
He is not committed to the evangelization of the world
in this generation--*unless* Mr. Roosevelt is committed to
it."[3] This reputation as Roosevelt's chameleon, which
at first blush seemed to disqualify Rosenman as a Truman
advisor, ultimately endowed him with influence over the
enunciation of post-war domestic policy he would not have
exercised had Roosevelt survived.

        In retrospect numerous parallels between Rosenman's
1928 assignment to Roosevelt and his tasks as Truman's
caretaker Counsel suggest themselves. Neither as Senator
nor as Vice President had Truman had the opportunity to
familiarize himself with the detailed operations of the
executive office, and although he might begin his administration with "never mind me let's work for Roosevelt"
exhortations, he could never maintain a government solely
by that strategy. Rosenman, by virtue of his experience
and personality, emerged as the White House staff member
most useful in assisting Truman maintain continuity with
his predecessor. Yet contrary to his later extravagant
claims for Truman's Senate record,[4] the new President was
an unknown quantity to him. Certainly, after working with
Roosevelt, he would be a letdown. Nonetheless the Counsel
was prepared to place his technical skills at Truman's
disposal--should they be requested.

        The decisions of the first weeks of the Truman ad-
ministration were invariably the products of momentum:
actions already initiated by the President's predecessor
requiring further implementation. Truman would intention-
ally undo nothing toward which Roosevelt had worked. The
war, of course, would continue to be prosecuted on both
fronts, and "as President Roosevelt had directed," the
United Nations conference would be held within the month.[5]
"Those ideals which have been so eloquently proclaimed
by Franklin Roosevelt," Truman pledged to defend "with
all my strength and all my heart."[6] The new President
had, as he later wrote, become inexorably caught up in

"an immense administrative operation. There had been a change of executives, but the machinery kept going in its customary routine manner, and properly so. It would have been nonsense to expect anything else."[7]

Truman's choice of the terms "customary" and "routine", though perhaps descriptive of the manner in which the executive office responded to events, is wholly inadequate in describing the events themselves. Actions that in less harried days would develop into prime national issues were unable to compete successfully for even short term attention against such considerations as the imminent collapse of Nazi Germany, forthcoming international conferences, reconversion, and the impending invasion of Japan. The fate of the Rosenman Mission report is a case in point.

Soon after Roosevelt's funeral, the Judge briefed the President on his activities. The food report could be completed in a few days, but the war crime issues had been postponed until the San Francisco Conference. Truman, prompted by Secretary of State Stettinius, authorized Rosenman to continue his war crimes assignments, and to facilitate matters designated the Judge his personal representative at San Francisco.

The Rosenman Mission report had been formally presented to President Truman on April 26, the day after the San Francisco Conference convened. Concluding that the "immediate and long-range economic situations of [the] liberated countries are extremely serious," it offered a series of recommendations predicated on the assumption that "the responsibility for providing a substantial share of most civilian supplies will rest with the United States," and urged the President enunciate such a policy. Needs were

> grave, not only from a humanitarian aspect,
> but because they involve internal and inter-
> national political considerations. The future

> permanent peace of Europe depends largely
> upon the restoration of the economy of these
> countries, including a reasonable standard of
> living and employment. United States economy,
> too, will be deeply affected unless Northwest
> Europe again resumes its place in the interna-
> tional exchange of goods and services. Further-
> more, a chaotic and hungry Europe is not fer-
> tile ground in which stable, democratic and
> friendly governments can be reared.[9]

Although there is probably no direct causal relationship, many of the long-range policy recommendations in the
report were ultimately implemented. Tragically, the short-
range relief activities received only token support.
Rosenman himself had qualified any United States commitment toward feeding Europe with assurances it would be met
"as fully as the successful prosecution of military operations and the maintenance of our essential domestic economy will permit."[10] When President Truman announced the
commitment "as the established policy of Government," he
reiterated these reservations.[11]

There was no rush to implement this commitment.
Even if Rosenman's analysis of the European situation was
accepted, his proposals were politically suspect. The
Judge had anticipated that the allocation of civilian
supplies to Europe would "in all probability cut into the
ration of the American consumer," and suggested an immediate "widespread official and public campaign to educate
the American people on the gravity of the needs of our
allies in liberated Europe."[12] Indiana Congressman George
W. Gillie was representative of the opposition. He had
read the Mission report with great interest. *"Perhaps*
Mr. Rosenman's report is true," but if it were, he believed the American people would still object to it.
"They are sympathetic to the people of the world who face
starvation...But they disagree...that this nation must be
denied food so that the world can be fed." Gillie's
solution was not "belt tightening" but replacing acreage

controls and providing new farm equipment.[13] Whatever
its merits, an effect of Representative Gillie's proposals
was to downgrade the urgency of European relief and subordinate it to longer range domestic political objectives.

Although the Judge directed a series of conferences
"with a view of seeing to what extent, if any," the needs
outlined in his report might be met,[14] the proposed campaign to educate the American public on the gravity of the
situation was never mounted. There were too many other
projects requiring simultaneous attention.

The San Francisco Conference was not the least of
these. Although war trial negotiations were not on the
official agenda, the international conference provided an
excellent opportunity for discussion of the issues. Specifically, Rosenman hoped to organize an international
military tribunal to try the major Nazi leaders and adopt
a procedure for the trials. Stalin had indicated his approval of such a policy, when on April 23, Sir Alexander
Cadogan of the British Foreign Office presented Rosenman
an *aide memoire* reaffirming the basis for British opposition.[15] The note included no new information and Rosenman
proceeded as if he saw no obstacles to settlement. President Truman had agreed to the appointment of a Chief
Prosecutor to the proposed International Military Tribunal
and Rosenman phoned Supreme Court Justice Robert Jackson,
a vocal advocate of war trials, to ask if he were willing
to take on the assignment. Jackson was indeed interested
and after Rosenman briefed him on the state of affairs,
the two judges worked out the details of Jackson's acceptance letter.[16]

Jackson delivered his final draft to the Counsel,
Sunday evening April 29, and on May 2, Truman made the
appointment official. He further revealed that Jackson
had already assembled a staff to help gather and examine
evidence. Both the President and Jackson justified the
appointment by emphasizing that speed in establishing an
international tribunal was of the essence. Furthermore,

since "we know some kind of military tribunal must be
set up," we should "be ready to begin presentation of
evidence as soon as the tribunal can be ready to hear
it."[17]

Rosenman arrived at San Francisco armed with this
fait accompli and a letter from the President specifically
rejecting British proposals "to dispose politically of the
top ranking Nazis and Fascists--without any trial." On
May 3, he presented the U.S. protocols to the Foreign
Ministers of Great Britain, Soviet Russia and France, and
waited. Rosenman feared that if agreement were not reached
early, all discussions regarding war trials would become
merely academic. Negotiations had already been initiated
for Germany's surrender, and unless special provisions
were made relating to the imminent capture of Nazi leaders,
it was probable that they would be disposed of in a manner determined by the caprices of whichever government
seized them first.

In an important sense something not unlike that had
already occurred: the execution of Mussolini by Italian
partisans on April 28, and the suicides of Hitler and
Goebbels the day following. This highly significant at-
trition of enemy leadership made the U.S. position seem
less risky to the British, and they relented sufficiently
to encourage Rosenman to cable the President: "We are
making progress."[18]

The negotiators routinely submitted the U.S. proposals for instructions to their home governments, but
despite the advent of V-E Day and the cajoling of the
State Department there were no immediate replies. The
negotiators spent some time tinkering with delicate
amendments defining criminal acts,[19] but in the absence
of further instructions came to no definitive conclusions.
After a week, Rosenman, noticeably disappointed at the
impasse, returned to Washington to deal with "pressing
matters." He hoped that when word arrived from the other

governments they might meet again. Either Washington or
San Francisco would be suitable.[20]

  Foreign Minister Eden was in Washington on the 14th,
and Rosenman urged him not only to "expedite action in
reference to our memo," but further requested that the
British government appoint a prosecutor with powers similar to Jackson's. A more formal request of this nature,
he revealed, would be made through the State Department.[21]
There was still no visible progress when on May 24, Heinrich Himmler escaped possible trial through suicide.
Senator Scott Lucas voiced dismay at the administration's
inability to conclude the pretrial negotiations. Rosenman replied that although Jackson was already in Europe
to collect evidence, there had been no answer "as yet"
from the other governments on the U.S. "proposals."
Under these circumstances the Counsel thought it appropriate for Lucas to call "to the attention of the Senate
and of the nation," that if the other nations "don't soon
come to an agreement with us on a speedy procedure, we
expect to proceed ourselves and try the top criminals now
in our possession ourselves."[22]

  Lucas' assistance was not necessary. That same day
the British submitted a counter proposal recommending
London as the negotiation site.[23] American public opinion
strongly endorsed the trial policy and Rosenman still
thought "it would be wise to have the final negotiations
in Washington since our Government has been taking the
lead in the matter." Nonetheless "it seems that they
prefer London." Other obligations militated against
Rosenman's attendance. Justice Jackson was then in London
and the Counsel advised that the prosecutor be given the
assignment. Within days after the American agreement to
the British site, His Majesty's Government "accepted in
principle" Rosenman's San Francisco draft proposal. The
French and Soviet approvals followed shortly.[24]

It had required about six weeks for the Counsel to complete those missions assigned him by the late President. During that time Truman had systematically replaced Cabinet and personal staff holdovers, and Roosevelt's Counsel prepared his own imminent departure. Foremost in his plans was to augment his income. Since leaving the bench Rosenman had supplemented his salary with personal savings that, by 1945, were exhausted. Visions of a high paying private law practice had become almost irresistible --especially after one potential client extended the offer of a $25,000 annual retainer, a single fee in excess of twice Rosenman's government salary.[25] Uncertain as to when he would be free to leave Washington and reluctant to dismiss so lucrative an opportunity, Rosenman discussed the matter with Truman directly.

Assuming that the President intended to appoint Hugh Fulton, the former Chief Counsel of Truman's Senate War Investigating Committee as his successor, Rosenman suggested Truman make the appointment immediately to allow time for him to "break in" the new Counsel before leaving Washington.[26] Truman's reply was not at all what Rosenman had anticipated. The President had not yet decided upon the Judge's replacement. He had looked, but he had not as yet found anyone whom he considered as capable. He wanted, Truman concluded, Rosenman to stay on at least until after the war. The Judge acquiesced. "When the Commander in Chief asks there can only be one answer-- Aye, aye, Sir."[26]

The private conference had an unusual public sequel. The President formally declined Rosenman's resignation by means of a letter which extolled, among other qualities, his "self-effacing zeal and patriotic devotion" which could not "yet be spared" by either the "Chief Executive" or "the welfare of our country." Rosenman wrote in turn of his own gratitude for Truman's "generous expressions of confidence." He "had about completed arrangements to go back to private life," and relinquished "those plans with some regret." Nonetheless he would be "delighted to serve with one who has so thoroughly demonstrated a desire and ability to carry on in the great traditions of liberal democracy and of cooperation for world peace." At the conclusion of a press conference on June 1, the President announced he had "persuaded Sam Rosenman to stay with me for another year," and Press Secretary Charles Ross distributed mimeographed copies of their correspondence.[27]

The President had not fired his Counsel, and to the uninitiated it seemed an extraordinary amount of sound and fury by which to mark a non-event. For Washington officialdom, however, the connotations were quite clear. Truman's elaborate display of appreciation and praise would help cement Rosenman's personal loyalty to the new President while underscoring Truman's intention to maintain Roosevelt programs. The reaffirmation of Rosenman, this time to specifically serve Truman, established the Counsel's credentials as a *bona fide* conduit directly to the new President. At least one of the established routes to the White House would remain open.

Whatever the consequences of Truman's decision, it had originated as a spontaneous rather than a deliberately calculated maneuver. The proprieties of war crime negotiations had necessitated that Rosenman retain his White House office, and the President had had little opportunity or inclination to ponder his subsequent usefulness. In bringing his personal situation to Truman's direct attention, the Judge posed a dilemma for which the President was not prepared. Beset by mass resignations, he may simply have grasped at an opportunity to preserve something of the administrative *status quo*. Truman did not know precisely how or where he most needed help, but he knew he was going to need it. He had, for instance, brought no speechwriters with him into office, and Rosenman's speechwriting prowess was legend. Furthermore, while after Roosevelt's death the administrative "machinery had kept going in its customary routine manner," it would be useful to have someone close by who knew its workings.[28]

Whatever considerations prompted the President's request that Rosenman remain, the request occasioned genuine surprise. Although Truman had facilitated his efforts to complete the tasks Roosevelt had assigned the Judge, he had not taken him into confidence. Having decided to retain Roosevelt's Counsel, however, Truman drew him immediately into the vortex of White House operations.

The decision to discard Rosenman's lame duck status coincided with a virtual cessation of press accounts of his international activities. Not only had his glamorous assignments requiring foreign missions and conferences been terminated, but his attention was redirected toward routine White House operations where public notice is focussed upon the President himself, and Presidential aides labor to keep it that way. If there was a visible aspect of Rosenman's official presence, it was through Truman's public papers and messages. There was relatively little speculation on their authorship. It was simply assumed that the principal responsibility for literary draftsmanship would remain with the President's Counsel. Rosenman fulfilled those expectations, and from mid-May, 1945 until February, 1946 when he left Washington, the preponderance of documents ultimately published in Truman's *Public Papers* were either composed or edited by the Judge.[29] Yet as a speechwriter he was never as effective working for Truman as he had been for Roosevelt. In part attributable to the differing oratorical styles of the two Presidents, Rosenman also never completely adjusted to Truman's speechwriting techniques. Under Roosevelt, while contributions to a message might come from many quarters, seldom did more than two or three individuals work on the final drafts. Under Truman, Rosenman was usually forced to work with a far larger number of collaborators. He found this an inhibiting experience.

His effectiveness as a speechwriter diminished in direct proportion to the size of the team with which he was expected to work. Large groups resulted in too much discussion of the substance and too little attention to

form. Furthermore, a sizeable group editing the final
drafts tended to preclude the development of a single
distinctive style. With rare exception Rosenman had been
most valuable to Roosevelt as a compiler and dispassionate
editor rather than as a phrasemaker. Under Truman the
physical presence of interested parties intruded upon the
final editing and dulled the Judge's pen. Rosenman would
have experienced similar inhibitions had Roosevelt regularly employed such speechwriting strategies, but the
matter was complicated by the fact that the Judge's association with other members of Truman's personal staff
was seldom intimate enough to permit relentless compres-
sion or other revisions without offending personal sensitivities. The Truman staff was not only larger than
Roosevelt's, but it had of necessity been hurriedly assembled and had not developed a sense of collective elan.[30]
While Rosenman became a fast friend and ideologic ally of
Press Secretary Charlie Ross, his relationship with other
participants was at best harmonious. Under these circumstances it was politically and personally expedient to
strive for consensus rather than effect. In addition, and
this was the fundamental consideration, the President
seemed to prefer it that way.

Rosenman's prime contributions to the Truman administration were his detailed knowledge of specific programs, his prodigious capacity for work, and his general
views on the role of government. During the early months
these views were not as commonly shared as they had been
among the Roosevelt staff, and Rosenman became their
gentle but determined advocate.

Once designated Truman's Counsel Rosenman wasted
no time in reasserting his prerogatives of office and
then enlarging it into a more powerful administrative ad-
junct than it had ever been under Roosevelt. While not
an inevitability, circumstances were propitious to the
process. The President thought it essential he be spared
routine problems while he gave "his attention to more important matters."[31] The conduct of the war, the formation

of the United Nations Organization, the Polish crisis, and
international conferences which by their very nature required his immediate and studied attention, basically com-
prised the latter category. Yet the surrender of Germany
and the imminent Japanese collapse produced questions of
demobilization, reconversion, and longer range domestic
objectives that also required immediate decisions. During his first months in office the President did not de-
vote extensive personal attention to these matters and
guided himself almost uncritically by his advisors's recommendations. Rosenman was only one such advisor, but
he exhibited a wider range of interests and expertise
than most others and in the event of conflicting advice,
the President was prone to turn to him for resolution.[32]
Not even during Roosevelt's gubernatorial administration
had Rosenman handled so large a volume of details or were
his recommendations so readily accepted.

Some recommendations were intended solely to enable
the President to stay clear of impending dispute. Senator
Claude Pepper, for instance, had solicited Truman's approval for a bill compensating hotel and apartment building owners who had leased their properties to the Army.
Rosenman studied the bill, anticipated it might stir controversy, and advised the President "that you do not get
into it in any way while it is in Congress."[33] After
examining both Senator Pat McCarran's proposals on international air transportation and an adverse report, Rosenman concluded the adverse report was "correct and represented the best views," but he doubted Truman "would want
to get into this controversy at this time."[34]

On some wider issues the administration was reluctant to encourage congressional initiative even when it
reflected general policy aims. There was agreement that
some adjustment in the unemployment compensation laws
was desirable "for workers temporarily unemployed during
the transition from war to peace," and the administration
had prepared a message for Congress urging such action.[35]
The Bureau of the Budget previewed the message and while

approving the phraseology cautioned against proceeding
further without first preparing a draft of legislation
that would implement the proposal. "If a member of Congress were to introduce his own bill on this very technical subject," the Budget Director warned, "it might be
more difficult later to effect the necessary administrative improvements to carry out your concepts effectively."
Truman passed the Smith memo along to Rosenman inscribed
with the request "could you do this for me?"[36]

The Counsel also undertook tasks without requiring
a specific presidential directive, and he seldom ever
relinquished his official interest. After Justice Jackson took on the principal war trial responsibilities,
Rosenman served as his liaison with the White House. His
duties ranged from reviewing the final protocol draft for
"objectionable" features to clearing German speaking lawyers for the prosecutor's staff.

Most Americans who had ever heard of the Rosenman
Mission report soon forgot it. When Republican Representative Everett Dirksen returned from a European tour with
recommendations similar to those Rosenman had earlier advanced, the Counsel drew the President's attention to
Dirksen's report and recommended a commendatory letter.[37]
In this instance Rosenman was motivated more by the hope
of drawing bipartisan publicity toward the European plight
than cultivating individual congressmen. In numerous
other instances, however, this latter objective was paramount.[38]

Rosenman thrived on the varied activities and also
developed a deep personal affection for the President.
Truman reciprocated. He was gratified by Rosenman's willingness to assume additional duties, and his reliance and
confidence in his Counsel fed upon each other and grew
along with the duties of the Counsel's office.

These early months in office--Truman's apprentice-
ship--were complicated by the President's disquietude over

the prospect of serving almost four years without some
office corresponding to that of Vice President. Rosenman
and others could familiarize him with the routine and
mechanics of office, and Rosenman especially, could in-
doctrinate him with the presumed legislative intent of his
elected predecessor, but Truman's view of his larger responsibilities did not end there. The vice-presidency
would remain vacant for almost four years with the Secretary of State in the line of succession. Truman deplored that he personally--or any Vice President upon becoming president--could select his own successor without
a public mandate and urged legislation to change the
presidential succession laws. As a temporary corrective
the highest ranking cabinet posts would be staffed by
men having formerly held high elective office. If Truman
were to be succeeded by an appointive officer, this would
at least assure that the successor would at some previous
time have demonstrated approval of his person through the
electoral process.

        Rosenman was never as convinced of the wisdom of
this strategy as the President. Furthermore, Truman's
anticipated choice of Jimmy Byrnes as Secretary of State
was displeasing to Rosenman. Nevertheless when called
upon to assist in implementing Truman's succession plans,
his personal loyalty held precedence over other considerations. He and the Solicitor General foresaw numerous
constitutional questions. Indeed the original statute of
succession of 1792 had provided for the President Pro
Tempore of the Senate and then the Speaker of the House--
a line of succession similar to that being proposed by
Truman--and "one of the reasons for the change in 1886 to
the present statute was the constitutional doubt about
whether these men are 'officers' within the meaning of
the Constitution." There were other questions as well
but the Counsel thought "the message ought to go as you
originally suggested." He just wanted to warn the President he would "get a lot of people claiming it is unconstitutional."39

Duly warned, Truman released his message on June 19,[40] and then proceeded to arrange the relevant cabinet appointments. Jimmy Byrnes was nominated Secretary of State on June 30, and received Senate confirmation two days later. The second ranking cabinet post, Treasury, also aroused the President's succession sensibilities, and in the midst of preparations for a big three conference in Potsdam he announced his intention to accept Henry Morgenthau's resignation after the European meeting concluded.[41] Fred Vinson, Director of War Mobilization and Reconversion and a former congressman and judge, would replace him at that time.

Just prior to embarking for Potsdam, however, Truman had second thoughts. Byrnes and Vinson were both scheduled to accompany him to the conference, and in the absence of the President and the Secretary of State the Treasury Secretary would be the ranking official remaining in the United States. Truman, alleging that this was an intolerable situation in which to leave a lame duck minister, instructed Vinson to remain in the United States and Rosenman to secure Morgenthau's immediate resignation.

Rosenman thought Vinson's an appropriate appointment,[42] but did not approve treating Morgenthau so cavalierly. His personal association with Morgenthau dated back to Roosevelt's gubernatorial administrations. Furthermore Rosenman and Morgenthau both believed that Truman's concern had been heightened by promptings from Byrnes, whose ambitions they suspected and with whom they had frequently clashed. The Judge resented being used but knowing that if Morgenthau sent in his immediate resignation "it would make the President very happy" he was compelled to secure it.[43]

He and Morgenthau agreed upon a series of three letters. In the first Morgenthau ostensibly reversed his decision not to leave office until after Truman's return because by then the Senate might have recessed and Vinson's nomination would not be confirmed before October.

The second was to be Truman's conventional acceptance of
Morgenthau's resignation and notice of Vinson's nomination.[44] The third letter was also to be from the President and named Morgenthau as Governor of the World Bank
and the International Monetary Fund; honors to which he
aspired. The first two letters were not contingent upon
the Bank or Fund appointment;, but Rosenman encouraged
Morgenthau in the belief that Truman would be obligated
for his prompt resignation, and likely to go along with
it.[45] The Judge could make no definite promises, however, and the inability to secure Vinson's prior endorsement was an ominous portent. All three dispatches were
cabled to Truman aboard the cruiser *Augusta*, but the President, concurring in the exchange of the first two, specifically instructed against release of the third. The
Counsel failed to secure even a symbolic reward for Morgenthau, although from Truman's view he had succeeded
admirably.

An admirable success was also credited to a team of
scientists who on July 16, exploded an atom bomb at a
test site near Alamogordo, New Mexico. The cable confirm-
ing Morgenthau's resignation had made the President "very
happy," but verification of the explosive force of the
new bomb made him jubilant. When on July 26, Rosenman
left Washington to join Truman in Germany, the Judge knew
almost nothing of this development. He had heard vaguely
of some "very special project", but the details had not
been revealed to him. Furthermore his own thoughts were
on details of the Big Three conference. His assignment
was to return home on the *Augusta* with the President to
assist him in preparation of a conference report. To
avoid any repetition of the disorientation that had accompanied the Yalta preparations, Rosenman arrived before
adjournment to sense the tone of the deliberations, collect data, and consult directly with the participants.
The Potsdam conference adjourned August 2, and the report was completed while the *Augusta* was still out at
sea.[46] The most memorable moments of the voyage related
to other matters.

News that the United States had dropped an atom
bomb on Hiroshima reached the *Augusta* August 6, the fourth
day of the journey home. Truman "could not keep back
[his] expectations that the Pacific war might now be
brought to a speedy end,"[47] determined to undertake immediate preparations to enunciate a domestic program before
Congress reconvened. To confront the first postwar session of Congress without some legislative program would,
he feared, surrender executive to legislative initiative.

Truman discussed the matter with Rosenman while
they were completing the final draft of the Potsdam report. According to the President's account he told his
Counsel that "one of the first things I want to do after
we get home...is to get busy on my domestic program." He
wanted "to submit most of it at the same time instead of
on a piecemeal basis." It was to take the form of a
State of the Union message except the President did not
want to wait until January to deliver it. They would
send the message up to Congress as soon as they could
put it together. "Will you," he requested of his Counsel,
"start to get together the material and perhaps get up a
rough draft?" Rosenman's conditioned response was to
solicit a general statement of "the things you would like
to say", and Truman has recalled with evident pride how
during his response Rosenman leaned forward and "eagerly"
revealed that the President's proposed program was "the
most exciting and pleasant surprise I have had in a long
time." He had, he confessed, been hearing from some of
Truman's "conservative friends" and "former colleagues
up on Capitol Hill...that the New Deal [was] good as
dead," and that the "conservative wing of the party had
taken charge." Rosenman asserted that though he had
"never really believed" such rumors, the proposed message
would settle the matter. It would, he predicted, provide
a "Progressive political philosophy and a liberal program
of action that will fix the theme of your whole term in
office."[48] Rosenman's delight over Truman's plans was
doubtless sincere, his prediction was probably calculated.

The message was ultimately organized into twenty-one interrelated groupings, most dealing with reconversion issues and advocating retention of government controls. Furthermore, the most detailed of these proposals were invariably restatements of existing policy that had crossed Rosenman's desk prior to the *Augusta* conference.[49] For the President not to have supported these established programs would have necessitated a spectacular reversal. More significant to long range policy than the points themselves was the tone of the message. Too long for Truman to deliver in person, most Congressmen learned its contents from personal copies that had been sent them. "We know," the President was to remind some skeptical former colleagues, "that by the investment of Federal funds we can...provide for our citizens new frontiers-- new territories for the development of industry, agriculture and commerce."[50] Housing, public works, scientific research, and educational activities were only some of the more obvious areas for public expenditures.

Truman's program was phrased as the enactment of Franklin Roosevelt's economic bill of rights, enunciated by the late President in his 1944 State of the Union Message and reaffirmed during the subsequent campaign.[51] Rosenman was Truman's closest personal tie to speculation as to what Roosevelt had hoped to accomplish, and Truman, as heir of the late President, was anxious to follow the Counsel's expertise in these matters. With Truman's knowledge and consent, Rosenman had been working on various programs implied in the Roosevelt message since Truman's first days in office. Especially active in preparing an education message, the Counsel had assumed even before the *Augusta* conversation that Truman intended to deliver it after his return from Potsdam.[52] Though aware of Truman's support for specific programs, he did not at first appreciate the depth of the President's commitment to social welfare principles. He also failed to anticipate Truman's willingness to ignore legislative realities which might have inhibited Roosevelt.

The twenty-one points constituted a call for more extensive reform than Truman's predecessor had ever made at a single moment. That the President seemed willing to propose such an ambitious program at a time many observers anticipated a trend toward normalcy delighted Rosenman. There is, however, even in Presidential messages, a long journey from original intentions to the final draft, and the Judge's prediction that the proposed message "would fix the theme for [Truman's] whole term in office" was the first deliberate step in that journey. Truman was later to write that the "twenty-one point message marked the beginnings of the 'Fair Deal'" and its September 6 delivery date "symbolizes for me my assumption of the office of the President in my own right."[53]

Rosenman began work on the message immediately after his return to Washington. Employing procedures similar to those he had developed for State of the Union messages under Roosevelt, the Counsel collected materials from numerous Departments and individuals. The resultant collection, which in this particular instance included some independent studies by the Judge, provided a summary of government operations and plannings.[54] In effect, the final draft was the product of further summary and selection from the mass of materials Rosenman had gathered. Because much of the message involved reconversion policy, it was necessary to have the Office of War Mobilization and Reconversion share in its development. In Rosenman's view that was an important obstacle; for if the President could be dissuaded from his *Augusta* sentiments OWMR Director John Snyder was the man who could do it.

Snyder, who had succeeded Vinson as Director was an old Missouri friend and political confidant of the President. A fiscal conservative with a fierce, almost literal, dedication to private enterprise, it seemed to Rosenman that he sometimes regarded him as a "Communist influence" upon the White House.[55] It was apparent he despaired at his "Harry being taken over," and he voiced his vehement opposition privately to Truman in "the frank-

est and most explicit terms."[56] Press Secretary Charlie
Ross, an even older friend, used every opportunity to
disparage the Director's fears. They were, he assured
Truman, extravagant exaggerations. Charlie Ross approved,
and he too was from Missouri.

Unable to elicit aid from Truman's personal staff,
Snyder was also thwarted in securing ideological support
from his own office. Relatively new to Washington and
very recently appointed to the directorship, he had to
rely upon an inherited staff for specific planning and
technical data. Circumstances dictated that Robert Nathan
as Deputy Director for Reconversion would be chief among
such lieutenants, and Nathan was among the least likely
men in Washington to implement Snyder's view of fiscal
responsibility. A Keynesian economist who had come to
Washington during Roosevelt's first administration, his
dealings with Rosenman dated back to the defense reorganization days when Nathan had emerged as Donald Nelson's
most controversial assistant. A former chairman of the
War Production Board's planning commission and a continued
advocate of Federal planning, Nathan and his staff were
the principal authors of the OWMR draft for the President's
message. Despite Snyder's personal reservations, he felt
obliged to submit the Nathan draft to Rosenman almost
without change.[57] The inability to convert his own aides
to his view effectively neutralized Snyder's subsequent
opposition to Rosenman's final drafts.

Truman presented the message to a special session
of Congress convened during the week after the formal
Japanese surrender. His general commitment to the New
Deal record was anticipated, but the degree to which he
appeared to favor Federal controls and extension of social
welfare principles was a genuine disappointment in some
quarters. It was, they warned, evidence that the President was "being captured by extreme New Deal leftovers,"
and one observer commented it must have made the Counsel
"gulp slightly" to watch Truman swallow his handiwork.[58]

The Judge dismissed such musings as nonsense. There was, he insisted, nothing in Truman's message that had not previously been enunciated by Roosevelt or implied in the 1944 Democratic platform upon which Truman had been elected Vice President.

Neither disingenuous nor a political neophyte, Rosenman did not always insist upon consistency for its own sake, and on occasion even advised substantial departures from specific planks.[59] Yet he had been adamant over the literal reaffirmation of the economic bill of rights. When translated into legislative terms it was precisely the sort of program the former Tammany Assemblyman could have sponsored. Not only might it be successful in effecting practical remedies, but it would also be successful in getting votes.

Harold Smith had objected to the message because it "shoots in many directions without a clear sense of the target," and advised that Truman "save as much of his ammunition as possible for times when particular targets are clear."[60] Presumably he would get more from Congress by requesting less and by delaying his requests until more propitious moments. The ultimate domestic legislative record of the Truman administration is not impressive, and measured against such traditional standards Smith's warnings appear prescient. As the President perceived matters, however, the flaw in Smith's reasoning was that more propitious moments were unlikely to occur without extraordinary Presidential proddings. Retreat toward normalcy was an everpresent threat to national security; yet it was an almost predictable "reaction...from the tremendous war effort. Everybody feels like letting down, and that has been the case after every war we have ever fought." The loss of overtime opportunities and a corresponding reduction in many workers take home pay had contributed "to some extent" to labor-management unrest, but according to Truman, the particular issue really did not "make any difference because it would be the same whether

there was a reduction in pay or not." Since the United
States had just concluded the greatest war in its history
it was "going to have comparatively greater difficulty in
getting people to realize the readjustment job is their
job."[61] Defining readjustment broadly, the President
coupled long range programs to immediate demobilization
programs, and insofar as he was able, determined to publicize both as public issues. The twenty-one points were
a salvo in that campaign.

To translate and expand the various points into
more specific legislative requests was the purpose and
joy of Rosenman's remaining months in Washington. Within
less than eleven weeks Congress was bombarded with ten
major "supplementary messages," all of which were reas-
serted in the Combined State of the Union and Budget Message of 1946. While in such areas as atomic energy control the Judge could lend no particular substantive
expertise to his drafting efforts, on most subjects which
the President pressed on Congress he possessed extensive
grounding. His direct involvement with plans for a St.
Lawrence power project predated Roosevelt's gubernatorial
administrations, and his initiation into the intricacies
of other "Points", although more recent, had also occurred prior to Truman's administration. The only supplementary message based unequivocably upon Rosenman's
cherished economic bill of rights, however, was one requesting enactment of a health and medical care program.

F.D.R. had anticipated his own message on the subject and had assigned Rosenman to get the material together. The Judge doubted Roosevelt would announce for a
comprehensive medical care program. He had failed previously to convince the President to take a deliberate
stand on the issue and attributed Roosevelt's lack of
response to his being "too political minded." Anticipating vocal and well financed opposition, the President had
been in no mood to risk losing a fight. The matter was
in limbo when he died, and after the Judge reported to
Truman that he had been collecting materials for such a

message, he was instructed to continue. While eschewing
specifics, the President concluded his September 6 message
with notice that he would soon be recommending a national
health bill to Congress.

Many of the specifics were derived from a report
by Vannevar Bush, Director of the Office of Scientific
Research and Development which the Judge had shepherded
through to publication the previous July.[62] OSRD recommendations included a Federal program to augment and balance the number and distributions of doctors and hospitals;
further extension of public health services; and Federal
aid to medical research and education. A fourth and fifth
recommendation, outside the scope of the Bush report, were
for programs of prepaid medical insurance and "protection
against loss of wages from sickness and disability" in
the form of cash benefits. These two final recommendations were the most politically controversial, with the
medical aid program most controversial of all. Conditioned
by Roosevelt's political realism, Rosenman's earliest
drafts consisted largely of "pious observations that the
subject was important and that it merited Congressional
study." The President "reacted quite vigorously by saying
that the message did not say anything, and that he would
favor health insurance, and that the Judge and the others
who were working on it should say so in unmistakable
terms."[63]

The Judge followed his instructions with a vengeance.
The President had seemed unequivocal, but the twilight
zone separating policy enunciation from policy formulation was still a wide one, and details such as the level
of benefits and how universal the coverage should be were
still to be agreed upon. Privately, and in alliance with
Charlie Ross and Dr. Wallace Graham, the President's physician, Rosenman urged a broad program,[64] and the message
approximated an agenda of maximum demands.

Despite obvious rhetorical efforts to soften anticipated attacks upon the program as socialized medicine,

such charges inundated the administration. Those portions
of the message requesting a compulsory insurance plan were
more vulnerable to this criticism than recommendations
for Federal aid to research, and while a National Science
Foundation was established in 1950, a compulsory medical
insurance plan was not enacted until 1965, and then in
very restricted form. If Rosenman conceived the message
primarily for the record rather than as an immediate legislative target, he nonetheless hoped to generate public
pressure in support of its provisions. Newspaper ads and
committee efforts were encouraged by the White House and
Rosenman continued an official interest even after his
return to private life.[65]

In a personal sense, however, the message served as
the capstone of his career in Washington. The eight months
between Truman's assumption of the presidency and the
health message were a period during which military and
foreign policy occupied the principal attention of the
administration. Yet with its enunciation, Truman had
further delineated and publicy committed himself to the
last remaining documented Roosevelt contemplations on
post war socio-economic programs. It was conceivable
that Roosevelt himself would not have been willing to
move so quickly on so broad a front, and the Judge prided
himself on being the technical and ideological catalyst
for Truman's feat. During the week just prior to release
of the health message, and after its contents were assured,
it was revealed he would leave the White House February
1 to resume private law practice in New York City.[66]

The Judge harbored few illusions that he had fulfilled a mission, nor was he pleased to leave. His loyalty to Truman was as profound as it had been to Roosevelt,
and perhaps surprisingly, his personal affection even
deeper. Yet he was leaving before anything important of
the highly vaunted domestic reform program became law,
and even the Full Employment Bill, the most universally
acceptable of the twenty-one points, was encountering
serious problems in Congress. Furthermore, proximity

to the President breeds opportunity for influence, and,
by leaving Washington for New York, subsequent opportunities would be sorely restricted. It was more difficult
to voluntarily relinquish the privileges and exercise of
power than the Judge had imagined it would be. Nonetheless he possessed no other practical option. During his
years on the Federal payroll his financial condition had
deteriorated to where he was less well situated than he
had been while Governor's Counsel seventeen years earlier.
On his salary of $12,000--$2,000 above his 1929 New York
State stipend--he had systematically consumed his savings.[67] With one son in college and a second son soon to
enroll, he simply could no longer afford to indulge himself in the luxury of public service.

There was no evidence of his private decision from
his official routine, and the quantity and tone of his
activities remained constant until almost the day of his
departure. His most delicate interim assignment concerned
armed forces unification.[68] Faced with divergent Army
and Navy views, Truman had ordered Rosenman "to make a
thorough study of the pros and cons of the unification
proposal."[69] The Judge favored the Army plan and after
an almost five month effort to reconcile the Navy to the
Army program, and the Navy's own counterefforts to convert
Rosenman to its own plan,[70] there was no visible progress.
The President was determined to send a unification message to Congress, however, and Rosenman assumed Truman
would "wish to adopt the Army view."[71] The forthcoming
message, unacceptable to the Navy, Congress, and substantial elements within the administration, failed to generate reorganization in any form.[72]

At the time the unification proposal reached
Congress, Rosenman had already started on his final State
of the Union Message. Some of the early deliberation and
drafting sessions were conducted in a holiday atmosphere
aboard the Presidential yacht *Williamsburg* to which Truman had invited a sizeable cortege of advisers, but the
greater part of the *Williamsburg* drafting sessions were

devoted towards a radio address for January 3.[73] Only
after this had been completed could work on the State of
the Union proceed in earnest. On January 9, the President
further complicated the task by deciding to combine the
State of the Union and the Annual Budget into a single
message.

Although Smith confided to his diary that "Apparently it was the President who suggested the two messages be
combined,"[74] the Budget Director had persistently advocated such a course. He had protested to both Truman and
Rosenman that the Counsel's system for designing messages
was too haphazard. The various departments which submitted materials did so "largely with the view of committing
the President to programs without regard to the relation
of these programs to others in the Government [and] without...respect to national economic health."[75] Furthermore the then current House hearings on the Full Employment Bill revealed Congressional enthusiasm for the establishment of a Council of Economic Advisers which neither
Truman nor Smith shared and whose usefulness might be
obviated by a more comprehensive Budget Measure. Representative Carter Manasco, presiding over the House hearings, had offered such a suggestion, and the President
agreed "we ought to go just as far as we could in the
direction of presenting a national budget in our Budget
Message." In Truman's opinion the most formidable obstacle was the Treasury Department's objection to estimat-
ing treasury income.[76]

Despite the President's foreboding the Treasury
Department acquiesced and Rosenman completed the first
reading draft within four days after the decision to
merge the two messages. It had been "a somewhat hasty-
shotgun wedding," and the Counsel's hopes that they would
be able to "smooth it out a bit" in the short time that
remained to them before the rescheduled target date[77]
were only partially realized. A near violent controversy
over the appropriateness of including provision for an
excise tax cut consumed much of the administration's re-

maining time and energy.[78]   The messages were never truly
integrated, the budgeting was not comprehendible to a
wide audience, and the sheer bulk of the message discouraged careful perusal.   As for its tactical success, the
Council of Economic Advisers became law along with the
Employment Act.

On the occasion of the President's first press conference after the omnibus message, he announced with "deep
regret" that Samuel I. Rosenman, his "friend and special
counsel," was leaving Washington to reenter private law
practice.   He had, however, agreed to return "from time
to time, without compensation, to render whatever assistance and advice he can," and Truman expected "to call on
him frequently."   The previous June the President had
written the Judge that "some day, when accurate history
is written you will receive the credit which is your
due...The months since then," Truman now added, "have
materially swollen that account."[78]

Later that morning scores of Rosenman's friends and
co-workers unobtrusively filtered through a side door
into the President's office.   At exactly 11:30 Truman
pressed the buzzer calling together his staff.   As Rosenman entered the President beckoned him closer and began
reading a prepared statement.   It was, Rosenman quickly
recognized, a citation accompanying the Medal for Merit.
The Judge was being honored for his "exceptionally merito-
rious conduct in the performance of outstanding services
to the President of the United States and his country."
The citation concluded with the observation that he had
"brought to his office not only high professional attain-
ments, but a marked devotion to duty, great perseverance,
outstanding administrative ability, and a deep sense of
public service."   Visibly affected by the proceedings,
the Judge mumbled some appropriate comments, accepted
the congratulations of the assembled well-wishers and
left the President's office.[79]

Truman had commended him for rendering "sound advice on many matters of national and international policy,
legislation and government administration." He had also
lifted "from the shoulders of the President many vexatious
problems...permitting him to give attention to more important matters." The citation included all the facts and
provided great personal gratification to Rosenman. The
prose, however, was stilted. Roosevelt would have insisted it be compressed, enlivened, and simplified.[80]

The Judge did not offer his own emendations until
after Truman left the presidency. "I," he then suggested,
"put him on the path of New Deal thinking from which he
never strayed."[81]

Chapter Thirteen

ATTORNEY AT LAW

In February 1946, Sam Rosenman at the age of fifty
returned to New York City to seek his fortune. A prudent
man, he had never seriously considered setting up practice anywhere but New York where his experience in all
three branches of state government could be capitalized
upon most readily. Augmenting his professional qualifications were such intangibles as having served as legal
counsel to two presidents, one of whom was still in
office. Also of significance was that New York provided
an arena in which Rosenman might renew old acquaintances.
The most notable of these turned out to be Robert Moses,
and Rosenman's personal and professional association with
Moses and his public works empire lasted until the
Judge's death. Most immediately apparent in 1946, however, was his rapport with William O'Dwyer, the newly
elected Democratic mayor of New York City. Rosenman,
while Counsel, had been the then Brigadier General
O'Dwyer's political liaison with the White House, and
simultaneously with Rosenman's return to New York the Mayor
signaled Tammany's congeniality by appointing him to a
special transit committee formed to avert a strike.[1]

Although such corporations as Seagrams, Columbia
Broadcasting Company, Twentieth Century-Fox (which Rosen-
man served for a time as Board Chairman), and the New
York Life Insurance Company ultimately numbered among
Rosenman, Goldmark, Colin and Kaye clients, Rosenman's
practice always included significant political components.
This was not merely because such a practice could be
highly remunerative; the Judge was incorrigibly addicted

to politics. His withdrawal from Washington was particularly painful and during the first few months he returned
so frequently that he attended to his "own office matters
more or less between trains." It wasn't until November
that he symbolically relinquished the captaincy of
Truman's speechwriting corps by turning the 1946 State
of the Union address file over to Clark Clifford.[2]

   Rosenman's "office matters" did not suffer from in-
attention, for within a very short time financial success
eroded any lingering ambition for public office. In May
1946, he was regarded as a "certain nominee for the New
York Court of Appeals," and despite having eagerly pursued the nomination in 1944, he now shunted it aside.
His decision was reported as having been "based largely
on the necessity for recouping through the private practice of law some of the financial loss he incurred when
he resigned from the State Supreme Court,"[3] an objective
he attained with remarkable dispatch. In 1951, after
Learned and Augustus Hand retired from the United States
Court of Appeals, Truman called Rosenman and Robert
Patterson to Washington to offer them the second circuit
appointments. The President was especially ambitious to
replace the retired jurists with "outstanding nominees,"
but despite the high honor and flattering circumstances
neither Rosenman nor Patterson would leave their private
practices.[4] Truman did not give up completely, however,
and in April 1952 turned again to his former Counsel.
This time he wanted Rosenman as Attorney General, but
Rosenman again declined.[5]

   Rosenman's unwillingness to accept public office
was in sharp contrast to his readiness to undertake
public service assignments. He accepted appointment to
presidential boards and commissions with alacrity, and
there was no dearth of opportunities during the remaining years of the Truman administration. The first such
commission was the President's Advisory Commission on
Universal Military Training. Truman had urged a postwar
military training program, but Congress instead voted to

discontinue all mandatory service. It was apparent that
Congress accurately reflected public opinion, and in
December 1946, the President attempted to redirect that
opinion by appointing a nine-member civilian commission
to study "the basic need as well as various plans for
universal military training in relation to overall planning for the national security."[6] The commission was
made up of representatives from business and professional
groups; all of whom were proponents of universal military
training.

As the commission member most familiar with the
President's views, Rosenman took a particularly active
role in the deliberations. During its six-month existence
the commission met on sixteen separate occasions and
consulted with over two hundred persons. Its 448 page
report drafted largely by Rosenman and Commission Chairman Karl T. Compton of the Massachusetts Institute of
Technology[7] was a studied elaboration of the President's
views. Truman had hoped that "publication of this report
by a group of distinguished and representative Americans
would move Congress to action."[8] It had no such effect.

The Judge hardly served as a disinterested member
on such commissions. The interests of the President
were clearly his paramount concern, and although he denied
any semblance of an attorney-client relationship, he
deliberately helped mold the recommendations and provided
the rhetoric the President would use. Since what the
President wanted was invariably in the public weal, or
so Rosenman would argue, ethical conflicts never arose.
His loyalty to Truman was never challenged. Occasionally,
when the cause was particularly worthy, even reasoned
logic was subordinated to "political hokum."

A 1949 steel strike provided the scenario for one
such instance. On July 15, with a strike scheduled for
the following day, Truman announced the appointment of a
three-man steel fact-finding board, that included Rosenman, to review and make recommendations in regard to

United Steel Worker wage-pension demands. The board was
to report to the President within forty-five days. Management and labor had agreed to a sixty-day non-stoppage
pledge thus leaving the disputants fifteen days to accept,
reject, or use the board's recommendations as a basis for
further negotiations before they were free to strike or
lock-out.

To many observers this presidential board seemed an
artifice designed primarily so that Truman might avoid
invoking provisions of the Taft-Hartley Act. The Act had
been passed over Truman's veto and he had pledged continuing efforts to secure its repeal. Under such circumstances the political constraints against appointing a
Taft-Hartley fact-finding board appeared prohibitive.
At the very least it would have been regarded as a be-
trayal by organized labor. As the most conspicuously
political member of the presidential board, it fell to
Rosenman's lot to rationalize this political expediency
into an act of statesmanship.

It is probably impossible to reconstruct Rosenman's
private views of the issues raised through the steel
dispute. Doubtless they were evolving; that he advocated
Truman invoke the Taft-Hartley Act in a 1951 steel dispute or proposed compulsory labor court decisions in 1967
is hardly evidence that he advocated such procedures in
1949. He probably simply assumed it impractical to invoke the Taft-Hartley and was predisposed toward the
Union gaining some substantial benefit. Fearing both
the real and perceived impact of an inflationary settlement, he preferred the Union gains be other than wage
raises. Rosenman's first felt obligation, however, was
to answer criticism both from those who argued against
any government intervention in the dispute and from those
who thought the President should have invoked the mech-
anisms provided for by the Taft-Hartley Act. To the
former he suggested it foolish to maintain that the
government had no direct interest in a basic industry
upon which national interest was so dependent. "It has,"

he asserted, "an interest deeper than the employers or
employees." The incantation "a peril to national health
and safety," through which Truman might have invoked the
Taft-Hartley was studiously avoided, and against those
who would nonetheless interpret his remarks as the Act's
justification, he argued that the President's fact-finding board had been accepted voluntarily and therefore was
more conducive to collective bargaining than one imposed
by law. Fact-finding, he insisted with a "solemn face
and without a smile," was designed to promote collective
bargaining. It should not be suspended nor should the
recommendations of a fact-finding board be imposed by
law.[9]

The board met in New York City throughout the summer, but despite its efforts the steelworkers struck in
October. Its recommendations nonetheless continued to
have interest. Asserting that "the organizational phase
of union activities has been passed," the board suggested
there be a reexamination "to see whether the public interest requires any modification in the definition and
theories of collective bargaining in...industries where
varying kinds of industry-wide rather than individual
collective bargaining have grown up." Having gone as far
as they dared, they then affirmed that the study "should
be made by the appropriate body which we think is the
Congress itself." The board "must limit ourselves to the
functions as directed by the President."[10]

On specific issues the report rejected Union demands for a general wage-rate increase while supporting
those for health insurance and a pension plan.

> ...although immediate and generally foreseeable
> ability to pay is very important in wage-rate
> determinations, it is not as important in the
> questions of social insurance and pensions.
> Here the more important consideration is the
> social obligation which the Board finds rests
> upon industry to provide insurance against the

economic hazard of modern industrial life....[11]

There might be, the board opined, "advantages to
the economy as a whole if the Government were itself to
extend the field of security.... It would certainly be
more just." But in the board's judgment "the date of
passage of such measures by the Congress is still far
off." Until that time the burden fell to private industry. "So long as Government does not provide any security at all, we believe that industry should. So long as
Government fails to provide an adequate amount, industry
should take up the slack."[12] When on November 11, the
United Steel Workers signed a contract with United States
Steel that provided a pension program similar to what the
board had recommended, Rosenman sensed victory. Presidential boards, he concluded, could serve long-term educational purposes as well as promote collective bargaining.

During the Eisenhower years Rosenman's services
were not solicited and he had not expected they would be.
Once the Democrats reoccupied the White House the appointments were resumed. In June 1961 John F. Kennedy named
him to a Taft-Hartley board in a national maritime strike
and in 1963 chose him chairman of an emergency board under the Railway Labor Act. Presidential appointments
exhilarated the Judge, and Dorothy Rosenman noted her
husband's greater buoyancy whenever one was tendered.
Apart from this, however, the boards achieved little
else.

Attributing much of their failure to systemic problems, Rosenman concluded that the public interest did require modifications in collective bargaining. "With
labor equality insured by our many labor laws, the right
to strike should be curtailed when it is in conflict with
the public interest." In such instances "some form of
final compulsory decision must be provided." Rejecting
compulsory arbitration by ad-hoc appointed boards, he
recommended "a separate system of labor courts and a
separate labor judiciary with the sole function of

deciding labor disputes."[13]   Shortly after Rosenman made
this proposal public this author engaged him in conversation on the seemingly irreconcilable views on labor-
management relations he had presented over time.   "Many
of the statements attributed [to him] by the press," he
agreed, "were political hokum."   Political hokum, he added smiling, was usually most effective when chanted with
"a solemn face and without a smile."   Other statements he
could not dismiss so easily.   "Perhaps we should attribute them to the fact that I was much younger and have
learned a great deal since then."

The rejection of comfortable and formerly operational assumptions can seldom be ascribed simply to personal
growth.   More realistically it reflects an awareness that
acting upon former assumptions have ceased to produce
desired outcomes.   Rosenman's responses to the "Jewish
question" suggest this.   His repeated insistence that
there was no inherent social, political, or economic distinction between American Jews and other Americans militated against his early support for Zionism.   It was precisely to demonstrate that discriminations were unwarranted that he resisted policies that might identify Jews
everywhere with a Jewish nation.[14]

In assessing his own career Rosenman might well assume that discriminations were not disabling.   They could
be overcome.   Discrimination did not keep him from being
admitted to Columbia College, although it would, he assumed, keep him from being admitted to the Columbia University Club after graduation.   Having graduated law
school with highest honors he never considered making
the effort to apply to "leading" New York law firms.   It
would have been a waste of a nickel subway fare to go
down there to ask them for a job.   It simply was not a
career option then open to Jews.   But discrimination had
not precluded his eventual acceptance into the professional mainstream; it has merely circumscribed the route he
followed.

Of eastern-European stock, Rosenman's Jewish models and professional associates had usually been of German descent, and, as was common to ambitious young men of his generation, he shared their values and practices as more fully consistent with American society than those of the more recently arrived eastern Europeans. This macrocosmic view of the Rosenmans' San Antonio community might have been maintained indefinitely, except as he later explained "Herr Hitler erased all differences between Eastern and Western Jews."[15]

Hitler's gas chambers rendered gradualism physically, politically, and emotionally irrelevant, and left Rosenman and his like-minded associates without a viable alternative to Zionism. The American Jewish Committee's concern for maintaining the civil and religious liberties of Jews throughout the world was all well and good, but it no longer held promise as an alternative to a Jewish homeland.[16] Human and political circumstances had evolved to where alternatives to the establishment of Israel constituted not only the abandonment of Palestine as a haven for displaced European Jewry, but also posed a serious threat to the continued welfare of those Jewish colonists already there. The Committee gradually relinquished its opposition to the creation of a Jewish national state. "Since we hold," a delegation of its draftsmen that included Rosenman wrote:

> that in the United States as in all other
> countries Jews, like all others of their citi-
> zens are nationals of those nations and no other,
> there can be no political identification of
> Jews outside Palestine with whatever government
> may there be instituted.[17]

Having made the point clearly and without reservation, the Judge both identified increasingly with the Israeli cause and advised the President to do likewise. Truman's support of immigration quotas for Palestine provided a public illustration of this. Under pressure

from their Arab clients the British had curtailed immigration despite forceful protests elsewhere. These protests ultimately became inextricable from American domestic politics, and in October 1946, Truman urged the
British to admit an additional 100,000 European Jews.
Rosenman, along with David Niles, was considered chiefly
responsible for the statement. According to Jimmy Byrnes
they had "told the President that New York Governor Thomas
E. Dewey was about to issue a statement favoring the
Zionist position on Palestine" advocating unlimited immigration, and had "insisted that unless the President anticipated this movement New York State would be lost to
the Democrats."[18] A few days after Truman's statement
Dewey announced that he favored admitting several hundred
thousand European Jews into Palestine.

Truman's recommendation, Rosenman alleged in his
own frequent public pronouncements, was based on a real-
istic estimate as to the number of refugees the Palestinian economy could then afford. The refugee problem could
not be solved simply by opening the gates to Palestine,
and it was "the duty of the United States Congress" to
admit to this country a limited number of refugees,
"Christians and Jews alike." Furthermore since it was
the duty of the United Nations to find a way to give
Palestine to those who wanted to go there, United States
policy on Palestinian immigration would be a concern only
until the United Nations established a portion of that
area as a Jewish homeland.[19]

With the British mandate drawing to an end, in February 1947 the Palestine problem was turned over to the
United Nations, and the central preoccupation became how
the international organization might elect to implement
the Balfour Declaration. The Declaration allowed for
varying interpretations, but on November 29, the General
Assembly approved a special committee recommendation to
partition Palestine into separate Arab and Israeli sec-
tors and asked the Security Council to implement the
decision. Two weeks later the British announced that on

May 14, 1948 they would regard their mandate at an end
and withdraw all civil and military forces.

The United States had lobbied mightily for UN adoption of the partition plan and critics sometimes depicted
Rosenman as "dictator" of that policy.[20] His most significant efforts were, however, as a liaison between Truman
and Chaim Weizmann, both of whom accepted Rosenman as a
person who would not betray their separate interests.

The Arabs, who had proposed a single Arab state in
which the Jews would live as a minority, declared they
would not be bound by the UN decision, and once the British withdrew their troops it was expected that Arab forces
would overrun the Jewish sector. The Palestinian Jews
first argued for an international force to implement the
partition and then pleaded for arms to defend themselves.
Acts of terrorism against British, Arab, and United
Nations personnel further complicated matters when on
March 19, 1948, the United States ambassador to the United
Nations Warren Austin proposed a State Department authored
resolution that Palestine be placed under a United Nations Trusteeship until a peaceful transition to partition could be achieved. The proposal, which would have
postponed the partition of Palestine indefinitely, appeared a major reversal of United States policy.

Truman had neither anticipated nor explicitly approved the announcement, but despite his personal commitment to partition he could not publicly disavow it.
Rosenman was at the White House the following morning.
The Judge, Truman carefully recorded, "called to see me
on another matter." Nevertheless, before the visit
ended their conversation turned to Palestine.[21] Rosenman
was already on record criticizing the State Department
for its dilatory attitude towards Israel. He wanted the
United States to "allow arms to be sent to the pioneers
of Palestine, who are ready and willing to defend themselves against attack." Unless the partition decision
of the United Nations was implemented, "unless we refuse

to sacrifice the settlers of Palestine as the League of Nations sacrificed the people of Ethiopia, Albania, and China, then the very life of the United Nations will be in danger and the consummation of peace perhaps forever frustrated."[22] Truman needed no such prepping. During the day immediately prior to the trustee resolution he had met privately with Chaim Weizmann and promised his continued support for partition. The UN resolution mortified him. Find Weizmann, he ordered Rosenman, and "Tell him I meant every word of what I said."[23]

Truman's convictions, Mrs. Rosenman has written, "could be turned away by excessive pressure and retained by unpressured advocation." The President deemed the trustee resolution an instance of excessive pressure by the State Department, but the constant hammering of such Zionists as Rabbis Hillel Silver and Steven Wise for alternative policies was no less irritating.[24] Rosenman, more sensitive to Truman's personal style--and keenly concerned for his political future--fit the role of confidential courier most comfortably. On one occasion in late April, after he had hand-carried a letter from Weizmann to Truman containing a request with which the President chose not to comply, Truman confided that "if a Jewish State was declared...he would do everything in his power to see that the United States recognized it as soon as it was proclaimed." Rosenman was pledged to repeat that promise only to Weizmann. Weizmann in his turn made it known to the Jewish governing body empowered to declare Israeli independence just prior to its decision.[25] On May 13, "exactly eleven minutes [Washington time] after Israel had been proclaimed a state," Truman wrote with evident pride, "Charlie Ross, my press secretary, handed the press the announcement of the *de facto* recognition by the United States of the provisional government of Israel."[26]

A few days later Weizmann wrote Rosenman that "even in this moment I must ask you again to be so good and impress upon the President the necessity of two additional

steps..." He hoped the United States would lift its arms
embargo and "warn the Arab States that they should stop
their destructive and murderous attacks...." This was,
Weizmann revealed, the first letter he had written since
learning he had been named President of Israel and it was
"only proper that it should be addressed to you who have
contributed so much of your effort and wisdom towards
bringing about some of the happy results during the past
few days."[27]

The very nature of Rosenman's effort obliged Weizmann to reserve expressions of his gratitude to private
communications. Rosenman's usefulness would have been
compromised if his activities were assessed publicly, and
in Weizmann's autobiography, published in 1949, he failed
to mention the Judge. Weizmann's was an extreme effort
to preserve Rosenman's anonymity, yet it conformed with
Rosenman's public image. He was an influence, some observers purporting to see him always in the background
labeled him ubiquitous, but precisely how or when he
asserted his presence was seldom clear. This was hardly
because Rosenman was spotlight shy. He cultivated anonymity when it served his political and professional purposes. At other times, especially after Truman left the
presidency, he welcomed celebrity status, for though retaining a becoming modesty, there was no longer need nor
profit in self-effacement. Indeed, visible trappings of
influence provide a source of power few attorneys would
profitably conceal, and by the mid-fifties Rosenman had
become one of the most eminent lawyers in New York.

Senior member of the firm of Rosenman, Goldmark,
Colin, and Kaye, his offices were located at Five Seventy
Five Madison Avenue, a post World War II vintage, twenty-
five story office building situated between Fifty-sixth
and Fifty-seventh Streets in Manhattan. His spacious private office was on the twentieth floor and constituted a
miniature gallery. Pictures, cartoons and letters from
prominent and formerly prominent persons adorned an entire
wall. All were inscribed, usually with "admiration" or

"affection." A brown leather chair opposite his desk had
been Harry Hopkins' during his years in Washington. The
bookshelves brimmed with volumes devoted to recent history,
and in almost all of them Rosenman was mentioned. The
Judge volunteered few comments on his memorabilia, but
whenever he was called from his office the visitor was
encouraged to peruse.

The office was most visibly connected to the outside
world by a color coded telephone panel. It might have
been installed because the Judge was becoming increasingly
hard-of-hearing, or perhaps because he preferred that his office conferences not be jarred by a ringing phone. In
any event its utility was obscured by the Judge's usual
practice of sitting with his back to the panel. Anyone
facing him could not fail to notice the blinking lights,
but anyone unfamiliar with the code would not have known
what they signaled. On occasion a secretary would appear
to "remind" the Judge that someone was "returning an important call." The panel served as a conspicuous accoutre-
ment of power that endowed the memorabilia a pertinence
they might not have possessed otherwise.

My own first meeting with the Judge was in 1957,
and during the course of an hour interview our discussion
turned to presidents and presidential politics. Rosenman's enthusiasm for the subject never waned. The previous year he had spearheaded New York Governor Averell
Harriman's unsuccessful drive for the Democratic nomination. Harriman, he had asserted, was an aggressive
champion of New and Fair Deal principles, while Adlai
Stevenson, the party's 1952 standard bearer, provided no
trace of this fighting spirit in his speeches.[28] Harriman
lost to Stevenson in 1956, but they would, Rosenman assumed, try again in 1960.

Harriman's defeat by Nelson Rockefeller in 1958
shattered those hopes. Nineteen forty-eight, it became
increasingly apparent, had been Rosenman's last opportunity to provide major assistance in a presidential campaign. That year he had helped prepare the party platform

and Truman's acceptance speech, and by accompanying the
President to the nominating convention served notice he
intended to work closely with him throughout the campaign.
Subsequent participation was not, however, as extensive
as either he or the President had anticipated. Both expected that Rosenman would be included among the campaign
entourage, but it had been discreetly arranged, presumably
by Matthew Connelly, that he not be invited. Drew Pearson
reported that Truman was not aware of Rosenman's absence
until his train was about to leave Washington. "What's
happened to Sam," he queried, "why isn't he here?" Clark
Clifford, privy to the connivance, suggested perhaps "Sam
doesn't have time for us anymore."[29] Efforts to keep
Rosenman from the campaign were moderately successful,
although he did contribute to two major addresses Truman
delivered in New York during the final days.[30]

        Despite these complications, personal relations be-
tween Truman and Rosenman flourished; nurtured by mutual
respect and pleasure in each other's company, it also
yielded mutual benefits. Rosenman was particularly helpful in November 1953 when the then former President was
served, while in New York City, a subpoena to testify before the House Committee on Un-American Activities. Upon
learning of the subpoena the Judge hastened to Truman's
hotel to provide the welcome advice that he decline to
appear, and then with Truman's concurrence prepared a
lengthy brief elaborating upon the contention that the
subpoena was improprietous. At a "tense and crowded" news
conference Truman declared that in spite of his own "personal willingness to cooperate" with the Committee, he
was "constrained by [his] duty to the people of the United
States to decline to comply with the subpoena." Later
that same day a spokesman for the Committee announced it
would make no further efforts to have Truman appear.[31]
Sometime afterwards Truman sent Rosenman a photograph of
the two men in hurried consultation during the press conference inscribed "I'll always be grateful for your help
and advice on this." Deriving tremendous personal satisfaction from Truman's "very thoughtful gesture," Rosenman

hung the picture in his apartment. He regarded it inappropriate to display so cherished a memento in his office.

Truman, in his turn, was a willing asset to Rosenman in Democratic state politics. A constant companion
of the ex-President during frequent meetings with New York
politicos, he was credited with gaining Truman's support
for Harriman's presidential candidacy during the 1956
Democratic National Convention.[32] Truman might well have
endorsed the New York Governor without Rosenman's unpressured advocacy, and even with Truman's support the Harriman boom could not head off an Adlai Stevenson victory on
the first ballot; nonetheless the situation worked to
Rosenman's advantage. Already closely associated with
the Governor, the Judge had aided significantly in Harriman's 1954 electoral victory, the staging of the Truman
announcement further enhanced Rosenman's status.

His political intimacy and easy access to Harriman
was most dramatically illustrated in a 1957 dispute over
negotiations for the sale of St. Lawrence power by the New
York Power Authority. Late in 1954, prior to Harriman's
election, Robert Moses, chairman of the state commission,
called on Rosenman to assist the Authority in contracting
for the sale of its power. The Judge of course was familiar with the general situation, having worked on various
aspects of the St. Lawrence project since before Franklin
Roosevelt had been elected Governor and having helped
draft the legislation that established the Power Authority. As originally conceived, a primary purpose for the
State developing St. Lawrence power was to have a yard-
stick against which to measure private utility charges and
insure reasonable rates to consumers. Rosenman and Moses,
asserting that this 1928 concern was no longer the paramount public need, arranged for the sale of more than half
the St. Lawrence public power to the privately owned
Niagara-Mohawk Corporation, the Aluminum Company of America and the Reynolds Metals Company.[33]

Rosenman was accused by groups such as the CIO and

the Liberal Party and individuals such as Eleanor Roosevelt and Senator Herbert Lehman of selling out Franklin
Roosevelt's program, but most disturbing was Governor
Harriman's threat to disapprove the St. Lawrence project
because of the preferential contract terms it had negotiated with the aluminum producers. On the same day Harriman
made his threat public, Rosenman flew to Albany and successfully persuaded the Governor not to exercise his
veto.[34] The State, he argued, would benefit most by the
sale of public power to industry. It would help to bring
needed new manufacturing into New York and bolster the
depressed economy of the St. Lawrence valley. In his judgment developing the industrial potential of the St. Lawrence was in the greater public interest than providing
the cheapest possible consumer rates.

     Harriman's prudent retreat forestalled serious dif-
ferences with Rosenman, but the political plans they
shared for the future were shattered by the 1958 New York
election returns. That year, with Harriman assured renomination, Democratic leaders focussed their attention
upon an "attractive personality" to run for the U.S. Senate. A strong, united ticket they confidently assumed,
would insure a victory in November. Edward R. Murrow, the
television and radio correspondent, was heralded as the
ideal choice until Rosenman reported that he had given a
"cool reception" to overtures of a political career.[35]
Harriman forces finally settled upon former Air Force
Secretary Thomas Finletter, but despite support from New
York City Mayor Robert Wagner and Eleanor Roosevelt they
were unable to obtain his nomination. Tammany leader Carmine DeSapio insisting upon Manhattan District Attorney
Frank Hogan, secured his nomination after a divisive contest.

     In an attempt to reunite the Harriman and DeSapio
forces Rosenman was named Hogan's campaign manager. Dutifully labeling widely circulated charges that Hogan was a
Tammany dominated candidate as a "deliberate and willful
attempt to mislead the voters," he countered that "if

there is a bossed candidate" Hogan's opponent Kenneth Keating "is it."[36] As campaign manager Rosenman performed com-
petently if not spectacularly. He did all that was expected of him, but his principal commitment remained to Harriman. On election day he was far less disappointed by
Keating's triumph over Hogan than Nelson Rockefeller's
landslide victory over Harriman.

The elections dashed Rosenman's last tangible hope
for influencing the highest levels of national politics,
but there were no debilitating professional repercussions.
Rosenman was too firmly ensconsed. As counsel to various
Robert Moses and Moses-related projects he continued to
represent their interests to state government without un-
toward effects.[37] Working with the Rockefeller administrations ultimately proved so comfortable that in 1970
the Judge supported the Governor for reelection. It was
the "first time he had ever publicly espoused the election
of a Republican," but the Democratic candidate Arthur J.
Goldberg, he alleged, patently lacked the "experience,
training and know-how in what it takes to be a Governor."
Rockefeller, in contrast, was a fighting liberal who had
amassed a "vast record of achievement" demonstrating his
"skill and know-how in the affairs of state government."
The Judge felt so strongly about this, he revealed at a
press conference called in the Governor's New York City
office, that he was going to head up an organization of
Democrats for Rockefeller. The Governor thanked the Judge
and attested to his "intelligence, ability, and dedication
to public service."[38] He also, as was evidenced from his
overwhelming victory, gained from Democratic support at
the polls.

To an important extent Rosenman had been spokesman
not merely for a Democratic establishment but for the es-
tablishment-at-large. Having been active so long at the
confluence of political, economic, and legal power enhanced his credibility. But his most incontrovertable
claim to such lofty eminence was his election, in 1964,
as President of the Association of the Bar of the City

of New York, the most august and prestigious of all legal
guilds whose leadership was traditionally vested in legal
luminaries who exemplified solid conservative values.
Rosenman's immediate predecessor was Herbert Brownell, and
the roster of former Presidents reads as if from a who was
who of American lawyers; Elihu Root, George W. Wickersham,
Charles Evans Hughes, C.C. Burlingham, John W. Davis,
Henry Stimson, and Samuel Seabury among them. Reflecting
upon his own election by senior members of many of the
same firms that fifty years earlier had regarded him as a
social and professional untouchable, Rosenman took a quiet
but fiercer pride in his designation than he did most
other forms of recognition.

     Since returning from Washington he had devoted sub-
stantial effort to Bar Association projects with his chief
interest being in reform in the judicial selection process. As chairman of the judiciary committee he articulated the formal judgment of the Association on judicial appointments. Most frequently these were ceremonial assertions of the Association's approval, but on occasion he
testified against the appointment of nominees as unqualified. The latter were usually exercises in futility.
The difficulty, as Rosenman viewed it, was that once a
nominee had been announced publicly, concern over his
qualifications were too easily subordinated to other matters. Rosenman had testified, for example, against the
appointment of Irving Ben Cooper to the federal bench,[39]
but had the Senate accepted Rosenman's judgment as compelling it they would have had to vote against President
Kennedy's appointment. Some senators who were reluctant
to confirm Cooper were even more reluctant to vote against
the President.

     Rosenman was disturbed. Professing that it was im-
perative that no person be elevated to the bench who was
not rated as qualified by his fellow lawyers, he further
insisted that the evaluation must occur prior to any public announcement if it were to be politically feasible.
Mayor Robert Wagner was receptive to the idea and agreed

bar organizations should formally assist judicial selection. Since the Mayor of the City of New York possessed the power to appoint or influence the nomination of more judges than any individual save the President, this was a highly significant concession. Wagner established the Mayor's Committee on the Judiciary to submit to him lists of qualified lawyers from which he would make his appointments, and Rosenman resigned his chairmanship of the City Bar Judiciary Committee to accept, at the Mayor's request, its co-chairmanship. Rosenman resigned in turn from the Mayor's Committee when elected City Bar president, but returned after his two year term was completed.

Given the vast number of judicial appointments affected by the Mayor's Committee and its subsequent incarnations, Rosenman's labors on local selection were his most constructive efforts toward judicial reform;[40] his most celebrated, however, was his opposition in 1970 to the nomination of G. Harrold Carswell as an Associate Justice of the United States Supreme Court. Although the efforts of both Rosenman and the City Bar Association were important factors in Carswell's rejection, neither had any formal role in the confirmation process. In so far as any bar organization had an assigned role it was the American Bar Association's twelve man Committee on the Federal Judiciary that unanimously endorsed Carswell as qualified in January, and then exited from the proceedings.

In subsequent months as Carswell's record was analyzed and made public, his nomination became increasingly unpalatable to members of the legal fraternity. The case against him, Richard Harris has written, "began to clearly demonstrate his dismal record in the field of human and civil rights and his lack of judicial stature in general."[41] Rosenman was incensed at the perfunctory manner in which the ABA had endorsed Carswell's qualifications to serve on the Supreme Court. It seemed clear to him that Carswell was unfit to sit on any court. Gathering together Bethuel M. Webster, like Rosenman a former City Bar Association President, Francis Plimpton, the current

President, and Bruce Bromley, a former Justice of the New York Court of Appeals, they agreed to publicize their personal opposition through full-page advertisements in newspapers throughout the country. Their original intention was to place an open letter attesting that "Judge Carswell does not have the legal or mental qualifications for service on the Supreme Court," but other Carswell opponents convinced them the letter would be more effective if signed by other leading attorneys as well.

Senator Birch Bayh's legislative assistant recalled that he and others working against Carswell "were stunned" when they first heard of Rosenman's plan. "About the last thing we expected was that men who were so much a part of the Establishment--in fact they are the legal establishment--would be willing to attack a Supreme Court nomination without any prodding from anyone."[42] The letter was ultimately published with over three hundred and fifty signatures of distinguished jurists, law school deans and professors, and attorneys from throughout the nation. Its impact was as great as its authors had hoped. It discredited the ABA endorsement and legitimized non-partisan opposition to Carswell based on his lack of judicial competence. In states where Senators were especially vulnerable to anti-Carswell arguments the ad helped mobilize local bar organizations and lawyers to work directly on their Senators. In a number of instances it was the latter that turned individual Senators around.[43]

Marshalling the opposition of his profession was Rosenman's most significant contribution to Carswell's defeat. It was also, except for his participation in Nelson Rockefeller's gubernatorial campaign, his last major contribution to public affairs. "Nicely rounding out his credentials as elder statesman, long-time leader of the New York Bar and as a man who had his finger in a chunk of the history of the 1930s and 1940s," Columbia University awarded him an honorary doctor of laws degree in May 1973.[44] Six weeks later, on June 24, after being admitted to Lenox Hill Hospital for treatment of lung congestion and a heart ailment, he died in his sleep.

NOTES ON FOOTNOTES

Some information in the text has been gathered from personal interviews. Other than interviews with the Rosenmans all are cited with the date of the interview. Discussions with the Rosenmans were numerous and often informal, and although I have copious notes from some meetings, others, dinner conversations for example, are undocumented. Furthermore since some details became apparent after a series of interviews, to indicate any particular date would be arbitrary. The bulk of our conversations took place from 1959 through 1964, although some information is from subsequent interviews.

Some documents noted as from the Rosenman Personal Collection which was stored in their New York City apartment have since been deposited with the Roosevelt and Truman Libraries. I have made no systematic effort to uncover which. On those occasions when I encountered a document previously viewed in the Rosenman Collection I cited the Library as the repository. Despite attempts to keep citations as current as possible, the exigencies of dealing with growing collections has sometimes required libraries to slightly alter classification systems during the time this biography was researched and written. As a result there may be some minor inconsistencies in footnoting; I am confident, however, that this will impose no difficulty to anyone attempting to locate the sources cited.

CHAPTER ONE

1.   Franklin D. Roosevelt Library, Papers of Louis
     McHenry Howe, Louis Howe to Franklin D. Roosevelt,
     October 2, 1928. Franklin D. Roosevelt Library here-
     after cited as R.L.

2.   Samuel I. Rosenman, *Working With Roosevelt* (New York:
     Harper and Brothers, 1952), 13.

3.   Mrs. Perry Kallison to author, April 2, 1967. Mrs.
     Kallison, a resident of San Antonio and a student of
     the Jewish community, has supplied much of the above
     general information.

4.   Interviews with Samuel I. Rosenman have been a chief
     source for the personal details. Much of the infor-
     mation can be found in the *New York State Red Book*
     1923, 117. His undergraduate resentments are quoted
     from a letter to Rexford Tugwell, January 16, 1969,
     Rosenman papers, R.L. The references to his Colum-
     bia professors and quotations as to their influences
     can be found in the Rosenman Memoir of the Columbia
     Oral History Project. The *Columbia Law Review* lists
     Rosenman as an editor as of November 1916. Samuel I.
     Rosenman hereafter cited as SIR.

5.   Interview with Dorothy Rosenman. Their engagement
     was not formally announced until May 30, 1924. *New
     York Times*, May 31, 1924. They were married a few
     months later. *New York Times*, September 16, 1924.

6.   *New York Times*, November 4, 1920.

7.   Interview with Joseph Shalleck, September 15, 1959.

8.   *New York Times*, February 26, 1939.

9.   Mrs. Rosenman believes this is the first time any
     candidate had utilized the system of soliciting per-
     sonal letters sent out on the writer's own stationary
     to his own friends. This has since become a common
     political practice. Details of the 1921 campaign are
     taken in part from Joseph Israels II, "The Saga of
     Sammy the Rose," *Saturday Evening Post*, December 5,
     1942, 63. Mr. Israels was the son of Belle Mosco-
     witz. This article contains many inaccuracies.

10. Rosenman Personal Collection, New York City, 1921
     campaign literature. The Lusk Acts were passed by
     the New York State Legislature in 1919 over the veto
     of Governor Al Smith. Directed primarily against
     Socialists, they were an extreme example of attempts
     to suppress unpatriotic and subversive activities
     following World War I. The Rosenman Personal Collec-
     tion is hereafter cited as R.P.C.

11. *New York Times*, November 9 and 10, 1921. In retro-
     spect Rosenman has credited his victory as much to
     John F. Hylan as to his own effectiveness as a cam-
     paigner. Hylan was elected by such a large majority
     that he was able to carry almost every other candi-
     date on the ticket into office with him.

12. *New York Times*, November 6, 1925. Assemblymen were
     elected to one year terms.

13. Interview with Robert Moses, March 26, 1964. Mr.
     Moses, who although a Republican eventually served
     as Smith's Secretary of State, was useful in re-
     cruiting able assemblymen to active leadership in the
     Governor's cause and claims credit for having first
     introduced Rosenman to Governor Smith. Rosenman at-
     tributes the initiative for cultivating young Assem-

blymen more to Smith's lieutenants than to Smith himself and during this period had no direct association
with the Governor. In addition to Moses he also
worked with Smith aides Belle Moscowitz and Bernard
Shientag.

14. Frances Perkins, *The Roosevelt I Knew* (New York: Viking Press, 1946), 23.

15. Alfred E. Smith, *Up To Now* (New York: Viking Press,
1929), 268-271.

16. *Laws of New York*, 1920, Chapter 944.

17. *Levy Leasing Co.* v. *Siegal*, 230 N.Y. 634 (1921).

18. *New York Times*, May 20, 1923.

19. *Ibid.*, May 23, 1923. For an elaboration of this type
of thinking upon Smith's subsequent political behavior see author's "Al Smith, FDR and the New Deal,"
Historian, May 1965.

20. *New York Times*, May 23, 1923.

21. *Ibid.*

22. *Ibid.*, June 3, 1923.

23. *Ibid.*, June 10, 1923.

24. *Ibid.*, June 27, 1923.

25. *Ibid.*, October 25, 1923.

26. *Ibid.*, June 17, 1923.

27. *Ibid.*, November 12, 1923.

28. *Ibid.*, January 19, 1924.

29. *Ibid.*

30. *Nod Away Co.* v. *Carroll*, 240 N.Y. 252 (1925), affirming *Nod Away Co.* v. *Carroll*, 290 A.D. 907 (1924).

31. *New York Times*, February 13, 1924.

32. *Ibid.*, February 10, 1926.

33. *Ibid.*, February 15, 1923 and February 7, 1925.

34. Margaret Sanger to SIR, October 3, 1941, R.P.C. See also Margaret Sanger, *An Autobiography* (W.W. Norton and Co., 1938), 292, 293, and Lawrence Lader, *The Margaret Sanger Story* (New York: Doubleday, 1955), 162.

35. *New York Times*, February 27, 1927. Also interview with Robert Moses, March 26, 1964.

36. Straus represented the 15th Senate District in which the 11th Assembly District was located. He was a member of a prominent merchandising family whose holdings included R. H. Macy and Abraham and Straus.

37. *New York Times*, January 9, 1924.

38. *Ibid.*, March 10, 1923.

39. *Ibid.*, August 11, 1925.

40. *State Bulletin*, 1923.

41. The New York State Bill Drafting Commission consisted of two attorneys, one chosen from each of the major parties. They were expected to serve from December until the end of the legislative session and draft, as well as advise on the effects and constitutionality of, any proposed legislation.

A vacancy had developed when Democrat William J. Mc-Cormick resigned to accept a similar but higher paying post with the New York City Municipal Assembly.

42. *New York Times*, November 22, 1926.

43. Joseph A. McGinnis to SIR, August 25, 1926, R.P.C.

44. *New York Times*, April 19, 1929.

45. Belle Moscowitz to SIR, November 10, 1924, R.P.C. This is a note congratulating Rosenman on his reelection.

46. Samuel I. Rosenman, *Working With Roosevelt*, 16.

47. *Ibid.*, 15.

CHAPTER TWO

1. *New York Times*, October 17, 1928.

2. Rosenman, *Working With Roosevelt*, 16, 17.

3. *Ibid.*, 18.

4. *Ibid*.

5. Rosenman, *Working With Roosevelt* (New York: Harper and Brothers, 1952).

6. Raymond Moley, *After Seven Years* (New York: Harper and Brothers, 1939), 65.

7. Raymond Moley, *27 Masters of Politics* (New York: Funk and Wagnalls, 1949), 139. See Alfred B. Rollins, *Roosevelt and Howe* (New York: Alfred Knopf, 1962), for the definitive study of Louis Howe.

8.   Rosenman, *Working with Roosevelt*, 25.

9.   *Ibid.*, 26.

10. *New York Times*, November 29, 1928. Other conferees
     were Maurice Bloch and Bernard Downing, Democratic
     leaders of the State Assembly and Senate, and William
     Bray, the Democratic State Chairman.

11. *Ibid.*

12. *Ibid.*, December 1, 1928.

13. *Ibid.*

14. *Ibid.*, December 19, 1928.

15. *Ibid.*, December 2, 1928.

16. *Ibid.*

17. SIR to FDR, December 8, 1928, Governor's Personal
     Papers, Rosenman File, R.L.

18. *New York Sun*, December 29, 1928.

19. Rosenman, *Working With Roosevelt*, 31.

20. *Ibid.*

21. In August 1929, Roosevelt issued a statement written
     "wholly" by Rosenman, setting the reasons for the
     commutation of the death sentence for a convicted
     slayer. The complete statement can be found in the
     New York Times, August 29, 1929. Roosevelt's credit-
     ing Rosenman with its authorship is to be found in
     FDR to SIR, September 19, 1929, Gp. 12, R.L. Felix
     Frankfurter, then a member of the Harvard Law School
     faculty, predicted the statement "will have an
     honored place in the history of the exercise of par-

doning power." R.L. Gp. 12, Rosenman Files, Felix
Frankfurter to FDR, September 10, 1929. Roosevelt
forwarded Frankfurter's note to SIR and from this
exchange Rosenman and Frankfurter developed an association which terminated only upon Frankfurter's
death.

The commutation incident elicited a less academic
letter from the mother of the prisoner. "I thank
God," she wrote Rosenman, "that he saw fit to have
two such wonderful men as the Governor and yourself
to be the final Judge." Mrs. Frances Harris to SIR,
September 9, 1929.

22. *New York Times*, February 9, 1930.

23. *New York Daily News*, May 11, 1931.

24. FDR to SIR, November 13, 1931, Group 18, Records of
the Governor, R.L. Records of the Governor hereafter
cited as Gp. 18.

25. *Ibid.*, January 27, 1932.

26. *Ibid.*, May 30, 1932.

27. *Yonkers Herald*, February 29, 1932, and *Troy Times*,
March 9, 1932.

28. FDR to SIR, May 30, 1931, Gp. 12, R.L.

29. SIR to FDR, August 21, 1941, President's Personal
File 64, R.L. President's Personal File hereafter
cited as P.P.F.

30. Bernard Bellush, *Franklin D. Roosevelt as Governor
of New York* (New York: Columbia University Press,
1955), 205.

31. *The Jeffersonian* (New York State Democratic Party

publication), July 1931.

32. SIR to FDR, May 12, 1930, Gp. 12, R.L.

33. Dorothy Rosenman to President and Mrs. Roosevelt,
     September 17, 1933, P.P.F. 64, R.L.

34. Howe too resided at the Executive Mansion when in Al-
     bany. During this period he was usually in New York
     City four days, Monday through Thursday of each week
     and in Albany the other three. Rosenman's procedure
     was usually the reverse.

     Howe's views of the procedure can be gleaned from
     some humorous verse he penned as a placecard for
     Dorothy on FDR's fiftieth birthday celebration, Jan-
     uary 30, 1932.

     DON'T LET THE WILEY SAMUEL FOOL
     YOU WITH TALES OF "BETTER SCHOOL."
     DOROTHY ANOTHER REASON
     MAKES HIM KEEP YOU ALL THIS SEASON
     IN MANHATTAN FAR AWAY
     COME UP UNANNOUNCED SOMEDAY.

     This card, along with one for Sam, was framed and
     hung in the Rosenman's New York apartment.

35. Bellush, *FDR as Governor*, 247.

36. FDR to Hamilton Ward, June 29, 1929, Gp. 18, R.L.

37. *Ibid.*, SIR to James J. Mahoney, June 27, 1929.

38. *Ibid.*, Ward to FDR, July 29, 1929.

39. *New York Times*, August 1, 1929.

40. Interview with SIR.

41. Samuel I. Rosenman, "Governor Roosevelt's Power Program," *The Nation* (September 18, 1929), 302, 303.

42. *New York Herald Tribune*, December 6, 1929.

43. *New York Times*, June 13, 1930.

44. FDR to Alfred E. Smith, June 18, 1930, Gp. 18, R.L.

45. SIR to FDR, May 23, 1930, Gp. 12, R.L.

46. *Ibid.*

47. 1930 Election Materials, R.P.C. The most widely distributed campaign literature was a pamphlet contrasting electricity costs for specific household devices in various cities throughout New York with publicly developed hydroelectric costs in Ontario, Canada. For background on the development of the pamphlet see Leland Olds to SIR, July 30, 1930, Gp. 36, Papers of Louis McHenry Howe, R.L. That Canadian costs of operating waffle irons and similar appliances were significantly lower made so deep an impression on some constituents that the 1930 election was sometimes referred to as the waffle iron campaign. See Frank Freidel, *The Triumph* (Boston: Little Brown and Company, 1965), 160.

48. 1930 Election Materials, R.P.C.

49. *Public Papers and Addresses of Franklin D. Roosevelt,* Volume I, "The Genesis of the New Deal," ed. by Samuel I. Rosenman (13 vols; New York: 1939-1950). Hereafter cited as *Public Papers.* See also relevant chapters in *Working With Roosevelt* and chapter seven of this volume.

50. *New York Times*, March 24, 1931.

51. SIR to Frank J. Shaughnessy, April 3, 1931, Gp. 18,

R.L.   Also see SIR to Oliver Cabana, April 3, 1931,
and SIR to Harlan Riply, April 3, 1931.   In addition
to the obvious issue of executive control, the Governor insisted he had appointed the original board
to perform functions different from those envisioned
under the proposed Power Authority and thus the Power
Authority would require a membership with backgrounds
different from that of the St. Lawrence Power Authority.

52. *Ibid.*, Press release of Senator Knight, April 3, 1931.

53. *New York Times*, February 25, 1957.

CHAPTER THREE

1. Rosenman recorded some less restrained comments on
Curry's ability in his Oral History Memoir, Columbia
University Oral History Collection.   The Columbia
interviews were conducted from April through July
1959 by James N. Perlstein.

2. The unsuccessful efforts of so skilled an investigator as Samuel Seabury to uncover irregularities in
Curry's personal finances provide indirect testimony
to the Tammany chieftain's propriety in such dealings.   Rosenman Oral Memoir, Columbia Oral History.

3. *Ibid.*

4. Rosenman, *Working With Roosevelt*, 60.

5. The City Trust Co. was the bank under investigation
and Frank Warder was the indicted Superintendent.
He was defended in court by Max Steuer, who frequently served as defense counsel for indicted Tammany
officials during this period.

6.   The Bank collapse occurred when Roosevelt was out-of-
     state, and acting Governor Herbert Lehman at that
     time commissioned Robert Moses to make the investi-
     gation.

7.   Telegram, FDR to C.C. Burlingham, July 18, 1929, Gp.
     12, Mancuso Folder, R.L. Burlingham was President
     of the Association of the Bar of the City of New
     York. A similar telegram was sent to William N.
     Cromwell who was President of the New York County
     Lawyers Association. The Moses Report only inciden-
     tally discussed Mancuso. Its basic concern was rec-
     comendations for banking reorganization.

8.   That Rosenman helped frame the request for his pre-
     sence at the committee hearings is evident from a
     cover letter to FDR dated July 22, 1929, in which
     Rosenman reports "I am enclosing herewith prepared
     draft of a letter as you suggested." The draft con-
     tains the request Rosenman be permitted to sit in on
     the hearings. Group 12, Mancuso Folder, R.L.

9.   *New York Times*, March 3, 1931. The importance of
     Bertini's Italian ancestry is evident from a fascin-
     ating exchange of letters between Lieutenant Governor
     Lehman and an Assemblyman. Vincent H. Auleta to
     Herbert Lehman, October 10, 1929 and Lehman to Au-
     leta, October 18, 1929, Gp. 12, Mancuso Folder, R.L.
     Bertini was subsequently suspected of having purchased
     his office, but charges were dismissed.

10. The scandals involved Judges W. Bernard Vause, Joseph
     Force Crater, and George F. Ewald.

11. *F.D.R.: His Personal Letters*; 1928-1945, edited by
     Eliot Roosevelt (New York: Duell, Sloan and Pearce,
     1950), 136.

12. *New York Herald Tribune*, July 23, 1930.

13. *F.D.R.: His Personal Letters*, 136, FDR to Herbert Lehman, July 29, 1930.

14. *New York Sun*, August 19, 1930.

15. *New York Telegram*, August 21, 1930. In a letter dated September 13, 1930, Group 36, Howe Papers, R.L., William D. Guthrie informed Louis Howe that in the course of a long conversation with Rosenman, Guthrie had refused an appointment by the Governor to investigate the magistrate courts as he doubted sufficient gubernatorial jurisdiction in the affair. He had instead, he reported, suggested the Appellate Division conduct the investigation.

16. *New York Times*, September 24, 1930. Seabury had resigned from the Court of Appeals to accept the 1916 Democratic gubernatorial nomination. He had anticipated the support of Theodore Roosevelt who instead backed the Republican nominee. Seabury lost the election to incumbent Charles S. Whitman.

17. Dorothy Rosenman to FDR, November 29, 1930, Rosenman Papers, R.L.

18. *New York American*, January 13, 1931. Also appearing at this time were a series of news reports alleging Rosenman to be a prime Tammany candidate for the Manhattan borough presidency. His "candidacy" was first conceived by an Albany correspondent and persisted as a regular news item for a week. See for instance *New York American*, January 7, 1931, *New York Evening Journal*, January 7, *New York Times*, January 8 and 16, and *New York Herald Tribune*, January 16. Despite this wide attention to Rosenman's candidacy, there was never any substance to the reports.

19. *Albany Evening News*, March 3, 1931.

20. Samuel Seabury to SIR, March 11, 1931, Rosenman Papers, R.L.

21. *New York Tribune*, March 23, 1931.

22. *New York Telegram*, March 23, 1931.

23. *New York Evening Post*, March 23, 1931.

24. *New York Times*, April 27, 1931. Even more significant, although seldom as openly proclaimed as Walker's abortive anti-Communist crusade, was the sentiment that attacks upon Tammany were motivated by anti-Catholic, especially anti-Irish-Catholic sentiment. In this context the opening speeches of Roosevelt's 1928 gubernatorial campaign may have a greater significance than is usually accorded them. Rosenman and Maurice Bloch have indicated impatience with Roosevelt's ignoring state issues to combat anti-Catholic prejudices then facing the Smith candidacy. These statements did, however, help immunize Roosevelt against even whispering campaigns attributing personal anti-Catholic bias to *him*.

25. *New York Tribune*, March 23, 1931.

26. *New York Evening Post*, April 28, 1931. His defense of this action was in most respects well argued and emphasized the concept that "the greatest caution... must be used in the exercise either of the impeachment power by the legislature or the removal power by the Governor in order not to annul the deliberate decision of the voters." Roosevelt went on to express his fears that otherwise a "precedent might be established by which the will of the electorate might be set aside for personal or partisan advantages."

27. Raymond Moley, *After Seven Years*, 67.

28. It should be emphasized that the reply to the Holmes-

Wise charges included a refusal to remove Walker on
the basis of those charges as well as a refusal to
proceed further on the basis of those same charges.
That Roosevelt and Rosenman anticipated further legislative action is suggested by the otherwise gratu-
itous warning contained within the reply that the
impeachment power of the legislature must be exercised
with caution. The most damaging evidence eventually
presented against Walker was not contained within
the Holmes-Wise charges but rather collected by the
investigations of the Hofstadter Committee.

29. No practical politician would have committed the
grievous blunder to present charges against Walker
on St. Patrick's Day as Holmes and Wise did. Walker
chose a communion breakfast of the New York Fire
Department Holy Name Society to level his counter-
charges of communism.

30. *New York Telegram*, January 6, 1932 and August 9,
1930. For evidence that these were not spurious
comments see for instance *New York Sun*, September
20, 1929. In the midst of the Mancuso hearings Rosenman had also acted as Roosevelt's representative
at a hearing in Westchester County. The Board of
Supervisors had been accused of permitting the use
of excessive expenditures in the purchase of sites
for county construction. The incident was resolved
without direct gubernatorial intervention.

31. *New York Times*, March 31, 1932. Roosevelt's patience
seems to have been completely exhausted the following
year when in an official refusal to a Holmes-Wise
request for the removal of the recently elected Sheriff of Queens County, he included a reprimand to the
clergymen for spending so much time "asking your
Governor to perform unconstitutional functions and
to ignore the principles of representative government." It was the Governor's considered opinion
that civic leaders' time "could be better spent."

Rosenman did not assist in the drafting of this particular letter and first learned its contents from
newspaper reports.

32. *New York Times*, October 20, 1931. A subsequent investigation by Seabury (Hofstadter Committee) resulted in conclusions similar to those advanced by Rosenman.

33. *New York Times*, October 31, 1931.

34. Seabury to FDR, December 30, 1931, Gp. 18, Thomas
Farley Investigation, R.L.

35. *New York Times*, January 3, 1932.

36. Farley Investigation, R.L. Rosenman was beseiged
with letters from private citizens. Some, such as
Holmes and Wise believed to remove Farley would produce more honest and efficient government. Others
saw the affair as an opportunity to strike a blow
against Irish-Catholic dominance of New York City
politics and openly urged that the Governor act in
behalf of that cause. There was also some correspondence of churchmen of various faiths who expressed
great confidence in Farley as a public official.

37. Rosenman Memoir, Columbia Oral History. In speculating why Roosevelt chose this time to invite Rosenman
to live at the Executive Mansion, the thought occurred
that Roosevelt desired to facilitate contact with
Rosenman during the period of the investigations.
Another improbable prospect is that Roosevelt sought
to assure Rosenman's loyalty at a time when his
presidential and Rosenman's judicial ambitions might
have served to split them. I have discarded these
and similar speculations to conclude that it was simply a matter of Rosenman's having to live alone and
the Roosevelts believing he would be more comfortable
with them. Roosevelt's similar hospitality in the

cases of Howe and Hopkins seems to verify this. It
may also be pertinent that during Charles Poletti's
tenure as Lehman's Counsel, he lived at the mansion
along with his wife and child.

38. Interview with Samuel I. Rosenman.

39. Edward J. Flynn, *You're The Boss* (New York: Viking
     Press, 1947), 55.

40. *New York Times*, January 30, 1932.

41. FDR to SIR, April 14, 1932, Rosenman Papers, R.L.
     The letter is printed in *Working With Roosevelt*, 60,
     with the portion derogatory to the court deleted.

42. Interview with Rosenman.

43. Rosenman, *Working With Roosevelt*, 60.

44. Wise and Holmes to FDR, January 6, 1932, Gp. 18,
     Farley Invistigation, R.L.

45. *Ibid.*, SIR to Farley, January 23, 1932. On January
     10, Rosenman had instructed Farley to answer the Sea-
     bury charges at his earliest convenience. The Sher-
     iff failed to reply by January 23.

46. *New York American*, January 24, 1932. Louis Howe,
     Ed Flynn and James Farley were also present.

47. SIR telegrams to Farley, Seabury, and Seigfried Hart-
     man, February 11, 1932, Gp. 18, Farley Investigation,
     R.L. Hartman was Farley's attorney with whom Rosen-
     man had conferred earlier. SIR to Hartman, February
     10, 1932.

48. *Ibid.*, Farley Testimony Memorandum. See also *New
     York Times*, February 25, 1932.

49. Moley, *After Seven Years*, 67.

50. *New York Times*, March 12, 1932. Although Roosevelt
     did not usually describe his lieutenants as right
     arms, Rosenman was not the only associate he so des-
     cribed.

51. The confirmation proceedings have been reconstructed
     from a stenographic record, but most New York City
     newspapers and some upstate dailies such as the *Syra-
     cuse Post Standard*, March 14, 1932, carried accounts
     of the Senate action.

52. *New York Times*, March 14, 1932.

53. *Ibid.*, March 1, 1932. Control of the county sheriff's
     office could decide the control of the county organ-
     ization for there existed a large number of staff
     positions which the sheriff was authorized to fill
     without regard to civil service requirements. Edward
     J. Flynn, *You're the Boss*, 14, has described the men
     holding these positions as the backbone of a county
     political organization. Sheehy's appointment seems
     a graphic demonstration that Roosevelt had no immed-
     iate intention of fighting the existing New York
     County political organization.

54. *Bronx Home News*, March 13, 1932.

55. SIR to FDR, April 13, 1932, Rosenman Papers, R.L.
     Roosevelt replied that Rosenman's note was "the fin-
     est token of real personal and deep friendship I have
     ever had." FDR to SIR, April 14, 1932.

                         CHAPTER FOUR

1.   This account of the installation ceremony has been
     reconstructed from the *New York Times*, April 16, 1932,

and the New York *Law Journal*, April 16, 1932.

2.   Rosenman, *Working With Roosevelt*, 57.

3.   Joseph Proskauer, *A Segment of My Times* (New York:
     Farrar, Straus and Company, 1950), 7.

4.   Rosenman, *Working With Roosevelt*, 57, 58. Raymond
     Moley in *After Seven Years*, admits to the probability
     of such a conversation but "questions that such a
     conversation was anything more than an incident is a
     development wholly unrelated to Sam Rosenman's plan-
     ning or imagination.... The process of the formation
     of the brain trust [as the group was soon to be
     labeled] was smooth, unspasmodic, almost inevitable."
     5, 6. Moley also believed that even without Rosen-
     man's sponsorship he would have had an important role
     in the "almost inevitable" brain trust. Rosenman
     doubts this. See SIR to Tugwell, January 16, 1969,
     Rosenman Papers, R.L. This letter, four pages single
     spaced, comments upon points raised in Tugwell's *The
     Brains Trust* (New York: Viking Press, 1968), and
     Moley's memoirs.

5.   SIR to Tugwell, January 16, 1969, Rosenman Papers,
     R.L. Moley in *After Seven Years* wrote that "Sam...
     loved Columbia in a boyish and rather touching way
     and the fact that I [and the others?] taught there
     was a point in my favor." Rosenman has cited in the
     above letter his unhappy undergraduate experience to
     refute this point.

6.   Brains trust was coined by Louis Howe who first ap-
     plied it as a term of derision. It was eventually
     picked up by the press, James Kiernan, and popularized
     as the brain trust. Roosevelt originally referred
     to the group as his privy council.

7.   Rosenman, *Working With Roosevelt*, 61. The speech,
     delivered April 7, 1932, contains the much quoted

reference to the "forgotten man at the bottom of the economic pyramid."

8. *Ibid.*, 63.

9. *Today*, April 14, 1934. Moley wrote that "O'Connor and I regarded Rosenman as our chief and our means of contact with Mr. Roosevelt." Until after Roosevelt received the presidential nomination, knowledge of the brain trust's existence was kept from the public. Illustrative of this as well as Rosenman's pre-eminence within the group is that in May, 1932, he traveled to Warm Springs, Georgia, to inform Roosevelt of the brain trust's progress and deliver some memoranda it had prepared. Moley had hoped to make the trip but Roosevelt insisted that Rosenman come alone. Because he occupied judicial office, Rosenmann suffered some embarrassment from the ensuing publicity. Reports assumed he was advising on Walker. See SIR to Tugwell, January 16, 1969, Rosenman Papers, R.L.

10. Rosenman, *Working With Roosevelt*, 63.

11. Moley, *After Seven Years*, 28.

12. Interview with Dorothy Rosenman. Mrs. Rosenman attributed her reaction more to tension over the nomination than fears for her husband's safety and contrasted her own behavior to that of Sara Roosevelt, Franklin's mother. Sara Roosevelt and "Rosey" Roosevelt, wife of Franklin's late half-brother, were so distraught that "Jimmy" Gerard and others of "their circle" had voted against Franklin's nomination that they spoke of little else.

13. *New York Times*, July 2, 1932. Despite almost instant radio reporting on the progress of the flight, the Judge reassured Dorothy of his safety at every opportunity. From Buffalo he wired "Going swell. Please don't worry" and from Cleveland, the second

refueling stop on their journey he wired "Just landed at Cleveland. Love from all. Next Stop Chicago." Rosenman Papers, R.L.

14. *New York Times*, July 2, 1932.

15. In passing over recommendations for Shientag's appointment, Roosevelt instead decided upon Joseph Force Crater, a singularly uninspired choice.

16. Alfred B. Rollins in *Roosevelt and Howe* (New York: Alfred Knopf, 1962), 346, wrote that "Roosevelt himself arranged for Justice Shientag to go to Harmon to meet Al's train." This is true in the sense that Mrs. Rosenman, who phoned Shientag from the Governor's mansion shortly after Roosevelt *et al.* had left for Chicago, did so with the Governor's knowledge and consent. Neither Judge nor Mrs. Rosenman recall with whom the idea of calling Shientag originated, but doubt it was with Governor Roosevelt.

17. Moley, *After Seven Years*, 33.

18. Moley, *Twenty-Seven Masters of Politics*, 135, 136.

19. Roosevelt's handling of this situation may provide some insights into his attempts while president to achieve harmony among subordinates advocating different and at times irreconcilable views by suggesting they combine into a single program. Thinking more in terms of the individuals who presented the programs than the abstractions they were proposing, he expected he could resolve conflict by applying the technique he had adapted so successfully at the time of the 1932 convention.

20. *Public Papers* Vol. I, 659.

21. It is interesting to speculate as to whether the phrase would have produced the response it did had

Roosevelt not flown to Chicago. It is fascinating
to consider what might have occurred had Kirby chosen
the expression "new order" rather than "new deal"
from the peroration.

22.   There are numerous claimants to the honor of coining
the New Deal slogan. For instance according to a
story circulated by the late Robert (Uncle Bob) Smith,
he and the late Max Friedman, both Knoxville Tennessee Democrats, were visiting FDR in his office in the
Governor's mansion in Albany, New York, in August
1932. Roosevelt had been nominated the month before
and "opened a wire from Jim Farley, urging immediate
adoption of a campaign slogan. FDR declared we would
hold an election then and there. He asked us for
suggestions, I came up with 'Shareholders of America.'
FDR nodded, but Max said he would have to disagree.
He announced that what the American people wanted was
a New Deal. The next day medallions were struck carrying the slogan, which helped the Democrats oust the
Republicans in 1932." *Knoxville News-Sentinel*, May
4, 1966.

Raymond Moley also claims credit and to substantiate
his claim has produced the following sentence from a
"general philosophic statement that prefaced" a series
of preconvention memoranda: "It is not the pledge of
a new deal: it is the reminder of broken promises."
After Seven Years, 23, fn.

Since it was Rosenman rather than Moley who utilized
the phrase in the affirmative manner in which it was
popularized, and since Kirby took his inspiration
from the acceptance speech, most historians have
credited Rosenman with having "stumbled upon the most
potent political slogan of his generation."

Speculation as to where Rosenman may have drawn his
inspiration for the phrase persists among historians.
Arthur Schlesinger Jr., for instance, rejects Moley's

claim and suggests it came from a *New Republic* series
by Stuart Chase entitled "A New Deal for America."
Crisis of the Old Order (Boston: Houghton Mifflin
Company, 1957), 403. A Stuart Chase volume, *The New
Deal* (New York: Macmillan, 1932), appeared in August
and went through seven printings by November. It was
based on his *New Republic* articles and did not mention Roosevelt.

23. SIR to Tugwell, January 16, 1969, Rosenman Papers,
R.L.

24. Moley, *After Seven Years*, 7 and fn.

25. *New York Times*, June 16, 1932. Although Seabury has
been accused of submitting charges at this particular
time in order to embarrass Roosevelt, the Governor
was not an innocent victim of political maneuvering.
On June 3, approximately two weeks before Seabury submitted the charges against Walker, Roosevelt, in the
course of a press release, made the following statement: "In the case of Sheriff Farley, Judge Seabury
asked the Legislative Committee to present the evidence to the Governor, the Committee refused. Judge
Seabury sent it himself. I acted. If the evidence
in any case now before the Legislative Committee, in
their judgment or that of their Counsel warrants, it
is time for the Legislative Committee and their Counsel to stop talking and do something." Press Release, June 3, 1932, Gp. 18, R.L.

26. As stated in less detail earlier, all appointments
to the New York State Supreme Court are interim appointments, and if the vacancy occurs prior to October 15, the term of office expires at the end of the
calendar year. On January 1, a candidate chosen in
the November elections assumes the post for a full
fourteen year term. If the vacancy occurs prior to
January 1, but after October 14, the appointee holds
office until the general elections of the following

year. The local political organizations within the judicial district nominate the candidate for the elected office, but in 1932 it was without precedent for the Governor's own party to deny nomination to his appointee.

27. *New York Enquirer*, June 6, 1932.

28. *New York American*, July 4, 1932.

29. *Ibid.*, September 2, 1932.

30. *New York Times*, August 26, 1932.

31. Interview with Dorothy Rosenman. Mrs. Rosenman had indicated that as the Judge was not informed of his rejection until two weeks prior to the convention, the above account of his civil activities is irrelevant to the story of his rejection. I have chosen to include them nonetheless. Rumor of his rejection appeared in the *New York Times* over a month prior to the convention; or over two weeks before Rosenman received verification from Hines. It is, of course, possible that Rosenman did not encounter the article or if he did he may have regarded it as just another dope story. If Hines did provide Rosenman with the first real indication that he would not receive the nomination, the above enumerated civic activities still serve as illustrations of what is generally expected of a candidate anticipating judicial preferment.

32. *New York Times*, September 2, 1932. Rosenman was with Roosevelt in Albany when word was received of Walker's resignation. The hearing was formally adjourned the following day.

Walker's and Rosenman's paths continued to cross, and in 1937, while sitting as a Justice of the New York State Supreme Court, Rosenman decided a Walker muni-

cipal-employment date controversy in such a manner as
to deny the former Mayor a $250 per week pension.
The decision, *Welling* v. *Fullen* 299 N.Y.S. 86 (1937),
was upheld by unanimous vote and without comment by
the Appellate Division. In 1945, Rosenman secured
the appointment of Harry Hopkins to a sinecure abandoned by Walker for a better paying position.

33. *New York Times*, September 30, 1932.

34. F.D.R., *His Personal Letters*, 302. FDR to Curry,
     September 29, 1932.

35. *New York Times*, September 30, 1932. Confirmation
     that Steuer was among those suggested by Curry in re-
     gard to the Mullan vacancy is contained in a letter
     from SIR to author, November 13, 1963.

36. FDR to SIR, September 30, 1932, Halstead Collection,
     R.L.

37. *New York Times*, September 30, 1932.

38. *Ibid.*

39. *New York Sun*, September 30, 1932.

40. *New York Times*, November 8, 1932.

41. *Ibid.*, October 1, 1932.

42. *Ibid.*, October 3, 1932.

43. Minutes of October 6, 1932 of the Association of the
     Bar of the City of New York. See also minutes of the
     New York County Lawyers Association, October 20, 1932.

44. *New York Times*, October 1, 1932.

45. *Ibid.*, October 6, 1932.

46. *Ibid.*, September 30, 1932.

47. FDR to Herbert A. O'Brien, October 15, 1932, Papers of the Democratic National Committee, R.L.

48. Interview with Samuel I. Rosenman.

49. Rosenman, *Working With Roosevelt*, 87, 88.

50. *Bronx Home News*, September 12, 1925.

51. *New York Times*, January 23, 1933.

52. *Ibid.*, March 16, 1933.

53. *New York World Telegram*, March 18, 1933. Allan Nevins in *Herbert H. Lehman and His Era* (New York: Scribners, 1962), 138, 139, has pointed out that upstate legislators were most concerned over a centralized plan (subsequently compromised) which they feared would enable New York City to dominate the proposed liquor board. City legislators generated most of their excitement over the more immediate practical problems relating to liquor store locations and bar service.

54. *New York American*, April 10, 1933.

55. *New York Daily News*, April 10, 1933.

56. *New York Times*, April 28, 1933.

57. *Ibid.*, May 5, 1933. Maldwin Fertig, who had been Rosenman's successor as Counsel under Roosevelt, retained that position under Lehman. Charles Poletti succeeded Fertig in August 1933.

58. Interview with Samuel I. Rosenman.

59. During this period Rosenman was associated with the law firm of Weil, Gotshal, and Manges. (*New York*

Times, February 8, 1933). Although he received financial remunerations for public service and court assignments, they provided only a small portion of his
total earnings. On at least one occasion a court assignment backfired. George W. Alger (one of the two
Independent Judges Party candidates in the 1932 election) has related how he, Rosenman, and Philip J.
Junn had been appointed referees in a complicated
action involving the bankruptcy of the Motion Pictures
Operators Union. Rosenman expended such comprehensive efforts upon the assignment that Alger and Junn
regarded themselves as almost superfluous. Despite
legal opposition and threat of personal violence,
Rosenman was able to avert bankruptcy. At this point
the Appellate Division ruled that the referees had
been improperly appointed and could receive no fee.
Interview with George Alger, September 11, 1963.
See also *Herald Tribune*, June 22, 1933.

60. Joseph Israels II, "The Saga of Sammy the Rose," *Saturday Evening Post* (December 5, 1942), 62. Mr. Israels
served as a publicity man for Rosenman's 1933 judicial campaign.

61. *New York Herald Tribune*, August 15, 1933, and *New
York Times*, August 25, 1933. Rosenman returned to
the bench before the retail code was adopted. Other
codes drafted with his assistance include those for
the millinery trades, *New York Times*, July 6, 1933;
the upholstery industry, interview with Rosenman,
and the Metropolitan Dress Contractors Association,
New York Times, June 23, 1933.

62. *New York Herald Tribune*, July 20, 1933. News stories
alleging Rosenman's reappointment began to appear almost as soon as Lehman assumed office. See for example *New York Times*, January 4, 1933, and *New York
Herald Tribune*, March 13, 1933. *The Tribune* alleged
that Tammany Hall was then supporting Rosenman's
candidacy. Curry had reputedly reversed himself in

regards to Rosenman in a desire to placate Jimmy
Hines. Rosenman had retained an association with
Hines since the district leader had first endorsed
him for the Assembly, and soon after the 1932 elections the Judge brought his district leader to Hyde
Park to meet with the President-elect. *New York Sun*,
November 22, 1932. According to Judge Rosenman,
Roosevelt was pleased with Hines and would have supported him in a contest to unseat Curry as Tammany
leader. Hines, however, was content to remain as the
only Manhattan district leader endowed with substantial state and national patronage. For a view that
Curry did not reverse himself on Rosenman see foot-
note 64 below.

63. *New York Times*, July 22, 1933.

64. *New York Times*, October 4, 1933. In a personal interview, Joseph Shalleck has stated that even prior to
Rosenman's first appointment in 1932, Tammany had
agreed to support his candidacy in the 1933 election.
Vacancies were assured for the latter year as four
justices would then reach the statutory retirement
age. Rosenman, according to Shalleck, accepted his
appointment from Roosevelt possessing knowledge of
this agreement and without any indication he would
receive redesignation.

This author wonders, however, if the New York County
Democratic Organization had been successful in its
opposition to the gubernatorial nomination of Lehman,
and/or the 1933 mayoralty campaign had been the
usual certainty for the Democratic candidate, whether
Tammany would have so willingly endorsed Rosenman.
It would have been an even more colossal blunder
than it was for Tammany to antagonize Roosevelt and
an articulate segment of the New York City population
by rejecting Rosenman in 1932 if it anticipated supporting him the following year. While Tammany leaders may have believed the endorsement of Hofstadter

demanded immediate attention, the appointment of the
youthful Aron Steuer (Max Steuer notwithstanding)
could have been prudently postponed until the following year.

CHAPTER FIVE

1.   The State Supreme Court maintains a courthouse in
     every county and Judges are not limited to the county
     of their origin but may be regularly assigned anywhere
     within the judicial district from which they are elec-
     ted. Rosenman therefore sat in both Manhattan and
     Bronx counties, but the former was the scene of his
     more important judicial activities.

2.   LaGuardia, an independent Republican, had been decis-
     ively defeated by James J. Walker in the 1929 mayor-
     alty contest and had lost his congressional seat in
     the 1932 Democratic landslide. The Fusion candidate
     for the President of the Board of Aldermen was Bronx
     Democrat Bernard S. Deutsch, an Independent Judges
     Party candidate of the previous year.

3.   *New York Times*, October 3, 1933. The Fusion nominees
     included George Trosk, Robert McCurdy Marsh, and Ed-
     gar J. Lauer. Marsh had received mention as a pos-
     sible Independent Judges Party candidate the previous
     year.

4.   *New York Sun*, October 3, 1933.

5.   FDR to C.C. Burlingham, October 4, 1933, Rosenman
     Papers, R.L.

6.   C.C. Burlingham to FDR, October 5, 1933, Rosenman
     Papers, R.L.

     Rosenman has stated that Hines never made irregular

requests of him and in fact, since Assembly days had
shielded his "discovery" from the more pernicious aspects of clubhouse politics. Rosenman continued to
meet with Hines socially after becoming a Judge, but
ceased his visits to the Monongahela club house.
Interview with Rosenman.

In 1940, after a series of sensational trials, Hines
was convicted of being a paid protector of gangster
Arthur "Dutch Schultz" Flegenheimer and sentenced to
prison. For District Attorney Thomas E. Dewey, who
prosecuted Hines, the trials provided the springboard
to his subsequent political successes. Joseph Shalleck, Rosenman's original sponsor, was numbered among
Hines' defense attorneys.

7. *New York Times*, October 8, 1933. See also *Syracuse
Post Standard*, October 8, 1933, and *New York Daily
News*, October 9, 1933.

8. *New York Times*, October 9, 1933, and *New York Herald
Tribune*, October 9, 1933.

9. *New York Times*, October 25, 1933. Names were added
to the Recovery judicial ticket through petitions
until the number of candidates eventually exceeded
the number of vacancies to be filled. Seabury and
George Trosk contested this arrangement and requested
the Court to strike the entire Recovery judicial
ticket from the ballot. They contended that both the
length of the ticket and the methods by which the
candidates had been chosen were illegal. In a unanimous decision the Court of Appeals denied these con-
tentions. *Trosk* v. *Cohen* 262 N.Y. 430 (1933). See
also *New York Times*, October 21, 1933, and *New York
Evening Journal*, October 24, 1933.

10. R.P.C. Included in this collection is a scrapbook
devoted to correspondence, speeches, and other election materials of the 1933 judiciary campaign. The

greatest volume of correspondence was conducted by
Paul Kammerer.

11. *Ibid.* Among other names included on campaign station-
     ary, pamphlets, and newspaper ads were Susan Brandeis,
     A.A. Berle, George Gordon Battle, George W. Alger,
     Victor Dowling, and Richard Washburn Child.

12. The Citizens Union report was carried in the *New York
     Times* and *Herald Tribune* of October 18, 1933.

     Technically the voter could have chosen any five
     among the judicial candidates regardless of their
     row and column on the ballot with those five amassing
     the most votes being elected. In practice, however,
     those candidates appearing in the same column on the
     ballot compete directly with each other for votes.
     The Citizens Union recommended the five Fusion candi-
     dates as the most qualified to fill the five vacan-
     cies. It is not, however, unusual to recommend more
     candidates as qualified than there are vacancies.
     Both the City Bar Association and the New York County
     Lawyers did this while recommending both Rosenman
     and Trosk. Nathan L. Miller even went so far as
     serving on Trosk's committee simultaneously with per-
     sonally endorsing Rosenman. The judicial columns on
     the ballot were the thirteenth through the seven-
     teenth. It has been suggested that this system is
     too sophisticated for some voters.

13. *New York Times*, October 20, 1933.

14. *Ibid.*, July 22, 1933. This editorial was reproduced
     in full and included in the Rosenman campaign liter-
     ature.

15. *Syracuse Post Standard*, March 15, 1932.

16. Rosenman's campaign literature included both quotes
     along with their published source. The Roosevelt

quote was from the *New York Times*, March 12, 1932,
and Lehman's September 17, 1933, R.P.C. A Rosenman
flyer is also included among the Rosenman papers at
the Roosevelt Library.

17. The R.P.C. contains both 1933 Rosenman and 1930 Roosevelt campaign materials.

18. A number of individuals who wrote letters for Rosenman forwarded copies to campaign headquarters. These
have been preserved along with other campaign materials in the Rosenman Personal Collection. James J.
Rosenberg (November 2, 1933) was the individual soliciting Lehman's support. Mrs. Lehman conveyed her
husband's impressions to Rosenman in an undated letter.

19. For evidence on the nature of speaking engagements
see *Bronx Home News*, October 16, 1933, and George H.
Sims to SIR, November 3, 1933. R.P.C.

20. A transcript of *the* Rosenman speech is in the campaign collection. The Moley quote appeared in the
Herald Tribune, October 30, 1933. Its moderation
irritated and disappointed Rosenman. See chapter 6.

21. For example see Henry Wollman to SIR, November 1,
1933. R.P.C.

22. *Ibid.*, George Meany to SIR, October 20, 1933. In
order to assist Rosenman in compiling endorsement
literature, Meany was requested to enumerate some
Rosenman activities which had commended themselves
to the labor organization. A copy of a congratulatory letter sent to Rosenman on the occasion of his
judicial appointment by Governor Roosevelt was the
only material forthcoming. Meany was Ed Flynn's
brother-in-law.

23. *New York World Telegram*, November 3, 1933, and *New*

York Evening Post, October 27, 1933.

24. *New York Evening Post*, November 2, 1933.

25. *New York Times*, November 9, 1933. It should be re-
    emphasized that technically a judicial candidate does
    not run against any other particular judicial candi-
    date, but rather the voter selects the number of can-
    didates corresponding to the number of vacancies.
    Taking into account multiple endorsements, and con-
    sidering only the four most popular parties, in 1933
    there were eight candidates for five positions. Both
    McLaughlin and McCook enjoying the endorsement of all
    four parties polled over 800,000 votes. By adding
    Rosenman's to Trosk's votes a total only slightly
    greater than that of McLaughlin's is obtained. I
    mention this to support the belief that with very
    rare exceptions voters tend to choose among candidates
    listed in the same column. This election did supply
    one such rare exception when neither Marsh nor Coha-
    lan, both in the same column, were elected while
    Koch and Lauer also sharing a column were both elec-
    ted. Oddly enough when added together Koch and Lau-
    er's total is less than McLaughlin's or the Rosenman-
    Trosk total. This would indicate that rather than
    voting for two candidates in the Koch-Lauer column,
    approximately 200,000 voters refrained from making
    any choice between Cohalan and Marsh.

13 Cohalan	296,046	14 *Rosenman	534,219	15 *McLaughlin	
Marsh	327,147	Trosk	322,084		
	623,193		856,303		841,169

16 *Koch	512,337	17 *McCook		
*Lauer	328,770		*Elected	
	841,107	818,066		

Had 7,000 votes been cast for Trosk instead of Rosenman, both men would have been elected. This suggests

that Rosenman's intensive campaign was as detrimental
to Trosk's hopes as it would have been had they technically campaigned against each other.

A touch of irony may be found in that while the Tammany endorsed candidates all served creditably,
Lauer, the only candidate elected without Tammany
endorsement, resigned in 1939 because of alleged
smuggling activities. See *New York Times*, November
10, 1948.

26. SIR to FDR, November 9, 1933, P.P.F. 64, Rosenman
Papers, R.L. Rosenman took his results from the *New
York Sun*, November 8, 1933.

27. FDR to SIR, November 13, 1933, P.P.F. 64, Rosenman
Papers, R.L.

28. Samuel I. Rosenman, "The Way to Select Better Judges,"
an address before the American Judicature Society,
August 12, 1964.

29. Contrary to the practice of many state judges then
sitting, Rosenman insisted that his law clerk be
someone trained in the law. Conveniently, Milton
Shalleck, a nephew of Joseph Shalleck, had recently
been admitted to the bar and, given the exigencies
of the depression, was anxious for the clerkship.
Rosenman was prepared to appoint him when he discovered that despite the prominence of the Shalleck
name in local politics--another of Milton's uncles,
Benjamin, was a Municipal Court Judge--John Curry
opposed the appointment. As payment for Tammany support in the recent election, Curry expected the privilege of selecting Rosenman's law clerk; doubtless
regarding it as a routine prerogative. Curry's candidate had rendered greater service than Milton to
the Tammany organization but was without legal training. Rosenman insisted upon Milton's appointment
and after some controversy, Jimmy Hines interceded

to secure Curry's acquiescence. Rosenman has since
insisted he would have appointed Milton even had Curry not eventually concurred. Interviews with Samuel
Rosenman and Milton Shalleck.

Shalleck remained as Rosenman's law clerk throughout
the remainder of Rosenman's judicial career, and in
1962 was appointed a municipal court judge.

30. Seven State Supreme Court justices sitting in the
First Judicial Department and five justices in each
of the other departments are selected by the Govern-
or to serve as the Appellate Division. The Appellate
Division in each district assigns other State Supreme
Court justices to serve in the Appellate term. When
sitting as the Appellate Division or Appellate term
the State Supreme Court does not act as a court of
first instance. I have found it desirable, however,
not to qualify the Supreme Court with each usage,
and since it primarily serves as a court of first instance, it shall be meant as such unless otherwise
specified.

31. Advocacy of judicial restraint at a time when national, state, and local governments were enacting legislation with which Rosenman sympathized could serve
as an effective means to uphold the constitutionality
of such acts. There are, however, sufficient instances of the Judge sustaining legislative acts which
were personally distasteful to him, and occasional
instances of his striking down acts in accord with
his previously expressed socio-economic views to indicate judicial restraint was applied as a principle
rather than an expedient policy. There is also circumstantial evidence to support this view. Rosenman's closest social associates who during this period ascended the United States Supreme Court were
Felix Frankfurter and Robert Jackson, both strong
advocates of restraint, and Harlan Fiske Stone had
been Rosenman's dean at Columbia Law School. For

relevant writings by Rosenman see *New York Herald Tribune*, September 4, 1938, and November 5, 1939.

32. *Farulla* v. *Freundlich*, 274 N.Y.S. 70 (1934).

33. *New York Times*, August 29, 1934.

34. *Ibid.*

35. *New York Herald Tribune*, August 28, 1934.

36. SIR to FDR, August 28, 1934, Rosenman Papers, R.L.

37. *Ibid.*, FDR to SIR, September 6, 1934.

38. *Montreal Labor World*, December 15, 1934.

39. *A.S. Beck Shoe Corporation* v. *Johnson*, 274 N.Y.S. 946 (1934).

40. *Feldman* v. *Weiner*, 17 N.Y.S. 2d, 730 (1940).

41. *Session Laws of the State of New York*, 1935, Chapter 976.

42. Section 2 of the law read "Willfully and knowingly advertising, offering for sale or selling any commodity at less than the price stipulated in any contract entered into pursuant to the provision of Section 1 of this act, whether the person so advertising, offering for sale or selling is or is not a party to such contract, is unfair competition and is actionable at the suit of the person damaged thereby."

43. *New York Times*, November 19, 1935.

44. *Coty Inc. of New York* v. *Hearn Department Stores, Inc.*, 284 N.Y. 909 (1935). The principle that the state might set minimum prices was upheld. Rosenman cited *Nebbia* v. *New York*, 291 U.S. 697 (1931), a 5-4

United States Supreme Court decision as the controlling case.

45. *Hazzard v. Chase National Bank of the City of New
     York*, 287 N.Y.S. 541 (1936). Affirmations are *Ibid.*,
     257 AD 950 (1939), and *Ibid.*, 282 N.Y. 652 (1940). See
     also *New York Times*, April 16, 1936. The opinion sub-
     sequently became "sort of a leading law school case."
     See Frankfurter to SIR, undated memo R.P.C. A copy of
     the memo is also in the possession of the author.

     Soon after the Rosenman opinion representatives of
     the New York Stock exchange convened in the Judge's
     chambers to obtain his assistance in designing regu-
     lations increasing obligations of banks holding
     trustee indentures. After a series of meetings,
     measures were drafted which after their voluntary
     adoption by the Stock Exchange provided investors
     with additional protection. Interview with Milton
     Shalleck, January 21, 1960.

46. It might be assumed that *Coty* v. *Hearn* is an excep-
     tion to this rule, but even in that instance Rosen-
     man had upheld the state's right to establish mini-
     mum prices while finding the particular mechanism
     employed to set them defective. Furthermore there
     was extensive legal precedent for invalidating such
     broad grants of legislative power.

47. *New York Times*, June 21, 1938. Rosenman's decision
     was not officially reported. Reported affirmations
     are *Mullins* v. *Kern*, 8 N.Y.S. 2d 466 (1938), and
     Mongello v. *Kern*, *Ibid*.

48. *New York City Local Laws of 1937*, No. 40.

49. *New York State Constitution*, Article 1, Section 1.

50. Rosenman's broad view of legislative option should
     not be confused with extension of government powers

per se. In the case of *Levy* v. *Valentine*, 17 N.Y.S.
2d 768 (1940), he struck down a New York Police
Commissioner's directive on the grounds that such activities as provided for in the directive were permissible only through legislative authority. The
Lyons Law was repealed March 7, 1962, *New York Times*,
March 8, 1962.

51. *New York Law Journal*, August 13, 1936. Rosenman's
    decision was not officially reported.

52. *Osborne* v. *Cohen*, 272 N.Y. 55 (1936).

53. *Withrow* v. *The Joint Legislative Committee to Inves-
    tigate the Educational System of the State of New
    York*, 28 N.Y.S. 2d 223 at 229 (1941). The Holmes
    citation is from *Missouri Kansas and Texas Railway
    Company* v. *May*, 194 U.S. 267 at 270 (1904).

    The reference in the opinion, dated April 8, 1941, to
    a state of "unlimited national emergency" is of some
    interest in light of Roosevelt's subsequent (May 27)
    declaration that such a state did in fact legally
    exist. See Chapter 8 for additional details.

54. *Blaustein* v. *Pan American Petroleum and Transport
    Company*, 21 N.Y.S. 2d 651 (1940). The statistical
    byproducts of the trial have been drawn from the *New
    York Times*, December 20, 1941, and *Time Magazine*,
    June 17, 1940.

55. *Blaustein* v. *Pan American Petroleum and Transport
    Company*, 263 AD 97 (1941) and *Ibid.*, 293 N.Y. 281
    (1944).

56. *New York Times*, May 2, 1941.

57. *New York Daily News*, November 28, 1939. Knight had
    been enthralled by the "divine singing" of Elizabeth
    Rethberg.

58. *New York Law Journal*, December 2, 1941. *New York Times*, May 2, May 13, June 4, and December 2, 1941.

59. *In re Knight*, 34 N.Y.S. 2d 810 (1942).

60. By 1940 Rosenman was spending most of his weekends and vacations in Washington on special assignments. This part-time Washington career was facilitated by judicial assignment to the Appellate term which Rosenman assured the President would give him "more time" for FDR "until you find a way to use me full time after resignation from the bench." SIR to FDR, undated, White House File date December 12, 1942. Rosenman Papers, R.L.

     Indications of Rosenman's belated romance with Washington are apparent from numerous letters. On September 16, 1941, Rosenman wrote Steve Early that he was "back in the judicial job, but miss Washington very much." Rosenman Papers, R.L.

61. Joseph Israels II, The Saga of Sammy the Rose," *Saturday Evening Post*, December 5, 1942, 68, 69. See also *New York Times*, March 29, 1942.

CHAPTER SIX

1. The Unofficial Observer (John Franklin Carter), *Today Magazine*, February 13, 1937. The earlier work was *The New Dealers* (New York: Simon and Schuster, 1934).

2. FDR to SIR, March 9, 1933, P.P.F. 64, Rosenman Papers, R.L.

3. Morgenthau Diary, May 5, 1933, as cited in Arthur Schlesinger Jr., *The Coming of the New Deal* (Boston: Houghton Mifflin Co., 1959), 182.

Except for the tepid endorsement cited in Chapter 5,
Moley made no efforts to assist Rosenman. He had
been kept busy launching a new magazine (October 28,
1933) and assisted McKee because both Ed Flynn and
Jim Farley had requested his aid. Furthermore he had
taken Rosenman's "election for granted and the results showed how certain it was. Had there been any
doubt I [Moley] should have dropped everything else
and have done more than I did--which I realize was
small enough--or than I promised to do if you needed
it to make up the loss after election." Moley to
SIR, July 17, 1934, Rosenman Papers, R.L.

4.   SIR to FDR, undated. P.P.F. 64, Rosenman Papers,
      R.L. Rosenman often marked his letters with only the
      day of the week or no dating at all and exact dates
      must be ascertained from White House filing dates.
      Lacking the latter, approximate dates can usually
      be ascertained from the contents of the letter. This
      particular note was probably penned May 21 before
      F.D.R. released the message. It could not have been
      written after the 22nd.

5.   *Ibid.*, FDR to SIR, May 23, 1933. The veto produced
      a flurry of letters and telegrams to the White House.
      Included among these was a cable from a Samuel I.
      Rosenman (not the Judge) protesting the veto message
      as unfair and unjust. Roosevelt forwarded the cable
      to his recent collaborator with the comment he was
      only "somewhat surprised at its source."

6.   Rosenman, *Working With Roosevelt*, 99.

7.   In his Columbia Oral History Memoir, Rosenman recor-
      ded that with men such as "Louis Howe, Basil O'Con-
      nor, myself I think--or Morgenthau--I think the
      ability to work with these men was more important
      than the fact that these men were experts in any par-
      ticular field of government." The account of Mar-
      guerite Le Hand's telephone call can be found in

Working With Roosevelt, 100.

8.   Rosenman, *Working With Roosevelt*, 103. Senator Wag-
     ner was scheduled to become chairman of the conven-
     tion's resolution committee. Rosenman and High had
     complied with the President's only instruction; that
     the platform be kept short. Rosenman maintains addi-
     tional provisions were added at the convention so as
     to lengthen the original work significantly. Moley,
     After Seven Years, 347, maintains the only change in
     the platform as adopted was the splitting of a sen-
     tence. The adopted platform was longer than the
     1932 and about half the size of the 1940 platform.

9.   Rosenman has passed on some reflections as to Roose-
     velt's duplication of assignment techniques in his
     Columbia oral history memoir. His explanation of
     this particular incident is in *Working With Roosevelt*,
     104. Moley in *After Seven Years*, does not mention
     Rosenman as working either on the platform or accep-
     tance speech.

10. *Ibid.*, 105. In fairness to Moley it should be noted
     that even before Roosevelt's first inaugural he
     wrote, "I am essentially a conservative fellow. I
     feel no call to remedy evil. I have not the slight-
     est urge to be a reformer," *Fortune*, February, 1933.

11. For an account of the tearoom incident see Rosenman,
     Working With Roosevelt, 109. Rosenman assumed that
     Roosevelt and Moley discussed the forthcoming speech
     and wrote so in his memoir. After reading *Working
     With Roosevelt*, Moley wrote that he had been "com-
     pletely ignorant that any speech was in preparation"
     and had discussed only campaign generalities with
     the President. Moley to SIR, June 2, 1952. Rosenman
     Papers, R.L.

12. "The People Approve," Vol. V of the *Public Papers
     and Addresses of Franklin D. Roosevelt* (13 vols.;

New York: Random House, 1939-1952), 404-408. Rosenman's rigid commitment to traditional budgetary values is illustrated by the 1921 decision of Dorothy Reuben and himself that they keep their engagement secret until such time as Rosenman's income had become large enough to *properly* support a wife. While there is presently an "approved" differentiation between the objectives of personal and government budgets, individuals such as Rosenman and Roosevelt always found deficits morally as well as politically painful to justify. Their arguments in behalf of deficit financing provided greater assurances to their sympathetic audiences than to themselves. In such instances as the 1935 bonus bill veto, their selective moral outrage over such practices is evident.

13. SIR to Early, October 3, 1936. P.P.F. 64, R.L.

14. Rosenman, *Working With Roosevelt*, 118.

15. *Chicago Tribune*, October 9, 1936.

16. Rosenman, *Working With Roosevelt*, 133.

17. Joseph Alsop and Robert Kintner, *Men Around the President* (New York: Doubleday Doran and Co., 1939), 109. The vitriolic tone of the address was in large part precipitated by a then current practice of some employers to include within pay-envelopes leaflets denouncing the recently adopted social security program. In speaking of such employers, Roosevelt maintained "I welcome their hatred." He went on to assert that "I should like to have it said of my first administration that in it [they]...met their match. I should like to have it said of my second administration that in it these forces met their master." See Chapter 7 for further comments on this address.

18. SIR to FDR, undated. Probable date December 28, 1936.

P.P.F. 64, Rosenman Papers, R.L.

19.   Rosenman, *Working With Roosevelt*, 146.

20.   *Ibid.*, 147. See also Donald Richberg, *My Hero* (New York: J.P. Putnam's Sons, 1954), 221, 222. The plan which provided for the appointment of an additional justice, up to a maximum of fifteen, whenever a sitting justice attained the age of seventy and failed to retire, would have resulted in the immediate appointment of six new Supreme Court members. Ironically, Owen Roberts, the youngest member of the court at 56, often voted with the conservatives, while Louis Brandeis, the oldest at 80, was regarded as the court's outstanding liberal.

21.   Rosenman, *Working With Roosevelt*, 148.

22.   SIR to FDR, February 5, 1937. P.P.F. 64, Rosenman Papers, R.L.

23.   *Philadelphia Inquirer*, February 8, 1937. The Columnist was Paul Mallon.

24.   John T. Flynn, *The Roosevelt Myth* (New York: Devin-Adair, 1948), 108.

25.   *Christian Free Press*, March 1937, as cited in *The Day*, March 21, 1937.

26.   *New York Evening Journal*, March 4, 1937.

27.   *Herald Tribune*, February 6, 1937. See also *New York Evening Journal*, February 6, 1937. Throughout Roosevelt's administrations and most of President Truman's, a Supreme Court vacancy was invariably accompanied by speculation that Rosenman might receive the appointment. There is no doubt he aspired to such a position, but since this is an ambition endemic to lawyers, no special emphasis need be placed upon it.

In 1937, despite his services to Roosevelt, Rosenman was probably regarded as too youthful with too little experience upon too low a court bench to be given *immediate* consideration for a seat on the United States Supreme Court, even an expanded one.

28. SIR to FDR, undated. This was apparently written February 12, 1937. P.P.F. 64, Rosenman Papers, R.L.

29. *New York Times*, March 23, 1937.

30. *West Coast Hotel Co.* v. *Parrish*, 300 U.S. 379 (1937). This case had been decided prior to the announcement of the court reorganization plan and was the result of a change in position by Justice Owen Roberts. He adhered to his new liberalsim until after the Court was overwhelmingly populated with Roosevelt appointees.

31. *New York Times*, May 19, 1937.

32. Major legislation still awaiting review in the Supreme Court included the Social Security Act, the Wagner Act, and the Holding Company Act.

33. Roosevelt's plan for executive reorganization and his Wages and Hours Acts were both turned down later in the year.

34. Rosenman Memoir, Columbia Oral History.

35. SIR to FDR, July 13, 1937, P.P.F. 64, Rosenman Papers, R.L.

CHAPTER SEVEN*

1. Richard Crawley trans.; *The Complete Writings of Thucydides, The Peloponnesian War* (New York: Modern Library, 1951), 14.

2. Rosenman memoranda of telephone conversation with the President, March 10, 1937, Rosenman Papers, R.L.

3. Published reference to Roosevelt's proposed autobiography is in Rosenman, *Working With Roosevelt*, 193. The Judge also discussed it in greater detail during a personal interview.

4. *New York Times*, July 7, 1939.

5. *Public Papers of Franklin D. Roosevelt, Forty-Eighth Governor of the State of New York* (4 Volumes, Albany, 1930-39).

6. Samuel I. Rosenman ed., *The Public Papers and Addresses of Franklin D. Roosevelt* (13 Volumes, 1938-1950), Volume I, xv.

7. Rosenman, *Working With Roosevelt*, 339-340. These pages provide an instance of Rosenman resorting to this argument to gain FDR's concurrence with certain points in a Stabilization Program enunciated April 27, 1942. (See Chapter 9 for further details.) In a note on the message in the *Public Papers*, Volume XI, 226 Rosenman described the proposal as comprehensive, but criticized Congress for its failure "to legislate in response to two of the main points of the President's anti-inflation program--farm prices and taxes." Rosenman had urged the farm

*Substantial portions of this chapter have appeared in the *Journal of American History* (September 1968).

prices point upon the President, arguing Roosevelt should speak for the record "irrespective" of what Congress would do.

The reporter referred to in the text is George Durno, and the incident occurred at *Press Conference* 782, November 7, 1941. Despite Roosevelt's assurances to the contrary, neither this exchange nor any other portion of this particular press conference is included in "Sam's book."

8. *New York Times*, July 7, 1937. SIR to Author, August 5, 1966, includes the following: "The President and I--on *his* initiative--began to talk about putting the speeches and papers into book form some time about the first of the year of 1937."

During an interview with the Judge the author suggested that since inspiration for publication occurred about the time of the court debate and Volumes IV and V respectively, are entitled *The Court Disapproves* and *The People Approve*, it might be assumed that the court issue in large part inspired publication. The Judge denied this and insisted there was no relationship. He also pointed out that the titles had been selected well after publication and been decided upon. The introduction to Volume VI, which relates mainly to the court reorganization struggle, was not written until after publication of the first five volumes.

9. Rosenman, *Public Papers*, Volume I, xiv.

10. Rosenman, *Working With Roosevelt*, xiii.

11. *New York Times*, July 7, 30, 1937.

12. In the introduction to the first volume of Roosevelt's gubernatorial papers for 1929 (published in 1930), "The value of the record for future Governors and

other public servants" is offered as the principal
object of publication. In the 1931 volume (published in 1937 and containing the August 1931 message) the introduction explains that "it is perhaps
worthy of note that during that year certain principles, later to be nationally adopted, were set forth
and established in the State of New York." The
August message is cited as an example of such principles.

"My recollection is not clear as to who wrote the
introduction to the 1931 gubernatorial papers. The
fact is, however, that by the time of its writing
[April 26, 1937] I had already explored with the
President the idea of making the first volume of the
Presidential Public Papers a compilation of gubernatorial speeches, messages, etc., in order to show
that 'The Genesis of the New Deal'...consisted of
his four years experience as Governor. The introduction to the 1931 Volume of the gubernatorial papers
expounds the same idea, and I am sure, was written
after the President and I had agreed upon the substance and name of the first volume of the Presidential Public Papers. All of this seems to indicate
that although I had nothing to do with the gubernatorial public papers, I must have written the introduction to the 1931 volume because of the similarity
of ideas. But I am not sure." SIR to author,
August 5, 1966.

The 1932 Gubernatorial volume (published in 1939)
takes the position that the major outlines of the
New Deal are discernible from Roosevelt's record in
Albany. For a more recent restatement of the Genesis
theme see Samuel and Dorothy Rosenman, *Presidential
Style* (New York: Harper and Row, 1976), 294.

13. Eliot Roosevelt ed., *F.D.R.: His Personal Letters*,
     763, 764. FDR to Stephen Early, February 28, 1938.
     Early read the statement at a press conference,

March 1, 1938.

14. *New York Herald Tribune*, March 2, 1938.

15. *Buffalo Evening Post*, February 10, 1938. *New York Herald Tribune*, February 25, 1938 had reported Rosenman's share at $25,000.

16. SIR to FDR, March 3, 1938, Rosenman Papers, R.L. Disclosure that the "useful public service" was to be the Roosevelt Library was not made until December 10, 1938.

17. *Ibid.*, FDR to SIR, April 28, 1938.

18. *Saturday Review of Literature*, May 7, 1938, 3.

19. *New York Times*, December 21, 1941. The *American Historical Review*, July 1942, 907-909, in what seems an attempt to avoid political partisanship, selected a Canadian, Winnipeg editor J.W. Dafoe, as its reviewer. Dafoe thought the volumes revealed "Mr. Roosevelt as the only leader in the Democratic world who knew the realities of the situation and could foretell future events." Reviewer Dafoe also reported that the volumes reveal Roosevelt "to his times and to posterity as the Liberator and Defender of Mankind." For a review of the final four volumes the *Review* turned to an American, Frank Freidel, who though favorable, was decidedly more restrained.

20. *Press Conference* 389, August 9, 1937, R.L.

21. *Saturday Review of Literature*, May 7, 1938, 3.

22. Edgar E. Robinson, *The Roosevelt Leadership* (Philadelphia: Lippincott, 1955), 421-422. This volume contains a still valuable essay on Roosevelt bibliography.

23. Kenneth Hechler worked on Volumes VI through XIII, and Richard Salant assisted on Volumes X through XIII. Hechler later was elected to Congress from West Virginia. Salant became President of CBS News.

24. Rosenman Memoir, Columbia Oral History.

25. *Ibid.*, Volumes X through XIII were published in 1950.

26. For an example of quasi-public papers published in *Working With Roosevelt* see the President's proposed message to the 1940 Democratic Convention declining the presidential nomination should the delegates fail to nominate Henry Wallace as his Vice-presidential running mate, 218.

    Roosevelt's view as to the proper place to begin his autobiography comes from a personal interview with Rosenman. The Judge believed commentary on childhood years to be relatively unimportant, and after reading this study in dissertation form, indicated he thought the author provided too much such commentary.

27. This autobiographical quality is limited to how Roosevelt regarded a specific message or turn of events and not as to how Roosevelt would have regarded some subsequent event of personality. Rosenman's subsequent support of candidates or policies with the implication (and on occasion baldly stated premise) that Roosevelt would have done so had he lived may or may not be true. Such commentary does not, however, possess the autobiographical qualities referred to in the *Public Papers*.

    An illustration of the latter appeared in the *New York Times*, August 4, 1956. At that time Rosenman was supporting the candidacy of Averell Harriman over Adlai Stevenson for the Democratic presidential nomination. Rosenman saw in Harriman an aggressive champion of New and Fair Deal principles and purported to find no trace of those principles in Stevenson's speeches.

28. Richard Salant to Evan Thomas, January 24, 1949. Thomas was a Harper editor. Rosenman Papers, R.L.

29. See Robinson, *The Roosevelt Leadership*, 423, *New York Times*, November 4, 1932, Rosenman, *Public Papers*, I, 856-860, and *Gubernatorial Papers*, IV, 662-665.

30. Charles A. Beard to SIR, December 16, 1938, Rosenman Papers, R.L.

31. *Ibid.*, SIR to Beard, December 13, 1938. Raymond Moley, who worked closely with the President-elect on the inaugural, has also omitted the opening clause (This is a day of national consecration and) from his account of its preparation, Moley, *The First New Deal* (New York: Harcourt, Brace, and World, 1966), 121. Rosenman has noted the omission in *Working With Roosevelt*, 91.

32. Rosenman Memoir, Columbia Oral History. For a less homey account of the editing process see Rosenman, *Public Papers*, X, ix.

33. Grace Tully, *F.D.R., My Boss* (New York: Scribner's, 1949), 94.

34. Rosenman Memoir, Columbia Oral History.

35. To illustrate something of Judge Rosenman's editorial practices, I have reproduced a portion of Roosevelt's Madison Square Garden speech of October 31, 1936 from a recording. Washington Records, *F.D.R. Speaks*. Additions to the text as published in Rosenman, *Public Papers*, V, 568-569 are underlined. In this particular excerpt there are no words in the published text which were omitted in delivery, although this sometimes did occur. I have also added

some indications of audience reaction both for its own sake and to help explain some textual deviations.

"For twelve years this Nation was afflicted with hear-nothing, see-nothing, do-nothing Government. (roar) The Nation the Nation looked to Government but the Government looked away. Nine mocking years with the golden calf and three long years of the scourge! Nine crazy years at the ticker and three long years in the breadlines! Nine mad years of mirage and three long years of despair! And my Friends Powerful influences strive today to restore that kind of government with its doctrine that that Government is best which is most indifferent to mankind.

"For nearly four years you have had an Administration which instead of twirling its thumbs has rolled up its sleeves. (roar) And I can assure you that We will keep our sleeves rolled up.

"We had to struggle with the old enemies of peace--business and financial monopoly, speculation, reckless banking, class antagonism, sectionalism, war profiteering.

"They had begun to consider the Government of the United States as a mere appendage to their own affairs. And we know now that Government by organized money is just as dangerous as Government by organized mob. (roar)

"Never before in all our history have these forces been so united against one candidate as they stand today. They are unanimous in their hate for me--and I welcome their hatred. (roar)

"I should like to have it said of my first Administration that in it the forces of selfishness and lust for power met their match. I should like to have it said (roar) wait a minute, I should like to have it

<u>said</u> of my second Administration that in it these forces met their master. (roar)"

36. Rosenman Memoir, Columbia Oral History.

37. *American Historical Review*, April 1945, 578. A later effort by Rauch, an anthology of F.D.R. materials entitled *The Roosevelt Reader* (Rinehart: 1957), includes the *Public Papers'* incomplete version of the first inaugural.

For documentary collections borrowing from Rosenman, *Public Papers*, see *Development of United States Foreign Policy. Addresses and Messages of Franklin D. Roosevelt* (Government Printing Office, 1942) and Douglas Lurton ed., *Roosevelt's Foreign Policy , 1933-1941: Franklin D. Roosevelt's Unedited Speeches and Messages* (Wilfred Funk, 1942). For other titles see Robinson, *Roosevelt Leadership*, 432-437.

38. *Saturday Review of Literature*, May 7, 1938, 3.

39. Histories of the Truman administration have been hampered by the lack of an interpretive structure such as that provided by the *Public Papers* for the Roosevelt years. This has been a contributing factor accounting for the limited number of publications which emanated from the Truman Library during its early years as contrasted with the Roosevelt Library.

40. In 1941 Rosenman was named an original trustee, but his judicial office made him ineligible for the post. Roosevelt purposefully left the trusteeship vacant until 1943 when Rosenman resigned from the bench and could be formally designated. There is some confusion over when Rosenman actually assumed the trusteeship. *The Fourth Annual Report of the Archivist of the United States as to the Franklin D. Roosevelt Library* lists him as a trustee in 1943. Rosenman has confirmed February 1944 as the correct date.

Rosenman was disappointed by his initial ineligibility. See SIR to FDR, circa July 12, 1941 and FDR to SIR, July 14, 1941. Rosenman Papers, R.L.

41. Herman Kahn, "World War II and Its Background: Research Materials at the Franklin D. Roosevelt Library and Policies Covering their Use," *The American Archivist*, April 1954, 159-160.

42. *Press Conference* 508, December 10, 1938, R.L.

43. Instances of administrative personnel consulting with Rosenman include Robert Jackson who in a letter to Rosenman, elaborated upon his pedagogical intent in *The Struggle for Judicial Supremacy* (Knopf, 1941). Jackson to SIR, December 17, 1940, Rosenman Papers, R.L. See also Donald C. Stone to SIR, November 18, 1941. Stone, who was Assistant Director of the Bureau of the Budget in Charge of Administrative Management, informed Rosenman that he had recruited Pendleton Herring to prepare an administrative history of subsequent years. Stone wrote that he knew of Rosenman's special interest in such histories and hoped the Judge might assist Herring by providing background materials as to prior administrative reorganization activities. Herring eventually produced *The United States at War, Development and Administration of the War Program by the Federal Government* (U.S. Government Printing Office, 1946). When during 1945 the question of a suitable publisher for the Herring volume arose, Rosenman insisted upon the Government Printing Office so that Truman might write the foreword. See SIR to Truman, December 14, 1945, Truman Library. For evidence of Rosenman's *alter ego* activities see Gerald Johnson to SIR, March 8, 1941, and SIR to Johnson, undated reply, R.L. Johnson was then working on *Roosevelt: Dictator or Democrat* (Harper and Brothers, 1941).

CHAPTER EIGHT

1.   Frankfurter to SIR, September 26, 1940, R.P.C. A
      copy of the memo is also in the possession of the
      author.

2.   The trial, *Blaustein* v. *Pan American Petroleum and
      Transport Company*, lasted over seventy days and might
      have been expected to bring Stimson and Rosenman into
      intimate contact. Rosenman denied that any such con-
      tact developed, and explained that since the trial
      was extremely arduous, Stimson, who was then 73 years
      old, left most of the court work to a younger asso-
      ciate, Allen T. Klots.

3.   References to Rosenman's anonymity gained currency
      during the court reorganization struggle and the
      above representative appelations are culled from that
      period. *Boston Globe*, February 24, 1937; *Washington
      Star*, February 22, 1937; and the *Hartford Courant*,
      February 16, 1937. On occasion the Judge's picture
      would accompany a relevant article and in such in-
      stances either "invisible automaton" or "spotlight
      shy" was the usual caption. Some years later Rosen-
      man observed that "Anonymity can be built up like
      any other reputation through publicity." The Kil-
      gallen item was published in the *New York Journal
      American*, March 20, 1939. Winchell's item appeared
      in the *New York Daily Mirror*, March 29, 1939.

4.   Rosenman, *Working With Roosevelt*, 193.

5.   Interview with Samuel I. Rosenman.

6.   Harold Ickes, *The Lowering Clouds*, Volume III of the
      Secret Diary of Harold Ickes (3 Vols., New York:
      Simon and Schuster, 1954), 186. The void which La-
      Guardia's departure would leave in New York City
      politics was offered as another argument militating

against his appointment.

7.   LaGuardia revealed his awareness of Rosenman's op-
       position on numerous occasions. Dorothy Rosenman
       was active in city housing affairs and had a falling
       out with the Mayor over such issues sometime prior
       to the War Department incident. Dorothy neglected to
       attend a housing committee meeting, incidentally oc-
       curring after the announcement of Stimson's cabinet
       appointment, and the Mayor took the opportunity not
       only to berate her for being absent but also to
       chide her for apparently sharing her husband's view
       of his competence. Interview with Dorothy Rosenman.

8.   Evidence of public awareness of Frankfurter's sup-
       port for Stimson can be found in the *New York Times*,
       May 4, 1940. In the course of a foreign policy ar-
       ticle there is included mention of a Frankfurter-
       Stimson luncheon at the White House. Frankfurter,
       as spokesman for the luncheon group, described the
       conference as just a meeting among old friends. His
       explanation that his judicial office precluded their
       having discussed substantive matters was, by impli-
       cation, rejected by the press. Direct evidence for
       Frankfurter's support of Stimson is in the Frank-
       furter correspondence. See Max Freedman ed., *Roose-
       velt and Frankfurter, Their Correspondence 1928-
       1945* (Boston: Little Brown and Co., 1967), 521-530,
       for private letters on this matter. Frankfurter had
       anticipated arguments against Stimson's advanced
       age by coupling his appointment with that of Robert
       Patterson (49) as Assistant Secretary.

       Freedman also includes correspondence confirming
       Frankfurter's active interest in speechwriting ac-
       tivities. See especially Frankfurter to SIR, Octo-
       ber 7, 1940, 544-546. Most frequently the jurists
       conferred by telephone or at Frankfurter's Washing-
       ton home.

Joseph Alsop and Robert Kintner, *Men Around the President* (New York: Doubleday Doran and Co., 1939), 114, characterized the pair as "benevolent allies" to New Dealers.

9.   Frankfurter to FDR, September 10, 1929, and FDR to SIR, September 19, 1929, Rosenman Papers, R.L.

10. Interview with Rosenman. See Frankfurter to FDR, January 21, 1937, as quoted in Freedman, 379, 380, for the ultimate resolution of Frankfurter's sartorial dilemma.

11. Interview with Rosenman.

12. *New York Times*, July 14, 1940.

13. Robert Sherwood, *Roosevelt and Hopkins* (New York: Harper and Brothers, 1948), 177, 178.

14. Rosenman, *Working With Roosevelt*, 209.

15. *Ibid.*, 210. Farley was National Chairman and had spoken to Roosevelt from Chicago although they had not discussed the details of a third term announcement. In *Jim Farley's Story* (New York: Whittlesey House, 1948), 72, Farley has written "I did not ask him [Roosevelt] about the contents of the letter or how he was going to get it to me, because I gathered he had no intention of releasing it through me. I was sure it had been written by that time, because Sam Rosenman had accompanied him on the weekend cruise and Sam always turned up when there was an important letter, document, or speech to be written."

The cruise referred to above was a weekend Potomac jaunt that took place during the convention jockeying.

The text of the letter is included in Rosenman, *Public Papers*, IX, 292.

16. Rosenman, *Working With Roosevelt*, 206 ff. One Wallace biographer, Russell Lord, *Wallaces of Iowa* (Boston: Houghton Mifflin Co., 1947), 476, describes Rosenman as an active pre-convention Wallace supporter. According to the Lord account, Rosenman was so pleased with a particular Wallace speech that he "carried such word to the White House favoring Wallace and the Judge's word at the White House bore weight." Rosenman has subsequently denied this account.

    Roosevelt's declination statement, reproduced in *Working With Roosevelt*, 336 ff., suggests the President's ambition to establish a clearly liberal v. conservative two party system. He returned to this theme in 1944.

17. Rosenman, *Public Papers*, IX, 298.

18. Rosenman, *Working With Roosevelt*, 223.

19. Rosenman, *Public Papers*, IX, 481.

20. Rosenman, *Working With Roosevelt*, 223.

21. Stanley High, "Mr. Roosevelt and the Future," *Harpers Magazine* (September 1937), 337-346.

22. Rosenman, *Working With Roosevelt*, 117.

23. Sherwood, *Roosevelt and Hopkins*, 184. Sherwood had come to Hopkins' attention through his activities on the Committee to Defend America by Aiding the Allies, formed to counter America First groups which were highly vocal in opposition to Roosevelt's foreign policy. See also Rosenman, *Working With Roosevelt*, 232.

24. *Ibid.*, 248, 249. Included among Rosenman's correspondence are similar assessments of the Cleveland address. Lowell Mellett thought it "one of the finest

utterances...by a candidate I have ever read." Mellett to SIR, December 4, 1940, Rosenman Papers, R.L.

25. Rosenman, *Public Papers*, IX, 506.

26. Sherwood, *Roosevelt and Hopkins*, 190, provides the Willkie quote. The Barton comment was included in *Working With Roosevelt*, 241. Barton had been sponsored by Willkie in his contest for the Senate nomination. Joe Martin has also corroborated views that the phrase proved a significant political liability. He regarded it as a "political gimmick," however, and "felt no particular resentment over it." Joseph William Martin, *My First Fifty Years in Politics* (New York: McGraw Hill, 1960), 118.

27. The comments on Roerich are from Schlesinger, *The Coming of the New Deal*, 31. Rosenman and Hopkins' reaction to the Guru letters can be found in Rosenman's Columbia Oral History Interview, and has been supplemented in the above account with personal interviews with Rosenman.

   Contrary to the Judge's fears, the Guru letters did not become an important factor during the campaign. Rosenman attributed this to Willkie's "restraint," and speculated that Willkie perhaps feared that the questionable authenticity of some of the letters might boomerang against him.

28. The Early-Sloan incident has been reconstructed from the *New York Times*, especially the issues of October 29 through November 3, 1940. Formal statements by Sloan were printed on November 2 and 3. Grace Tully, *F.D.R., My Boss*, also includes an account of the incident, 152, 153.

29. *New York Times*, December 1, 1940. Sloan wrote this in a letter to Early dated November 22, 1940. He had "delayed" the letter until after the election to

assure it would not be "seized on for political purposes."

30. FDR to SIR, November 13, 1940, Rosenman Papers, R.L.
     The President was even then thinking toward his *Pub-
     lic Papers* and concluded his letter by suggesting a
     time for Rosenman to "work on the papers when I may
     be able to steal a few hours to help."

31. *Ibid.*, SIR to FDR, November 8, 1940.

32. Freedman, *Roosevelt and Frankfurter*, 482. Arthur
     Hays Sulzberger, the publisher of the *New York Times*,
     was among the delegates.

33. *New York Times*, September 25, 1940. In 1935 Rosenman
     had joined with 50 communal and religious leaders of
     three faiths in a plea for "the safeguarding of
     religious freedom as the foundation of democracy and
     all social, economic, and political liberty." *New
     York Times*, March 18, 1935. In an address reported
     in the *Times* of December 11, 1939, Rosenman declared
     "The people of the United States have become more
     conscious of religion, more dependent upon their
     faith and more interested in spiritual regeneration
     than they were during the two decades before,...
     One of the reasons for the return to religion has
     been the spectacle of those nations of the world that
     have ostracized religious faith from their borders."

34. SIR to FDR, December 2, 1938, Rosenman Papers, R.L.
     The memorandum was accompanied by a cover sheet at-
     testing that Rosenman had "talked at length with
     Bernie Baruch about parts of it." Rosenman thought
     Baruch could be encouraged to take the lead in rais-
     ing money as well as assume a principal part in the
     development. In an interview with the author (March
     25, 1964), Baruch recalled from memory that Louis
     Brandeis was to take the lead in fund raising and
     "John D. Rockefeller, Jr., had pledged five to ten

million dollars." The organizers anticipated the
operation would require approximately 500 million
dollars. Herbert Hoover was to be in overall charge
of the project and Hamilton Fish had agreed to serve
as a member of the executive committee. Lower California had also been considered as a potential site.
Baruch could not recall any specific reasons the
plan failed to become operational.

This is essentially the same plan Baruch discusses
in *Public Years* (New York: Holt Rinehart, 1960), 256.
Writing as late as 1960 Baruch referred to the "desperate plight of hundreds of thousands." This numer-
ical understatement is more than literary allusion
and provides a key to the limited (German) context
in which the problem was viewed.

35. David Brody in "American Jewry, the Refugees and Immigration Restriction," *American Jewish History Society Publications*, XLV (June 1956), 219-247, has
labeled colonization programs a "psychological compensation" for the inhospitality of American Jews
toward enlarged immigration quotas during this period.
After 1938, a "veritable flood" of colonization proposals appeared. They included settlements in the
Philippines, Alaska, Lower California, Australia and
the Dominican Republic.

36. SIR to A.A. Berle, October 19, 1939, and Berle to
SIR, December 9, 1939, Rosenman Papers, R.L. There
are additional letters on this and related matters
included among the Rosenman Papers. The "regret"
over following State Department advice was elicited
from an interview.

37. SIR to FDR, November 8, 1940, Rosenman Papers, R.L.

38. *Ibid.*, SIR to Marguerite LeHand, undated.

39. Rosenman, *Public Papers*, X, 7.

40. It is sometimes difficult to recapture the image of
     Willkie as a repentant isolationist. A reading of
     his campaign literature reveals that by mid-October
     he was referring to Roosevelt as a warmonger and sug-
     gesting that the President had made secret agreements
     calculated to bring the United States into the war.
     Whether Willkie believed this or not, he had taken a
     public stance which would require thorough and com-
     plete repudiation in order for him to support Lend-
     Lease. He eventually dismissed his isolationist
     preachings as "campaign oratory," but for some time
     Rosenman persisted in the belief that Willkie had
     been sincere during the campaign.

41. *New York Times*, May 25, 1941.

42. *Ibid.*, May 27, 1941. See also *Christian Science
     Monitor*, May 27, 1941.

43. Sherwood, *Roosevelt and Hopkins*, 296. Sherwood cites
     Hopkins as having instructed a "proclamation of Un-
     limited National Emergency," and explains "up to then,
     since September 1939, the emergency had been 'limi-
     ted'!" Rosenman, *Working With Roosevelt*, 283, pro-
     vides essentially the same account, but does not at-
     tribute any such special role to Hopkins. Rosenman,
     himself, had utilized the term unlimited national
     emergency in a judicial decision rendered the month
     previous. He had then written "in this period of
     unlimited national emergency every arm of the govern-
     ment must be especially vigilant..." *Withrow* v. *Joint
     Legislative Committee*, 28 N.Y.S. 2d 223 at 229.

44. Sherwood, *Roosevelt and Hopkins*, 297.

45. Ickes, *The Lowering Clouds*, 534. The press confer-
     ence is not included in the *Public Papers*. The speech
     and the proclamation are included: *Public Papers*,
     X, 181-195.

46.   Rosenman, *Working With Roosevelt,* 283. If one event
      can be singled out to have produced sufficient anxiety
      to permit the President to agree to the proclamation,
      it was the presence of the German battleship *Bismarck*
      loose on the Atlantic. The *Bismarck,* which had already
      sunk the British cruiser *Hood* and was believed headed
      for the Caribbean, was in itself a formidable menace
      to Allied and American shipping. Early probably had
      it in mind in his reference to "rapidly changing con-
      ditions abroad." The *Bismarck* was sunk by the British
      Navy only hours prior to Roosevelt's address thus mak-
      ing the proclamation redundant to the crisis the *Bis-
      marck* had evoked. The removal of this threat might
      help rationalize Roosevelt's apparent turnabout at
      his press conference the following day.

      For a different interpretation of Roosevelt's "turn-
      about" see Deborah Wing Ray, "The Takoradi Route:
      Roosevelt's Prewar Venture Beyond the Western Hemi-
      sphere," *Journal of American History* LXII (September
      1975), 240-358.

47.   *New York Times,* May 31, 1941.

                          CHAPTER NINE

1.   Committee of Records of War Administration, *The United
      States at War* (Washington, D.C.: U.S. Government
      Printing Office, 1946), 521-535.

2.   Rosenman, *Public Papers,* X, 357.

3.   SIR to FDR, September 5, 1941, Rosenman Papers, R.L.

4.   *Ibid.,* Forrestal to SIR, October 27, 1941.

5.   Executive Order 8629 of January 7, 1941. The OPM had
      been established as part of a streamlining of the

even more cumbersome Advisory Commission of the
Council of National Defense.

6.   Executive Order 8734 of April 11, 1941.

7.   *Washington Daily News*, August 19, 1941. See also
      Time, August 18, 1941.

8.   The amortization agreement cited above and concluded
      shortly after the establishment of SPAB is only one
      such instance.

9.   Although this sketch is admittedly a simplification
      it does provide a useful framework from which to
      view the politics of reorganization. Senator Harry
      Byrd, for instance, consistently coupled demands for
      an economic czar with the ending of the forty hour
      week. The CIO, on the other hand, passed resolutions
      in opposition to any economic czar. *New York Sun*,
      September 3, 1942. *New York Times*, September 2, 1942.

      Maintenance-of-membership agreements provided that
      new employees were not required to join a union as a
      condition of employment, but those employees who held
      union membership were required to retain their mem-
      bership during the life of the agreement. The union
      acted as the bargaining agent for *all* employees dur-
      ing the life of the bargaining contract.

10.   Leon Henderson to FDR, August 11, 1941, OPACS-OPM
      Folder, R.L.

11.   Ickes, *The Lowering Clouds*, 602.

12.   *Ibid*.

13.   *Ibid*., 608.

14.   Board members in addition to Wallace were Harry Hop-
      kins, Henry Stimson, Frank Knox, Sidney Hillman,

William Knudsen, and Leon Henderson. Donald Nelson
was named Executive Director.

The Nation, September 6, 1941, otherwise critical of
SPAB, noted that it was weighted four to three in
"favor of the New Deal." Those pro were Wallace,
Hopkins, Henderson, and Hillman. The antis were
Stimson, Knox, and Knudsen.

The assignment of the OPACS civilian supply responsibilities to the OPM resulted, among other things, in
some reinitialing. The emergent OPA remained as a
foremost control agency well into the Truman administration.

15. *Time*, September 1, 1941.

16. *Ibid.*, September 8, 1941.

17. *New York Times*, August 30, 1941.

18. *Ibid.*, September 5, 1941.

19. *Ibid.*, August 30, 1941.

20. *Portland Oregon Scribe*, August 27, 1941.

21. *The Nation*, September 6, 1941. Students of subse-
    quent federal agencies will perhaps view SPAB as a
    pioneering effort in the acronymic art.

22. Committee of Records, *The United States at War*, 79.
    See also William L. Langer and S. Everett Gleason,
    The Undeclared War (New York: Harper and Brothers,
    1953), 736, 737. Evaluation is complicated by the
    fact that this was a tooling period and construction
    of new plants and the production of machines to pro-
    duce war materials had little *visible* short term
    impact on increasing military production.

23.   Executive Order 9024 of January 16, 1942.

24.   Harold Smith to Eleanor Roosevelt, July 22, 1941,
      Housing Folder, R.L. It was not unusual for Mrs.
      Roosevelt to attempt to stimulate activities by first
      approaching members of government other than her hus-
      band. If the officials consulted concurred with Mrs.
      Roosevelt's opinion she would then approach the Pres-
      ident fortified with "expert" advice. At times Rosen-
      man served as Mrs. Roosevelt's "expert". See for in-
      stance, Rosenman Papers, Eleanor Roosevelt to SIR,
      April 26, 1944 and SIR to Eleanor Roosevelt, May 1,
      1944. Mrs. Roosevelt took an interest in Puerto
      Rican affairs and approached the Judge with an argu-
      ment to remove Rexford Tugwell as Governor and re-
      place him with Admiral William Leahy. Her position
      was anti-Luis Munoz Marin. Rosenman reviewed her
      argument and concluded it was too onesided to merit
      presidential action. Rosenman himself pushed for the
      extension of Puerto Rican self-government in August
      of that same year. (SIR to FDR, August 29, 1944.)
      His appeal was election oriented and emphasized the
      300,000 Puerto Ricans then living in New York City.

25.   Among the largest of these were: United States Hous-
      ing Authority, Federal Housing Administration, Federal
      Home Loan Bank, Home Owners Loan Corporation, Federal
      Savings and Loan Insurance Corporation, and the De-
      fense Homes Corporation.

26.   Dorothy Rosenman, *A Million Homes a Year* (New York:
      Harcourt Brace, 1945), 34. The Rosenmans' particular
      interest in housing is evidenced both by the inclusion
      of numerous housing documents and the frequent notes
      on them in the *Public Papers*. These notes are among
      the most extensive and heavily documented in the
      volumes.

27.   FDR to Eleanor Roosevelt, July 31, 1941, Rosenman
      Papers, R.L.

28. *Ibid.*, Eleanor Roosevelt to FDR, August 25, 1941.

29. *Ibid.*, FDR to SIR, August 30, 1941.

30. *Ibid.*, Grace Tully to SIR, September 26, 1941.

31. Rosenman, *Public Papers*, X, 211.

32. *Ibid.*, XI, 125.

33. Housing Folder, Rosenman appointment pad, R.L. The
    folder consists in large part of memoranda, some of
    which have lost their sense of urgency in the inter-
    vening years. My personal favorite is from SIR to
    David C. Stone, November 11, 1941. "Thanks very much
    for sending me those charts. They have renewed my
    faith in charts because they have pointed out some of
    the weaknesses in some of the memos."

34. Rosenman, *Public Papers*, XI, 125.

35. *New York Times*, December 4, 1941.

36. All legislation relating to defense housing was re-
    ferred to the House Committee on Public Buildings
    and Grounds.

37. Wagner to FDR, November 23, 1941. Housing Folder,
    R.L. Rosenman transmitted the letter to the Presi-
    dent. It was to be used at a conference Roosevelt
    had scheduled with congressional leaders to discuss
    the housing situation.

38. See *New York Times*, December 25, 1941, for signing of
    the appropriations bill, and January 6, 1942 for
    Straus's resignation. Rosenman, *Public Papers*, XI,
    125, discusses the reorganization changes. Rosenman
    had originally conceived of the NHA with one princi-
    pal division for all public housing functions and
    another to carry out all the functions of government

aid in private construction. The final form of the
reorganization order included these two divisions
plus an additional one to carry out the lending functions of government in housing.

39. *New York Times*, February 25, 1942. Executive Order
    9070 of February 24, 1942. The USHA became the
    Federal Public Housing Authority.

40. Smith to SIR, February 27, 1942, Housing Folder, R.L.
    Blandford, while serving as Secretary to the TVA
    Board, had been David Lilienthal's candidate for
    General Manager. The appointment was staved off in
    1934 by the board chairman who regarded Blandford as
    insufficiently sensitive to the needs of private
    power interests. In 1937, however, he secured the
    position as General Manager of TVA and served until
    1939 when he came to Washington as Assistant Director
    of the Bureau of the Budget.

41. *Ibid.*, Palmer to SIR, February 27, 1942.

42. *Ibid.*, Palmer to FDR, February 25, 1942.

43. *Ibid.*, SIR to Frankfurter, March 2, 1942.

44. *New York Times*, February 26, 1942, and *Time*, March 9,
    1942.

45. *New York Times*, February 26, 1942, (Arthur Krock).

46. Press Conference 929, December 28, 1943, R.L.

47. Committee of Records, *The United States at War*, 183.

48. Frances Perkins, *The Roosevelt I Knew*, 373. Miss Per-
    kins' account has Rosenman play the major role in
    setting up the commission.

49. Executive Order 9139. Anna Rosenberg was a Baruch

protégé and some contemporary accounts credit her
along with Harold Smith with suggesting McNutt as
Director (*Washington Post*, April 16, 1942--Drew Pearson). *The Nation*, June 22, 1942, reported that Rosenman chose McNutt. It would appear that McNutt had
always been the likely Director *if* the commission
should be established, and this probably influenced
Perkins and Hillman in their opposition to its establishment. William Hassett, *Off the Record With FDR*
(New Brunswick: Rutgers University Press, 1958), recorded in his entry for April 16, 1942, that "The
President had decided to make Paul McNutt chairman,
which will put Sidney Hillman's nose out of joint."
Hillman had hoped that, if the Commission was established, he would get the chairmanship.

50. *American Magazine*, July 1943, "Sammy the Rose," 109.

51. *New York Times*, May 22, 1942.

52. *Public Papers*, XI, 279-280. See also Sidney Weinberg,
     "What to Tell America: The Writer's Quarrel in the
     Office of War Information," *Journal of American His-
     tory*, LV (June 1968), 77.

53. Rosenman, *Public Papers*, XI, 281. See also the text
     of Sumner Welles's argument in behalf of Rockefeller
     in a letter to FDR, March 17, 1942, as cited in Com-
     mittee on Records, *The United States at War*, 221.
     Attending the above cited White House conference were
     Rosenman, Harry Hopkins, Sumner Welles, Francis Bid-
     dle, Cordell Hull, Frank Walker, Steven Early, and
     Harold Smith.

54. Rosenman, *Public Papers*, XI, 185. Other Rosenman ac-
     tivities during this period included quasi-legal mat-
     ters for which the President acted as a final court
     of appeal. The President, for instance, solicited
     and acted upon Rosenman's recommendations in regard
     to a presidential review of the sentences imposed

upon eight Nazi saboteurs who had been captured in
June 1942. Rosenman recommended that two of the
death sentences be commuted to long prison terms.
(*Public Papers*, X, 298 and memo to author.) Attorney
General Francis Biddle, *In Brief Authority* (New York:
Doubleday, 1962), 339, has written that the President
followed Biddle's recommendation in commuting the
sentences. It is probable that the President consulted both men.

Rosenman was also credited with "having a hand in the
release from prison of Communist Earl Browder," *News-
week*, June 22, 1942. Attorney General Biddle had
also recommended Browder's release but opposed Roosevelt's rationale that it be done "in the interests
of international unity." Biddle, *In Brief Authority*,
303. Biddle doubted that Rosenman had anything to do
with the commutation, but thought "Mrs. Roosevelt
probably did." Francis Biddle to author, April 21,
1967.

55. Rosenman, *Working With Roosevelt*, 339. Other than
Rosenman, the conferees included Vice President Wal-
lace who was chairman of the Board of Economic War-
fare and a member of the War Production Board; Henry
Morgenthau, the Secretary of the Treasury; Marriner
Eckles, the chairman of the Federal Reserve Board;
Harold Smith, the Director of the Budget; and Leon
Henderson, the administrator of the Office of Price
Administration.

56. Rosenman, *Working With Roosevelt*, 337.

57. The seven points were: to increase taxes and limit
profits, to fix price ceilings on commodities and
rents, to stabilize wages, to stabilize farm product
prices, to induce larger purchases of war bonds, to
provide for rationing, and to limit credit and installment buying.

58. Rosenman, *Working With Roosevelt*, 339.

59. Rosenman, *Public Papers*, XI, 222. See Chapter 7 for comments on the efficacy of the above sort of argument upon the President.

60. Press Conference 838, July 28, 1942, R.L.

61. *New York Times*, July 29, 1942. The Little Steel formula authorized higher hourly wage rates in situations where wage increases had not kept pace with the rising cost of living from January 1, 1941 to May 1, 1942, but drew the line at this latter date against further general wage increases.

62. *Ibid.*, July 28, 1942.

63. *Ibid.*, August 20, 1942. Preliminary reports predicted a seven man board.

64. Press Conference 842, August 21, 1942, R.L.

65. *New York Times*, August 22, 1942. The press continued to report Rosenman's activities as the most important clues to Roosevelt's anti-inflation program. By September 4, they published rumors of an economic czar, and by September 8, were speculating as to whether it would be William O. Douglas, Bernard Baruch, Herbert Lehman, or James F. Byrnes. See *New York Times* of above dates.

Rosenman was much disturbed by these and other leaks which were believed to come from the War Production Board and the Bureau of the Budget. According to Hassett, *Off the Record*, 118 (entry for September 5), Rosenman had "accused one important man by name."

66. James F. Byrnes, *Speaking Freely* (New York: Harper and Brothers, 1947), 17.

67. *New York Times*, August 28, 1942. The *Times* of August 29 reported a nine point increase in the farm price level during the last month.

68. Dean Albertson, *Roosevelt's Farmer* (New York: Columbia University Press, 1961), 299.

69. Rosenman, *Working With Roosevelt*, 356.

70. *Ibid*, 229. Rosenman has cited this as one of the few occasions in which Harry Hopkins agreed with him in conference and then in a later private conference with the President argued for a different course.

71. James F. Byrnes, *All In One Lifetime* (New York: Harper and Brothers, 1958), 154.

72. Rosenman, *Public Papers*, XI, 364.

73. Executive Order 9250 of October 3, 1942.

74. *New York Times*, November 24, 1942.

75. *Ibid.*, November 27, 1942. See also newspapers of following days. *Time Magazine*, December 7, 1942.

76. Executive Order 9279 of December 5, 1942. The following year Selective Service was restored to independent status.

77. Executive Order 9301 of February 9, 1943.

78. The bill was jointly sponsored by Republican Senator Warren Austin and Republican Representative James Wadsworth.

79. William Leahy, *I Was There* (New York: Whittlesey House, 1950), 150.

80. *New York Times*, March 7, 1943. This disclosure pre-

ceded formal submission of the report.

81. Leahy, *I Was There*, 150. The statement on the Roose-
     velt-Baruch positions is confirmed in Margaret Coit,
     Mr. Baruch (Boston: Houghton Mifflin Company, 1957),
     530. Miss Coit interviewed both Baruch and Rosenman
     on this point.

82. Press Conference 885, March 19, 1943, R.L.

83. *New York Herald Tribune*, April 11, 1943.

                        CHAPTER TEN

1. SIR to FDR, May 18, 1943, Rosenman Papers, R.L.

2. Rosenman, *Working With Roosevelt*, 378. Rosenman had
    been hospitalized the previous December after an at-
    tack of dizzy spells similar to ones he had suffered
    "six or seven years" previous. It was at that time
    (December 1942) that he informed Roosevelt of his ap-
    pointment to Appellate term which would facilitate
    "Washington work...until you want to use me full
    time after resignation from the Bench." SIR to FDR,
    undated, White House File date December 12, 1942,
    Rosenman Papers, R.L. In a memo to the author, how-
    ever, Rosenman has written that the President's
    decision to bring him to Washington (in some as yet
    undetermined capacity) was made in April 1943 and as
    a consequence of the eye disorder which was unrelated
    to the dizzy spells.

3. *PM*, November 17, 1944.

4. *Chicago Tribune*, September 24, 1943. *New York Daily
    News*, September 27, 1943. Rosenman, *Working With
    Roosevelt*, 408. Roosevelt delighted in the alleged
    revelation, and for sometime afterwards occasionally

greeted Rosenman with "I'm sorry Sam, I still have to
keep Marshall in as Chief of Staff--you can try again
some other day."

5.   Press Conference 917, September 27, 1943, R.L. Biddle has written that "The President took great personal interest in the pardon cases and although usually following the opinion of the pardon attorney
backed by me, he sometimes had suggestions as to how
they should be handled. That was his human side.
As to the draft deferments the President took those
over after an important meeting of the cabinet where
the President in substance announced that draft deferments must be stopped at once. I asked him who
would pass on the deferments and he said he would
personally--no wonder he needed Samuel Rosenman to
help him. But we avoided running into the situation
which the English had to face by first refusing draft
deferments in most cases of often very highly competent men." Francis Biddle to author, April 21, 1967.

6.   *New York Times*, September 27, 1943.

7.   The quotations in the above paragraphs are from a
letter from Francis Biddle to author, April 21, 1967.

For speculation as to administrative conflicts appar-
ent in the appointment of a counsel see *New York
Times*, October 5, and October 28, 1943 (Arthur Krock).
For specific instances of Rosenman's previous ac-
tivities in areas traditionally those of the Justice
Department see Chapter 9, fn. 54.

8.   Examples of reports of the Rosenman White House residency are to be found in the *New York Daily News*,
October 12, 1943, December 20, 1943, and March 13,
1944. See also *The Philadelphia Inquirer*, October
17, 1943. The reports begin by asserting that the
Rosenmans would move into a White House suite being
vacated by Harry Hopkins, then asserting they had

moved in, and finally through preparing to move out "sometime prior" to the 1944 Democratic convention. Leonard Lyons, a gossip columnist friendly to the Rosenmans, wrote that the Judge "clips all those repeated false reports about living at the White House and encloses them with his rent checks to the manager of the Wardman Park Hotel where he lives." *New York Post*, March 13, 1944. The Wardman Park Hotel has become the Sheraton Park.

9. Katherine Tubridy to author, February 18, 1960. Mrs. Tubridy (Kitty Gilligan) served as Rosenman's secretary from his appointment as Counsel in 1943 until after his resignation in 1946.

10. Interview with Milton Shalleck, January 21, 1960. Shalleck, who served as Rosenman's law clerk, came to Washington as attorney for the Office of Lend-Lease after Rosenman's resignation from the Bench.

11. During the summer of 1943 there was public speculation that Rosenman might be brought to Washington as "coordinator of planning for the return of the economy to a peace time basis in the post war period." *New York Herald Tribune*, August 27, 1943, *New York Times*, August 27, 1943, and *New York Daily News*, September 1, 1943.

12. Rosenman, *Public Papers*, XII, 497. This was the longest message Roosevelt ever sent to Congress.

13. Oscar Cox to SIR, January 8, 1944, Rosenman Papers, R.L.

14. For Rosenman's account of the negotiations see *Working With Roosevelt*, 389 ff. See also *Public Papers*, XII, 425, 426. Rosenman has described the negotiations as among the most dramatic episodes of his Washington experience.

15. Oscar Cox to SIR, October 27, 1943. The letter con-
     gratulated Rosenman for initiating the repeal of the
     Acts. Rosenman Papers, R.L.

     Other materials in the Rosenman papers relating to
     this period include memos on the Navy V 12 (Officer
     Training) Program, the United States-Mexican Treaty
     on water rights, Senator Wagner's 1944 campaign, a
     report for the President on Sumner Welles, *The Time
     For Decision* (New York: Harper and Brothers, 1944),
     views on post-war military training, and correspon-
     dence with congressmen.

16. Rosenman, *Working With Roosevelt*, 394, 395. See also
     Public Papers, XII, 454.

17. SIR to FDR, February 2, 1944, Rosenman Papers, R.L.
     The Rosenman Papers also contain correspondence on
     veteran's legislation with Senators Robert Wagner
     and Elmer Thomas, as well as individual members of
     the President's committee of educators.

18. See Chapter 9 for accounts of the Little War Cabin-
     et's deliberations. An anti-inflationary argument
     was that many workers were leaving war industries to
     accept better paying and more permanent jobs else-
     where. Unless a method could be devised to find
     additional workers for war industries without re-
     course to raising wages, costs of production would
     be significantly increased.

     The situation was complicated by the fact that some
     of the downturn in production statistics reflected
     a *curtailment by the government* of some war contracts.
     Thus some "war workers" were dismissed from their
     jobs which in turn influenced other workers in still
     essential industries to anticipate their own lay offs
     and seek more permanent employment. The situation
     was, of course, more serious in some areas than
     others.

19. Rosenman, *Working With Roosevelt*, 422, 423. Secre-
     tary of War Stimson had strongly urged such recommen-
     dations for a national service act.

20. The only Rosenman, Hopkins, Frankfurter triumvirate
     story which I encountered in the *New York Times* may
     be of some interest here. Dated July 1, 1943, six
     months prior to the above incident, it reported that
     "the prevailing theory on Capitol Hill...is that
     Mr. Byrnes carries the titular responsibility for
     the civilian side of the war, but it is the Hopkins-
     Frankfurter-Rosenman group, superior in its contacts
     both with the White House and the lesser administra-
     tive personnel that actually runs the show." For
     those Congressmen disposed to this theory the State
     of the Union message did nothing to dispel their be-
     lief. Rosenman's Columbia Oral History interview
     contains the observation that Assistant President
     Byrnes was "quite jealous and annoyed" he could not
     issue Rosenman orders.

21. Grace Tully, *F.D.R., My Boss*, 167-168 has commented
     extensively on the situation:

        ...in the rush of things, the Boss would channel
        the very same problem over to Sam Rosenman
        giving him the same instructions that had been
        sent over to Byrnes. Being a man of action,
        Sam would at once bulldog his way forward to
        get at the facts only to find that Jimmy was
        checking the same matter. Sam would at once
        step out of the picture. But in the meantime,
        the grapevine would carry the news of Sam's
        inquiry straight to Jimmy, and he would wonder
        why the new personality had been sent into his
        domain. Sam understood perfectly what had
        happened and explained to me the difficulty
        of carrying out the President's order. Yet I
        can remember the times the President rang for
        me and in a tired and rather pathetic tone

said, "Grace, call Jimmy Byrnes and ask him
if he can run right over. I hear he is all
upset over something I did. I don't know
what I've done now but get him in and I'll
see what I can do to smooth his feathers."

22. Interview with Bernard Baruch, March 25, 1964.

23. *Chicago Tribune*, February 21, 1944.

24. Rosenman, *Public Papers*, XIII, 80.

25. *Baltimore* [Maryland] *News and Post*, March 17, 1944.

26. *New York Times*, February 29, 1944. The veto message
     was authored in the Office of War Mobilization with
     Benjamin Cohen contributing the above quoted phrase.

27. *Washington Post*, March 3, 1944.

28. *Houston Post*, June 9, 1944 and *Austin Statesman*,
     June 16, 1944. A dispute over delegates to the Nat-
     ional Convention also ensued and was resolved at
     Chicago by dividing the seats between the rival dele-
     gations.

29. Johnson to SIR, September 23, 1944, Rosenman Papers,
     R.L. The Rosenman-Johnson correspondence over the
     incident consists of three short notes from Johnson
     meant to accompany enclosures such as newspaper
     clippings and a copy of the relevant Texas Supreme
     Court decision (*Seay* v. *Latham*). The correspondence
     from the Judge to Johnson related to a "Texas turkey"
     which Johnson had sent from his ranch for Rosenman's
     1944 Christmas dinner. The Judge alleged it was so
     large that he sprained his sacoriliac carrying the
     turkey home.

30. Dewey supported the United Nations concept and made
     almost no direct appeal to isolationist sentiment.

Roosevelt insisted, however, that a Dewey victory
with accompanying Republican Congressional majorities would provide important committee chairmanships
for opponents of an international organization.
Hiram Johnson, for example, as ranking Republican
member of the Senate Foreign Relations Committee
would presumably assume the chairmanship. Rosenman,
Public Papers, XIII, 348. The same situation would
of course have prevailed had Willkie been the Republican nominee.

31. Rosenman, *Working With Roosevelt*, 466. Although the
meeting was not revealed until 1952, a rumor that
Willkie might gain the Democratic vice-presidential
nomination through Roosevelt's support gained currency. Regarding this, Roosevelt wrote to George Norris,
who was unfriendly to Willkie's candidacy, that he,
the President didn't think there was any "possible
danger...though feelers were put out about a week
ago." The letter was written July 17, 1944, aboard
the presidential train upon which Rosenman was also
traveling. *FDR Letters*, II, 1522, 1523.

Philip H. Willkie, Wendell Willkie's son, upon being
interviewed at the time of the first public disclosure of the meeting, denied that his father had any
plans for party realignment and described Rosenman's
report of a meeting as "a great injustice to my
father." *New York Times*, April 30, 1952.

32. It was argued that those who supported Wallace were
unlikely to support a Republican candidate, while on
the other hand his "extremism" would serve to fright-
en away some voters who would otherwise support
Roosevelt.

Most men who advocated dumping Wallace also held
views as to an appropriate successor. Byrnes, who
was himself ambitious for the nomination, reported
that Rosenman supported Henry J. Kaiser, a spectacu-

larly successful Liberty Ship builder. James F.
Byrnes, *All In One Lifetime* (New York: Harper and
Brothers, 1958), 222. There is also circumstantial
evidence to indicate Rosenman's sympathy towards
Kaiser, although the *New York World Telegram*, July 10,
1944, reported he was booming William O. Douglas. The
decision in favor of Truman was not made in Rosenman's
presence.

33. Rosenman, *Working With Roosevelt*, 441, 442.

34. *Ibid.*, 440-445.

35. *Ibid.*, 446, 447. Rosenman maintains that Truman was
     selected at a White House conference of July 11, and
     that the decision was confirmed in an FDR memo to
     Hannegan postdated July 19. There has been specula-
     tion that the July 11 memo specified either William
     O. Douglas or Harry Truman in that order and that
     Hannegan did not get Roosevelt to issue a memo re-
     versing the order of acceptable candidates until the
     July 15 meeting (at which Rosenman was also not
     present).

36. Rosenman maintained a diary of this trip on deposit
     at the R.L.

37. *New York Daily Mirror*, July 24, 1944. See also *New
     York World Telegram*, July 28, 1944, and *New York
     Daily News*, July 29, 1944.

38. Interview with Rosenman.

39. R.P.C. During the campaign Rosenman compiled a
     scrapbook which included only two speeches by Roose-
     velt, a somewhat larger number by Truman, and a score
     of Republican campaign addresses.

40. Rosenman, *Working With Roosevelt*, 472.

41. *New York Times*, November 22, 1942. Rosenman's esti-

mate netted him $25 as the winner of an election pool
to which he, Roosevelt, Hopkins, Early, Sherwood, and
Pa Watson all contributed.

42.   FDR to SIR, November 25, 1944, Rosenman Papers, R.L.

CHAPTER ELEVEN

1.   Interview with Mrs. Samuel I. Rosenman.

2.   FDR to Jesse Jones, January 20, 1945, *FDR Letters*,
     II, 1566, 1567. The letter is also quoted and ac-
     companied by extensive comment in Bascom Timmons,
     Jesse H. Jones (New York: Henry Holt, 1956), 354.

3.   *New York Times*, January 4, 1945, reported that Wal-
     lace had requested the commerce post. Newspaper spec-
     ulation as to the Wallace-Jones future continued
     until notice of Jones's resignation.

4.   Grace Tully, *F.D.R., My Boss*, 190.

5.   Rosenman, in a separate context, has made passing
     reference to such Jones activities, *Working With
     Roosevelt*, 430. On 463 he refers to the Texas in-
     cident as a factor in the Willkie-Rosenman confer-
     ence.

     Although Timmons in *Jesse H. Jones*, 347-349, attempts
     to absolve Jones from any culpability in the Texas
     incident, his presentation produces a contrary ef-
     fect.

6.   Rosenman, *Working With Roosevelt*, 443. The appoint-
     ment would of course be popular with organized labor.

7.   *PM*, November 17, 1944. Rosenman was apparently dis-
     turbed by the "charge," and on December 2, I.F.

Stone retracted it.

8. During the Senate struggle over Wallace's confirma-
    tion, Rosenman was the only member of Roosevelt's
    staff still in Washington who was in a position to
    handle such matters. He has maintained that unless
    he supplied direction, the President would have been
    rebuffed in his selection of a cabinet appointee.
    To avoid this rebuff was, according to Rosenman, the
    motivation for his actions throughout the affair.
    Interview with Samuel I. Rosenman.

9. Byrnes, *All In One Lifetime*, 256. Had Wallace been
    able to retain control of the lending agencies, he
    would, as Secretary of Commerce, have been able to
    exercise a far larger influence over reconversion
    policy than he ultimately did.

10. *Ibid.*, 257. Leahy, *I Was There*, 293. Leahy has
    recorded that the first telegram was signed by Rosen-
    man and the second by Mrs. Roosevelt.

11. *Washington Star*, February 1, 1945. Truman has rela-
    ted, *Year of Decisions*, Vol. I of *Memoirs of Harry
    S. Truman* (2 Volumes; New York: Doubleday, 1955),
    195, that "Barkley was supposed to place the House-
    passed bill immediately before the Senate when it
    convened. With the bill passed, the way would be
    clear for Wallace's confirmation. But when I con-
    vened the Senate, Taft quickly demanded recognition
    and was prepared to move immediate action on Wallace's
    nomination before the Senate could pass on the sav-
    ing bill. I recognized Barkley first, however, and
    the agreed-upon procedure was followed. Otherwise
    Wallace's confirmation would very probably have been
    rejected."

12. FDR to SIR, January 20, 1945, Rosenman Papers, R.L.
    At the time of the public announcement Early read
    the first two, but did not disclose the third para-

graph of the appointment letter. The third paragraph referred to postwar considerations and possible legislation.

13. Rosenman, *Working With Roosevelt*, 518. Earlier that month Roosevelt had appointed Rosenman as his personal representative on the war crimes problem, and in that capacity the Judge had assisted in devising a scheme for an international trial which Roosevelt might discuss at Yalta.

14. SIR to FDR, January 22, 1945, Rosenman Papers, R.L. The magazine article referred to is Josef Israels, "The Saga of Sammy the Rose," 69.

15. *Washington News*, January 23, 1945.

16. *New York Post*, February 5, 1945. See also *Minneapolis Tribune*, December 12, 1944. Through much of 1943 and 1944 Rosenman received frequent mention as a possible New York City mayoralty candidate. See *New York Times*, March 30, 1943, and *New York Sun*, April 17, 1944.

17. Interview with Rosenman.

18. *Chicago Tribune*, February 12, 1945.

19. Rosenman Memoir, Columbia Oral History. Evidence of Rosenman's prior involvement with relief activities is provided by numerous letters and memos, most relating to Italy, among his papers at the R.L. The mission was, however, his only assignment which dealt with the problem directly. Presumably his research in preparation of FDR's message to Congress on the Food Program (November 1, 1943) had provided him with insights into America's productive capabilities and limitations.

20. *New York Times*, March 11, 1945.

21. *Business Week*, February 24, 1945. The Johnson Debt
     Default Act of 1934 provided that no loans be made
     to any nation in default or arrears to the United
     States in payment of their World War I debt. This,
     of course, would prohibit extension of credits to
     western Europe. During World War II Lend-Lease
     had been used to circumvent the restriction, but it
     was due to cease with the conclusion of the war.
     A pending bill sponsored by Representative Sol Bloom
     provided for modification of the Johnson Act.

     The Export-Import Bank was then operating under a
     $700 million ceiling and its president, Warren Lee
     Pierson, was calling for revision upwards to $2
     billion.

22. *New York Times*, January 23, 1945.

23. *Ibid.*, February 11, 1945.

24. Rosenman, *Working With Roosevelt*, 522.

25. *Ibid.*, 522-541. The fact that the United States had
     agreed to support the Soviet Union's request for
     three votes in the General Assembly of the United
     Nations was kept out of the speech at the President's
     insistence. This was one of the decisions Rosenman
     would have disclosed through the report.

26. *New York Times*, March 7, 1945.

27. *Ibid.*

28. *Business Week*, February 24, 1945.

29. *New York Times*, March 6, 1945.

30. Winston Churchill to FDR, March 18, 1945, as cited
     in Winston Churchill, *Triumph and Tragedy*, Vol. VI of
     The Second World War (6 Volumes; Cambridge, Mass.:

Houghton Mifflin Company, 1953), 430.

31. Rosenman, *Working With Roosevelt*, 542.

32. The French conferees provided a large sampling of future Prime Ministers: General DeGaulle, M. Bidault, M. Ramadier, M. Mendes France, and M. Pleven.

33. *New York Times*, March 25, 1945.

34. *Report to the President of the United States by Samuel I. Rosenman on Civilian Supplies for the Liberated Areas of Northwest Europe* (Washington, D.C.: Government Printing Office, 1945), 47. This is the official report of the Rosenman Mission and was released May 5, 1945. The *New York Times*, April 5, 1945 also reported on the tour.

35. Sherwood to SIR, March 28, 1945, Rosenman Papers, R.L.

36. Rosenman, *Working With Roosevelt*, 545.

37. British, Russian, and U.S. views were often revised and thus the "official position" of any of the three nations must be associated with some point in time. Prior to Rosenman's discussions with British officials it had been assumed the British were in favor of trials for the principal Nazi leaders. Their new views were officially set forth in an Aide-Memoire which was presented to the Judge on April 23, 1945. It is included as Document II in *Report of Robert H. Jackson United States Representative to the International Conference on Military Trials* (Washington, D.C.: Government Printing Office, 1949).

38. Perkins, *The Roosevelt I Knew*, 382. The President had advocated "a few drumhead trials in the field and have it over quick."

Rosenman's study appears to have commenced in December.

Green Hackworth to SIR, December 15, 1944, War Crimes File, Rosenman Papers, Truman Library (hereafter cited as T.L.). Hackworth, General Counsel of the State Department, conferred with the Judge and forwarded to him a British Embassy memo of August 19, 1944 and the United States reply of October 4. These were the then most recent position papers.

39. Henry L. Stimson and McGeorge Bundy, *On Active Service in Peace and War* (New York: Harper and Brothers, 1947), 586. The report was prepared as a guide for Roosevelt's use at Yalta, but no substantive decisions were reached there. It is included as Document I in Jackson, *International Conference on Military Trials*.

    The snag in trial negotiations turned out not to be over the trial of major Nazis but rather the definition of lesser war crimes and war criminals. Joseph E. Davies, after reviewing the above report, spelled out some of the difficulties Rosenman was to face. Davies did not even refer to the trials of top Nazis as it was assumed that Great Britain and the Soviets were agreed to them. Joseph E. Davies to SIR, January 22, 1945, War Crimes File, Rosenman Papers, T.L.

40. Rosenman, *Working With Roosevelt*, 545.

41. *Ibid.*, 548.

42. *New York Post*, April 15, 1945. See also *Washington Star*, April 14, 1945.

43. Rosenman, *Working With Roosevelt*, 551.

44. Rosenman, *Public Papers*, XIII, 613-616. This is the final entry in the last volume of the *Public Papers*. The draft contains, in Roosevelt's handwriting, the often quoted "Let us move forward with strong and active faith."

CHAPTER TWELVE

1. *Chattanooga News-Free Press*, April 16, 1945.

2. Press Conference of April 17, 1945, *Public Papers of The Presidents, Harry S. Truman, 1945* (Washington, D.C.: U.S. Government Printing Office, 1961), 8.

3. Stanley High, "The White House is Calling," *Harpers Magazine* (November 1937), 580-589. High believed that Rosenman had gone further left with Roosevelt than his own convictions and much further than he would be willing to go with anyone else.

4. See for example *New York Times*, April 7, 1946. Rosenman claimed that "Senator Truman's record in Roosevelt's opinion, showed him to be the man most certain and most able to carry on the policies and objectives of the Government of the United States as they had been laid down by a long line of action and declaration."

   On April 13, 1945, the Bureau of the Budget prepared a "Compilation of Information and Statements which may Indicate or Suggest Possible Policies of President Truman." Rosenman did not receive his copy until September. See Statements Made by Harry Truman as Senator Folder, Rosenman Papers, T.L. Harold Smith had alerted the President to the existence of this report on August 18. Smith Diary, R.L. Truman ordered copies for members of his White House staff.

5. *Truman Public Papers, 1945*, 1. Statement of the President after taking the oath of office, April 12, 1945.

6. *Ibid.*, 2. Address before a Joint Session of the Congress, April 16, 1945.

7. Harry S. Truman, *Year of Decision*, Vol. I of *Memoirs by Harry S. Truman* (2 Vols; New York: Doubleday & Co., 1955), 87.

8. Rosenman assisted Stettinius in preparing the Secretary's speeches to the impending United Nations Conference, and on April 21, the Secretary thanked Rosenman for his aid and predicted the international organization would be a "living memorial to President Roosevelt." The following day he wrote that he had cleared it with Truman to have Rosenman come to San Francisco to confer with the allied foreign ministers. Stettinius folder, Rosenman Papers, T.L. Truman's letter of authorization to Rosenman, April 30, 1945, is quoted in Truman, *Memoirs*, I, 110. The press release of the Rosenman Report is Press Release of April 30, 1945, White House Press Release Files, Truman Papers, T.L.

9. *New York Times*, May 1, 1945. The release was reprinted in its entirety.

10. *Ibid.*

11. *New York Times*, May 23, 1945. See also *Truman Public Papers*, 1945, 61, 62.

12. *Rosenman Report*, 82.

13. *Congressional Record*, 79 Cong., I sess., Vol. 91 Appendix Part II, A2053 (May 3, 1945).

14. *New York Times*, May 1, 1945.

15. Memoranda, SIR to Herbert Wechsler, SIR to John J. McCloy, April 23, 1945, War Crimes File, Rosenman Papers, T.L.

16. SIR to Jackson, April 27, 1945, War Crimes File, Rosenman Papers, T.L. Eugene Gerhart, *America's*

Advocate, Robert H. Jackson (Indianapolis: Bobbs-Merrill Company, 1958), 308-310, contains an account of the appointment based partially upon personal interviews.

17. Jackson to the President, April 29, 1945, War Crimes File, Rosenman Papers, T.L., Executive Order 9545. President Truman hereafter cited as HST. See also Press Conference of May 2, *Truman Public Papers*, 1945, 35.

18. Truman, *Memoirs*, I, 284.

19. SIR to S.A. Golunsky, May 9, 1945, War Crimes File, Rosenman Papers, T.L. Identical notes were sent to Sir William Malkin and Jules Basdevant.

Amendments discussed were not insignificant and often turned on the nature of national sovereignty. For instance: If certain German acts against German Jews in Germany were defined as war crimes, it would radically alter traditional concepts of national sovereignty which assumed a nation might treat its inhabitants in any manner it saw fit. See for example, "Soviet Intentions to Punish War Criminals," April 30, 1945, a one hundred page document prepared by the Office of Strategic Services. A copy is in Rosenman's War Crimes File. The Counsel hoped to avoid prolonged controversy at San Francisco by providing the International Tribunal with the jurisdiction to determine what acts were criminal within broad areas defined by the negotiators.

20. SIR to Malkin, May 10, 1945, War Crimes File, Rosenman Papers, T.L. Identical notes were sent to Golunsky and Basdevant.

21. SIR to Eden, May 14, 1945, War Crimes File, Rosenman Papers, T.L. That same day Rosenman initiated the State Department request to Eden. See SIR to Acting

Secretary of State Joseph Grew, May 14, 1945. The
Judge had made an earlier public plea for the appointment of prosecutors. *New York Times*, May 11,
1945.

22. SIR to Lucas, May 24, 1945, War Crimes File, Rosenman Papers, T.L.

23. Grew to SIR, May 22, 1945, War Crimes File, Rosenman
Papers, T.L. The conferees indicated they would prefer some place other than San Francisco if they were
to resume negotiations, and Rosenman requested that
Grew advise them to "send or delegate" someone to
Washington. He urged immediate action. Green Hackworth to Grew, May 24, 1945, reported the British
Foreign Office had cabled Malkin its reply "suggesting that since officials of the British Government
who would conduct the negotiations are in London and
would find it difficult to go to Washington, and
since officials of other governments would be more
easily available there, the negotiations should take
place in London." Hackworth countered that the Judge
preferred Washington and might not "be prepared to
go to London." The reports were forwarded to Rosenman without comment.

24. SIR to HST, May 25, 1945, War Crimes File, Rosenman
Papers, T.L. The American memo of April 30, was
"agreed to in principle" in an *aide memoire* dated
June 3. War Crimes File, T.L. On June 11, the
British Ambassador in Washington presented the Sec-
retary of State an invitation for a June 25 meeting.

25. *New York Times*, April 28, 1945. The retainer was for
service as impartial chairman of the National Suit
Industry Recovery Board. This sinecure was then held
by former New York City Mayor James J. Walker, who
had accepted a higher paying position elsewhere. At
Rosenman's suggestion, the chairmanship was awarded
to Harry Hopkins.

26.   Interview with Rosenman. The Fulton rumor was built
      upon such circumstantial evidence as Fulton having
      resigned as Chief Truman Committee Counsel to assist
      Truman in the 1944 campaign, and a celebrated walk
      with Truman from the President's hotel to the White
      House on the morning of Truman's first full day in
      office. (Truman, *Memoirs*, I, 13.) The President
      denied there was ever a basis to the rumor of Fulton's
      appointment. Interview with Truman, November 23,
      1960. George Meader, who served under Fulton as a
      Counsel to the Truman Committee, thought that during
      the 1944 campaign Fulton had demonstrated he was
      "not as good a politician as he was a lawyer."
      Transcript, George Meader Interview, June 12, 1963,
      4, T.L.

27.   HST to SIR and SIR to HST, May 31, 1945, as quoted
      in Press Release of June 1, 1945, White House Press
      Release Files, Truman Papers, T.L. See also *Truman
      Public Papers, 1945*, 82 and 99, and *New York Times*,
      June 2, 1945.

28.   Truman emphasized his dilemma in being "beset with
      resignations" in an interview with the author, Nov-
      ember 25, 1960.

29.   A comparison of *Truman Public Papers, 1945*, with the
      Rosenman file at the Truman Library reveals that with
      the obvious exception of press conferences the Coun-
      sel drafted or edited virtually all materials which
      ultimately appeared as the *Public Papers*.

30.   This reference is to Roosevelt's personal staff.
      Certainly there were intense rivalries among advisors
      of both Presidents, but members of Roosevelt's per-
      sonal staff (LeHand, Tully, Early, Hassett, and Rosen-
      man) tended to protect each other with a dedication
      unknown to the Truman administration. Katherine Gil-
      ligan Tubridy (Rosenman's personal secretary) has
      made similar observations in a note to the author.

31. Truman's announcement that Rosenman would remain in
     the White House followed the decision by almost a
     week. As early as May 25, Vannevar Bush indicated
     his pleasure the Judge was staying on. Bush to SIR,
     Health Message Folder, Rosenman Papers, T.L. Rosen-
     man's Papers indicate that on or about May 26, Tru-
     man began to earnestly route assignments through the
     Counsel's office. This may in part be due to Rosen-
     man's prior occupation with his mission report and
     war trial negotiations, although Rosenman's willing-
     ness to relinquish his role as chief United States
     negotiator for the war trials seems to have been in-
     fluenced by his readmittance into the White House
     routine. Another factor for his relative non-activ-
     ity is that his long absence from Washington neces-
     sitated Roosevelt cease relying upon him for daily
     support, and the Counsel had to reestablish his of-
     fice functions under Truman.

     General Harry Vaughan has described the first sixty
     days of Truman's administration as one large prepara-
     tion for the already scheduled Potsdam Conference.
     Transcript, Harry Vaughan Interview, January 14,
     1963, 36, T.L.

32. One such instance involved a suggestion by Secretary
     of Interior Ickes that coal production would be in-
     creased if experienced coal miners were granted pre-
     ferential discharges from the army. The War Depart-
     ment opposed this because it was inconsistent with
     the then existing "point system" for determining dis-
     charge priorities, and any exception for coal miners
     would lead to more demands for other groups such as
     railroad workers and copper miners. Rosenman recom-
     mended that the point system be left undisturbed and
     Ickes's letters proposing the coal miner exception
     be filed. See War Message to Congress Folder,
     Rosenman Papers, T.L. See also OF 175, Truman Papers.

     Other more prolonged controversies were over such

issues as the status of Puerto Rico and the Philippine Islands. See Puerto Rico Folder and Philippine Islands Folder, Rosenman Papers. Although there is no obvious pattern of preferment to Rosenman's recommendations, he exercised an important influence over who would be invited to various conferences held to iron out policy differences among administrative and at times legislative personnel.

33. Memorandum, SIR to HST, May 28, 1945, OF 677, Truman Papers, T.L. The War Department opposed this legislation.

34. Memorandum, SIR to HST, June 1, 1945, OF 249, Truman Papers, T.L.

35. *Truman Public Papers, 1945*, 72-75. The message was sent to Congress May 28.

36. Smith to HST, May 26, 1945, OF 121A, Truman Papers, T.L.

37. SIR to HST, June 13, 1945, OF 326A, Truman Papers, T.L.

38. Alben Barkley seems to have been a pet personal project of the Counsel. On one occasion the Judge "reminded" the President that Bernice Thielman, who had baked a cake they had eaten while cruising on the Presidential yacht, was Barkley's sister. Rosenman prepared a note to Mrs. Thielman for Truman to sign as he knew "it would please the Senator if his sister got this note of thanks from you." SIR to HST, October 11, 1945, Barkley Folder, Rosenman Papers, T.L.

39. Memorandum, SIR to HST, June 13, 1945, Presidential Succession Folder, Rosenman Papers, T.L.

40. *Truman Public Papers, 1945*, 128-131. The message was dated June 19. Rosenman kept an elaborate check

on public and press reaction to the message and for-
warded editorial comments to the President. SIR to
HST, June 20, 1945, Presidential Succession Folder,
Rosenman Papers, T.L.

41. *Truman Public Papers, 1945*, 161.

42. Rosenman and Vinson worked together on a number of
related matters. These include a determination of
the status of the Public Health Service (Memorandum,
SIR to HST, June 20, 1945, Public Health Folder, Rosenman Papers, T.L.), the decision *not* to dismantle
the OSRD (OF 53, Truman Papers), and preparations
for the release of the OSRD report, *Science--the Endless Frontier* (Washington, D.C.: Government Printing
Office, 1945). The latter provided a blueprint of
federal funding for the scientific community.

43. An account of the Morgenthau-Rosenman transactions
is in John Morton Blum, *From the Morgenthau Diaries*,
III, 468-473.

44. HST to Morgenthau, July 14, 1945, as cited in *Truman
Public Papers, 1945*, 170, 171.

45. Important differences between Truman and Morgenthau
over the tax program then before Congress augured
Morgenthau's dismissal and Rosenman had no questions
on Truman's judgment in this matter. He was, however, "uncomfortable" with the request that Morgenthau disregard the agreement to remain in office until after Potsdam and instead resign immediately.
He attributed this decision to Byrnes's influence,
and other observers shared his suspicions. The *Washington Post*, October 30, 1945, carried an account alleging that Byrnes had not only convinced Truman to
dismiss Morgenthau before Potsdam, but had also persuaded the President to use Rosenman to secure the
resignation. The Rosenman-Morgenthau long friendship
was broken as a consequence. See Rosenman, *Presiden-*

tial Style, 449.

The Morganthau plan for Germany had advanced recommendations at opposite poles from some Rosenman had
made in his own Mission report. The plan may also
have become a liability to Morgenthau's hopes to be
named Bank and Fund Governor. Most fundamental,
however, was Byrnes's opposition to his person. Rosenman was candid in acknowledging this.

In regard to the antagonism between Rosenman and
Byrnes, the author once inquired of President Truman
if it had been evident to him. Mr. Truman replied
that much of what Rosenman had "warned against" later
became evident, but that Mr. Truman had "to find out
by experience." Personal interview, November 20,
1965.

46. Truman, *Memoirs*, I, 482. Technically the message
should have been addressed directly to Congress, but
since that body was "anxious to recess," Rosenman
secured the approval of Speaker Rayburn and Majority
Leader Barkley to address the Potsdam report to the
nation. SIR to Ross, July 20, 1945, Report to the
Nation on the Potsdam Conference Folder, Rosenman
Papers, T.L.

47. Truman, *Memoirs*, I, 422.

48. *Ibid.*, 482, 483.

49. Examples are points relating to unemployment compensation, Federal salaries, executive reorganization,
war controls, veterans legislation, science research,
FEPC, housing, selective service, and education.

50. *Truman Public Papers*, *1945*, 301.

51. Rosenman, *Roosevelt Public Papers*, XIII, 41.

52. Evidence of such activities during April can be found in the Daily Reports, April 30, Smith Diary, R.L. On July 6, Rosenman drafted a letter from HST to Congressman Joe Bates which assumed "you [Truman] still wish to send a message to Congress on education some time after you return." Memorandum, SIR to HST, Bates Folder, Rosenman Papers, T.L.

53. Truman, *Memoirs*, I, 481.

54. September 6, 1945 Message to Congress Folder, Rosenman Papers, T.L. Individual and departmental contributors included Vinson, Snyder, E.S. Land, Harold Smith, Oscar Cox, Chester Bowles, Paul McNutt, Harold Ickes, Generals Marshall, Bradley, and Flemming, the Agriculture and State Departments, the OWMR and the FEA. The above is a representative and not an exhaustive list of contributors.

Also of assistance was Clark Clifford who had been brought to the White House by James K. Vardaman, a Missourian who served as Truman's naval aide. Clifford, also from Missouri, served as Vardaman's alternate while the latter accompanied Truman to Potsdam. Clifford rendered Rosenman informal assistance and it has been reported that at the Judge's request the President asked Clifford to remain in Washington. Edward A. Rogge, "The Speechwriting of Harry S. Truman," Ph.D. Dissertation, University of Missouri, 1958.

55. After reading an earlier version of this chapter Rosenman commented that Snyder was a "study in the effects of political success," and once a program had proven its political value he would cease his opposition to it.

Rosenman and Snyder had frequent official dealings. One example was the Committee on the Disposition of War Agencies. Snyder served as chairman and Rosenman

and Harold Smith were the two remaining members. The
committee was created at Rosenman's suggestion. Memorandum, SIR to Snyder, August 18, 1945, Reorganization of Government Departments Folder, Rosenman
Papers, T.L. The first meeting was on August 24,
and the committee, which Smith dubbed the Big Three,
met fairly regularly until November 19. Smith
Diary, R.L.

While acknowledging Snyder's official prerogatives,
Rosenman was nonetheless anxious to monitor their
exercise. On an issue relating to government research
activities, for instance, he recommended that the
Director "handle" the details, but invite the Counsel
to the meetings at which the details were decided.
Memorandum, SIR to Snyder, August 14, 1945, Research
Folder, Rosenman Papers, T.L.

56. Truman, *Memoirs*, I, 483.

57. For a close analysis of the OWMR and Rosenman drafts
     see Mary Hinchey, "The Frustration of the New Deal
     Revival, 1944-1946," Ph.D. Dissertation, University
     of Missouri, 1965.

58. *New York Herald Tribune*, September 12, 1945.

59. One important departure involved immigration and
     other positions in regard to Palestine. The 1944
     Democratic platform had advocated "the opening of
     Palestine to unrestricted Jewish immigration and
     colonization and such a policy as to result in the
     establishment there of a free and independent Jewish
     Commonwealth," and the Republican platform contained
     a similar plank. Despite pressures to reaffirm this
     plank (see Joint letter from Robert Taft and Robert
     Wagner to the President, December 6, 1945, OF 204,
     Truman Papers, T.L.), the President, with Rosenman's
     support, advocated a vaguer and more limited policy.
     (For evidence of Rosenman's assistance to Truman see

Memorandum, SIR to HST, December 10, 1945). A model
statement of Truman's position is in *Public Papers,
1945*, Items 187, 188. See also Chapter 13.

60. Smith to SIR, August 31, 1945, September 6, 1945 Message to Congress Folder, Rosenman Papers, T.L.

61. Press Conference of October 8, 1945, *Truman Public
Papers, 1945*, 383, 384.

62. *Science--The Endless Frontier*, see fn. 42. Bush to
SIR, May 25, 1945, Health Message Folder, Rosenman
Papers, T.L. Bush had written he was "very happy to
know you [Rosenman] are going to be here [Washington]
to see this report through to the President."

63. William Haber to Author, August 28, 1968. Haber was
an Assistant Director of the OWMR who worked with
Rosenman on the Health Message.

64. Interview with Rosenman. The Judge has suggested
that especially during the illness of the President's
mother, they frequently commented upon how heavy a
financial strain the required care would have imposed
upon a less happily situated citizen. This particular tactic would have been most effective *after* the
first health message.

65. The Judge's official exercise of this proprietorship
is apparent from correspondence at the Truman Library.
See for example Ross to Mrs. Raymond Clapper, June
18, 1945, OF 103 Misc. His continued interest in the
program during his post-Counsel years is evident both
from his files at the Library and a portrait in the
New Yorker, March 23, 1946.

66. *New York Times*, November 3, 1945. This report of
Rosenman's impending resignation is misleading. It
reveals he was to become counsel for the Associated
Fur Coat and Trimming Manufacturers at a $40,000

annual salary and implies it would provide full-time employment. Actually the Association was to be *one* of his clients, and one which his firm would soon relinquish.

67. The Judge frequently related how one day he reached into his safe deposit box and came up empty. He knew for certain then that the time had come to leave Washington.

68. Other major "interim" assignments involved details of Puerto Rican status, reconstruction and independence of the Philippines, an investigation of the Pearl Harbor attack, labor-management relations, and immigration and displaced persons.

69. *New York Times*, August 24, 1945.

70. H. Struve Hensel to SIR, December 7, 1945, Unification of the Armed Forces Folder, Rosenman Papers, T.L. Hensel to SIR, December 11, 1945, Hensel Folder, Rosenman Papers, T.L.

71. SIR to HST, November 13, 1945, Unification of the Armed Forces Folder, Rosenman Papers, T.L.

72. Admiral William Leahy to SIR, December 14, 1945, Unification of the Armed Forces Folder, Rosenman Papers, T.L. See also *Forrestal Diaries*, ed. by Walter Millis (New York: Viking Press, 1951), 118, and Smith Diary, December 13, 1945, R.L.

73. *New York Times*, December 29, 1945 and January 2, 1946. See also Truman, *Memoirs*, I, 550.

74. Smith Diary, January 9, 1946, R.L.

75. Smith to SIR, August 31, 1945, September 6, 1945 Message Folder, Rosenman Papers, T.L. Smith had also protested against the lack of "regard for the strategy

of Executive-Congressional relationships."

76. Smith Diary, October 30, 1945, R.L.

77. SIR to HST, January 13, 1946, 1946 State of the Union
     Message Folder, Rosenman Papers, T.L.

78. Smith Diary, January 15, 1946, R.L. Truman had indi-
     cated his approval of a probable excise tax cut and
     Smith insisted any decrease in revenues should be re-
     flected in the message. Treasury Secretary Vinson
     opposed both the cut and its inclusion in the mes-
     sage. Rosenman, who conceived his role as arbitor
     between the Treasury Department and the Bureau of the
     Budget, personally favored the inclusion of the ex-
     cise tax cut as a political reality. The issue was
     thrashed out at a White House conference at which
     Vinson was unusually aggressive in defense of his
     position. There was no discussion of tax reduction
     in the final message.

79. Press Conference of January 24, 1946, *Truman Public
     Papers, 1946*, 90. See also *New York Times*, January
     25, 1946.

80. The complete citation is included in *Truman Public
     Papers, 1946*, 95. The *New York Times*, January
     25, 1946, and *Newsweek*, February 4, 1946, also re-
     ported comments included in the text.

81. Joel L. Lefkowitz, "Louis McHenry Howe and Samuel
     Irving Rosenman--Intimate Presidential Advisers,"
     undergraduate essay, Syracuse University, 1958, 134.
     Mr. Lefkowitz quoted from an interview with the
     Judge.

CHAPTER THIRTEEN

1.   Rosenman's association with Moses is chronicled, un-
      sympathetically, in Robert A. Caro, *The Power Broker:*
      Robert Moses and the Fall of New York (New York:
      Alfred A. Knopf, 1974).   Letters and memoranda from
      1944 reflecting Rosenman's monitoring of O'Dwyer's
      quasi-military assignments are in the R.L.   For Rosen-
      man's transit board appointment see *New York Times*,
      February 27, 1946.

2.   SIR to Clark Clifford, November 29, 1946, 1946 State
      of the Union, OF 419F, Truman Papers, T.L.   Clifford
      had allegedly been kept on at the White House on
      Rosenman's suggestion.

      Rosenman's most reported appearance in Washington was
      during a May railroad strike.   Less apparent were his
      advisory notes to Truman.   The first such note, Janu-
      ary 29, 1946, T.L., suggested that Secretary of State
      Byrnes had lied to the press when he disclaimed know-
      ledge of a secret Yalta agreement that the United
      States would support Russian claims to the Kurile Is-
      lands.   "Why it was not released after VJ Day I do
      not know but certainly Byrnes knew it all along."

      An item on the Rosenmans in the *New Yorker*, March 26,
      1946 includes the "more or less between trains" ref-
      erence.

3.   *New York Times*, May 21 and July 17, 1946.

4.   Interview with Rosenman.   Patterson had resigned as
      a United States Court of Appeals Judge in 1940 when
      he went to Washington as Assistant Secretary of War.

5.   See for example Alonzo Hamby, *Beyond the New Deal*
      (New York: Columbia University Press, 1973), 463.

6.   *New York Times*, December 20, 1946.

7.   Advisory Commission on Universal Training, *Report to the President* (Washington: U.S. Government Printing Office, 1947), 103.

8.   Truman, *Years of Trial and Hope*, 55.

9.   See *New York Times*, July 16, 1949 and *U.S. News and World Report*, September 30, 1949. Carroll R. Daugherty was board chairman and David L. Cole the third member.

10.   Steel Industry Board appointed by the President July 15, 1949, *Report to the President of the United States on the Labor Dispute in the Basic Steel Industry* (Washington: U.S. Government Printing Office, 1949), 11 and 26.

11.   *Ibid.*, 6 and 7.

12.   *Ibid.*, 62. The report was submitted officially September 10.

13.   For an elaboration of these views see Samuel Rosenman, "A Better Way to Handle Strikes," *Newsday*, July 15, 1967. See also Rosenman's testimony before a sub-committee of the Senate Judiciary Committee, October 17, 1967 in support of S. 176, sponsored by George A. Smathers.

14.   See Chapter 8.

15.   Rosenman Interview, William E. Wiener Oral History Library of the American Jewish Committee. The interviews were conducted in July 1970 by Mitchell Krauss.

16.   See for example SIR to FDR, undated and FDR's reply January 7, 1938, P.P.F. 64, Rosenman folder, R.L. Reporting that the Roumanian government had violated

treaty and constitutional guarantees, the Judge asked
Roosevelt to intercede as "it was so helpful when
you did so in other situations." The President assured Rosenman "we are doing everything we can without actually declaring war on Roumania."

17. Joseph Proskauer, *A Segment of My Times* (New York:
    Farrar, Straus, and Company, 1950), 198.

18. *Forrestal Diaries*, 347.

19. *New York Times*, October 8, 1947. Chaim Weizmann re-
    garded the American Jewish Committee's support of the
    partition plan a "welcome and striking change in at-
    titude." Weizmann, *Trial and Error* (Philadelphia:
    The Jewish Publication Society of America, 1949), 457.

20. *New York Times*, May 5, 1948.

21. Truman, *Years of Trial and Hope*, 162.

22. *New York Times*, March 14, 1948.

23. Larry Collins and Dominique Lapierre, *O Jerusalem!*
    (New York: Simon and Schuster, 1972), 230. See also
    Truman, *Years of Trial and Hope*, 162.

24. Rosenman, *Presidential Style*, 510. Rabbi Silver
    was head of the American section of the Jewish Agency
    and Co-chairman with Rabbi Wise of the American Zion-
    ist Emergency Committee. Silver also served as an
    advisor to Senator Taft.

25. Collins and Lapierre, *O Jerusalem!*, 361.

26. Truman, *Years of Trial and Hope*, 164. In Rosenman's
    memoir in the William E. Wiener Oral History Library
    he speculates that Roosevelt would *not* have recog-
    nized Israel so promptly.

27. Weizmann to Rosenman, incorrectly dated March 17,
    1948 (probably May 17, 1948), R.P.C. References in
    this letter make it apparent that it was authored
    after May 14.

28. *New York Times*, August 4, 1956.

29. *Ibid.*, July 15, 1948. The Judge also participated
    in some strategy sessions, but he was *not* the author
    of an unsigned memorandum "Should the President Call
    Congress Back?" that was located in his Truman Lib-
    rary files. The idea, according to Rosenman, occur-
    red independently to a number of advisors and to the
    President himself. For the Pearson story see *Wash-
    ington Post*, October 1, 1948. Mrs. Rosenman suggested
    the Judge could tell me some "very amusing stories"
    about this, but when I queried the Judge he preferred
    to talk about "more important" matters.

30. *New York Times*, November 7, 1948.

31. *Ibid.*, November 11 and 13, 1953. It was alleged that
    at the time Truman appointed Harry Dexter White as
    Director of the International Monetary Fund he knew
    him to be a Russian spy, and the subpoena was issued
    in this connection.

32. *Ibid.*, August 12, 1956. See also October 14, 1954.

33. *Ibid.*, February 25, 1957.

34. Caro, *Power Broker*, 722.

35. *Syracuse Herald Journal*, March 19, 1958.

36. *New York Times*, August 29 and October 5, 1958.

37. In addition to continuing as Counsel to the Power
    Authority Rosenman represented the Triborough Bridge
    and Tunnel Authority and was a member of the executive

committee of the board of directors of the New York
World's Fair. His well remunerated efforts in behalf of Tammany sponsored slum clearance landlords
and ultimately Webb & Knapp, a real estate and investment firm, have been chronicled in Caro, who depicts
Rosenman as having come full circle from his youthful
efforts as champion of the rentpayers.

38. *New York Times*, July 29, 1970. See also September
20 and October 3, 1970. For an example of a Democrats for Rockefeller ad see *New York Post*, September
28, 1970.

39. *New York Times*, March 19, 1962.

40. See for example *New York Times*, December 26, 1965.
This author, although having strong reservations
about the overall advantages of judicial selection
boards, believes they work best when applied to inferior court appointments. They are better equipped
to weed out the incompetent than attract exceptional
men.

41. Richard Harris, *Decision* (New York: Dutton, 1971),
94.

42. *Ibid*.

43. See for example *Burlington* (VT) *Free Press*, March 19,
1970. This particular advertisement energized Vermont lawyers to further pressure Senator Winston
Prouty to vote against confirmation. The author wrote
to Judge Rosenman the day before the Senate vote that
Prouty would nonetheless vote to affirm. Prouty voted
against Carswell the same day the Judge received my
letter, and in his reply suggested that if I wanted
to establish a reputation for sagacity it might help
if I waited a day before mailing letters.

44. *New York Post*, May 18, 1973.

INDEX

Aluminum Company of America
(ALCOA) 241
American Bar Association
245, 246
American Federation of La-
bor 82
American Jewish Committee
140, 234
Arnold, Thurman 162
Astor, Vincent 79
Association of the Bar of
the City of New York 41,
68, 243
Atlantic Conference 190
Atom Bomb 214, 215
Austin, Warren 236

Balfour Declaration 235
Bankhead, William 131
Barkley, Alben 131, 179,
189
Barton, Bruce 135
Baruch, Bernard 151, 152,
179, 197, 267, 277
Bayh, Birch 246
Beard, Charles A. 120
Berle, Adolf A. 60, 82
Bertini, Amadeo 41
Biddle, Francis 174, 191
Biel, Leonard 8
Black, Hugo 110

Blandford, John B. Jr. 157
Blaustein v. *Pan American
Petroleum* 93
Bloch, Maurice 2, 18, 21
Bohlen, Charles 193
Brain Trust 58-61, 65
Brandeis, Louis 110
Brandeis, Susan 18
Bromley, Bruce 246
Brown, Stewart 13
Brownell, Herbert 244
Bullitt, William C. 101
Bureau of the Budget 153,
162
Burlingham, C.C. 77, 244
Bush, Vannevar 221
Byrnes, James F. 166, 167,
178, 189, 191, 212, 213,
235

Cadogan, Sir Alexander 203
Capper, Arthur 180
Carswell, G. Harrold 245,
246
Carter, John Franklin (Un-
official Observer) 98
Charwell, Lord 196
Chase National Bank 90
Chattanooga News-Free Press
199
Chequers 196

Chicago Tribune   173, 179, 191
Childs, Marquis   180
Christian Free Press   199
Churchill, Winston   194, 196, 197
Citizens Union   16, 79
City College of New York 5, 130
Clifford, Clark   228, 240
closed shop   85
Cohalan, Denis O'Leary   74
Cohen, Benjamin V.   106, 134
Colby, Bainbridge   79
Columbia Broadcasting Company   227
Columbia University   5, 8, 59, 246
    Law School   6, 8
    Club   233
Commager, Henry Steele 116
Compton, Karl T.   229
Congress of Industrial Organizations (CIO)   241
Connelly, Matthew   240
Cooper, Irving Ben   244
Corcoran, Thomas   101, 102, 105, 106, 134
Coughlin, Father   44, 152
Council of Economic Advisors   225
Cox, Oscar   175, 191
Crain, Thomas C.T.   42, 44
Crater, Joseph Force   26, 41
Cummings, Homer   107
Curry, John F.   38, 39, 40, 41, 50, 51, 52, 53, 54, 66, 68, 69, 70, 76

Daniels, Jonathan   199
Davis, Elmer   116, 123, 161
Davis, John W.   79, 93, 244
Democrats for Rockefeller 243
DeSapio, Carmine   242
Dewey, Thomas E.   94, 181, 235
Dirksen, Everett   211
Donovan, William   161
Douglas, William O.   259
Dowling, Victor   57
Dulles, John Foster   79
Dunnigan, John J.   54

Early, Stephen   104, 116, 137, 144, 180, 185, 193, 199, 205
Eden, Anthony   205
Eisenhower, Dwight D.   195, 232
Eisenhower, Milton   160
Emergency Price Control Act   164, 165, 166
Ewald, George F.   41, 42, 43

Fair Deal   217
Fair Trade Law   89
Farley, James   131
Farley, Thomas   48, 49, 52-54, 61, 65, 77, 134
Farulla v. *Freundlich*   85, 86
Fearon, George   53
Finletter, Thomas   242
Fish, Hamilton   135
Flynn, Ed   50, 51, 54, 61, 67, 76, 134, 185, 186, 197
Foreign Economic Administration   192

Forrestal, James   148
Frankfurter, Felix   33, 125,
   127-30, 139, 172, 173,
   199
Full Employment Bill   222
Fulton, Hugh   206
Fusion Party (N.Y.C. 1933)
   76, 77, 82

GI Bill of Rights   176
Garner, John Nance   134
Genesis of the New Deal
   34, 115
Genung, George L.   68
George, Walter   189
Gillie, George W.   202
Goebbels, Josef   204
Good Neighbor League   100
Graham, Dr. Wallace   221
Griffin, Edward G.   25

Hayes, Carleton   5
Hand, Augustus   228
Hand, Learned   228
Handler, Morton   175
Hannegan, Robert   182, 184
Harriman, Averell   239,
   241-43
Harris, Richard   245
Hassett, William   199
Hazzard v. *Chase National
   Bank*   90
Healy, Martin J.   41, 42
Hechler, Kenneth   118
Henderson, Leon   149, 163,
   164
Herald Tribune   87
High, Stanley   100-102, 105,
   106, 134, 200
Hillman, Sidney   159

Himmler, Heinrich   205
Hines, James (Jimmy) 8, 17,
   66, 77
Hiroshima   215
Hitler, Adolf   126, 139,
   141, 142, 204
Hofstadter, Samuel   45, 54,
   57, 65, 67, 68, 70
Hogan, Frank   242
Holmes, Reverend John
   Haynes   44, 45, 46, 52
Holmes, Oliver Wendell   93
Home Rule Amendment   92
Hoover, Herbert   24, 36, 65,
   70, 125
Hopkins, Harry   29, 101,
   115, 132-37, 142, 144,
   152, 160, 163, 164, 166,
   167, 172, 173, 179, 185,
   193, 199, 239
House Committee on Un-
   American Activities   240
Howe, Louis   1, 23, 29, 52,
   61, 63, 64, 100
Hughes, Charles Evans   30,
   110, 244
Hull, Cordell   161
Hylan, John F.   9

Ickes, Harold   144, 151,
   152, 160, 166, 183
Independent Judges Party
   69-70, 76
Insull, Samuel   70
International Military
   Tribunal   203

Jackson, Robert   144, 203,
   205, 211
"Jewish problem"   141, 142,
   233-38

Johns Hopkins Hospital   169
Johnson, Hugh   86, 100, 149
Johnson, Lyndon   180, 181
Jones Beach   15
Jones, Jesse   156, 157, 188,
  189

Kamenets-Podalski, Ukraine
  2
Kammerer, Paul T.   78
Keating, Kenneth   243
Kennedy, John F.   232
Kilgallen, Dorothy   126
Kirby, Rollin   64
Kirsch, Benjamin   18
Knight, John   35, 42
Knight, Richard A.   94, 95
Knudson, William   149, 152
Koch, Edward R.   74
Krock, Arthur   160
Kupfer, Milton   8, 57

LaFollette, Robert   101
LaGuardia, Fiorello H.   76,
  81, 90, 127
Lanham, Fritz G.   156
Leahy, William   167, 173,
  193
Leary, Thomas   67
Legislative Bill Drafting
  Commission   17
LeHand, Marguerite (Missy)
  101, 106, 133
Lehman, Herbert   24, 54,
  69-72, 74, 80, 127, 242
Lend-Lease Bill   142, 143
Lex Amici   47
Liberal Party   242
Lindley, Ernest   112
Little Steel Formula   165

Little War Cabinet   167,
  177
Lucas, Scott   205
Lusk Laws   9, 92
Lydon, Richard P.   67, 68
Lyons Residency Law   90-92

McBain, Howard   60
McCarran, Pat   210
Machold, Edmund   16, 30
McCooey, John Jr.   47
McCooey, John Sr.   47, 69
McCook, Philip J.   74, 77
McGoldrick, Joseph   60
McKee, Joseph V.   76, 78,
  99
McKellar, Kenneth   129
McLaughlin, Charles B.
  51, 68, 74, 77
McNaboe, John J.   67
McNutt, Paul   159, 165, 167
Macy, William K.   68
Madison Square Garden   105,
  137
Manasco, Carter   224
Mancuso, Francis X.   40-42
Markham, Edwin   64
Marshall, General George C.
  173
Martin, Joseph   135
Massachusetts Institute of
  Technology   229
Metropolitan Opera House
  94
Miller, Nathan   9, 79
Moley, Raymond   45, 53, 59-
  63, 65, 71, 99-103
Mongello, Emmanuel   91
Monongahela Democratic
  Club   7

Moreland Act 42
Morgenthau, Henry Jr. 99, 213, 214
Moskowitz, Belle 2, 18, 25
Moskowitz, Henry 82
Moses, Robert 15, 16, 18, 24, 82, 227, 241, 243
Mullan, George V. 49-51, 67
Mullins, Robert 91
Murphy, Charles F. 8, 38
Murrow, Edward R. 242
Mussolini, Benito 204

Nathan, Robert 218
National Committee on the Housing Emergency 154
National Defense Housing Act 155, 156
National Housing Agency 157, 158
National Labor Relations Act 107, 108
National Public Service Corporation 90
National Industrial Recovery Act (NRA) 73, 85, 86, 89
National Science Foundation 222
National War Labor Board 165
Nelson, Donald 152, 153, 218
New York City Civil Service Commission 90, 91
New York County Lawyers Association 44
New York Daily News 173

New York Regional Labor Board 86
New York Life Insurance Company 227
New York State Association 16
New York State Liquor Control Board 71
New York State Power Authority 241
New York State Power Commission 33
New York State Public Service Commission 30
New York Sun 75, 84
New York Times 48, 54, 68, 69, 74, 79, 87, 104, 111, 145, 152, 155, 160, 174
Niagara-Hudson Power Corporation 30
Niagara-Mohawk Corporation 241
Niles, David 172, 173, 235

O'Brien, John J. 76
O'Brien, Morgan J. 78, 79
O'Connor, Basil 59
O'Donnell, John 173
O'Dwyer, William 227
Office of Economic Stabilization 166
Office of Price Administration and Civilian Supply 149
Office of Production Management 149
Office of Scientific Research and Development 221
Office of War Information 160, 161

Office of War Mobiliza-
tion and Reconversion
217
Osborne v. *Cohen*   92
Ottinger, Albert   24

Palmer, Charles F.   154,
157
Pan American Day Address
(1941) 143
Pan American Petroleum and
Transport Company   93
Patterson, Robert   148, 228
Pearson, Drew   240
Pepper, Claude   210
Perkins, Frances   10, 159,
166
Potsdam Conference   213,
214

Quincy (Battlecruiser)
193, 194

Railway Labor Act   232
Rauch, Basil   112
Recovery Party   26, 78, 81
Reed, Stanley   107
"refugee problem"   140
Reuben, Dorothy   *see*   Ros-
enman, Dorothy
Reynolds Metal Company
241
Richberg, Donald   101, 107
Rockefeller, Nelson   161,
239, 243, 246
Roerich, Dr. Nicholas   136
Rogers, Lindsay   58, 60
Roosevelt, Eleanor   57, 154,
156, 189, 242
Roosevelt, Eliot   197

Roosevelt, Franklin Delano
1928 gubernatorial cam-
paign   1, 19-24
1930 gubernatorial cam-
paign   33, 34
Gubernatorial administra-
tions: water power 30-
36; cabinet selection
24, 25; turkey cabinet
27, 28
presidential candidate:
1932 52, 61-64, 67, 70;
1936 100-106, 111; *1940*
131-138; *1944* 185, 186,
inauguration   187
attitude toward Rosenman
1, 21, 23, 29-33, 49,
51, 53, 68, 80, 98, 99,
101, 106, 114, 126, 137,
138, 148, 151, 152, 186
appoints Rosenman as
Governor's Counsel 25,
26; as Presidential
Counsel 96, 173, 174
published papers: guber-
natorial 113, 120; pres-
idential 112-124
selection of Rosenman as
editor   113, 114
Tammany Hall   37-41, 43-
46, 48, 52, 53, 65, 66,
69
presidential speeches and
messages   100, 132, 137,
142-44, 163, 164, 168,
176-79, 193, 194
Supreme Court reorganiza-
tion   107-110
last meeting with Rosen-
man   194

death 197, 198
legacy 119, 124, 200, 216
Library 112, 116, 118, 122, 123
Root, Elihu 244
Rosenberg, Anna 159
Rosenman, Dorothy Reuben 6, 8, 18, 54, 62, 154, 232, 237
Rosenman, Ethel Paler (mother) 2
Rosenman, Isaac (uncle) 2
Rosenman, James Saul (son) 29
Rosenman, Robert (son) 29
Rosenman, Samuel Irving
  Family: Parents 2-4; Wife *see* Dorothy Rosenman; Children, *see* James and Robert Rosenman; European cousins 141
  Early Life: San Antonio 2-4; New York City 4-6; Assemblyman 7-17; Rosenman Act 13-14; Bill Drafting Commissioner 17-19
  Counsel to the Governor: appointment 25; duties 26, 27, 54, 128; turkey cabinet 27, 28; resides in Executive Mansion 29, 30; waterpower article 32; liaison with Tammany 39, 40; Tammany scandals 40-55; resigns 59

Judicial ambitions and career 33, 49-52, 108; FDR appointment 53-55; denied nomination 67; Lehman appointment 74; election campaign 79-83; resignation 96, 172; judicial record 85-96; New York Court of Appeals 184, 185, 228; United States Court of Appeals 228
Tammany 2, 7, 33, 34, 37-40, 66, 69, 76, 77, 227, 242
Attitudes toward FDR 2, 19, 21, 53-55, 106, 114, 127, 139, 179, 188, 198
Attitudes toward Truman 200, 210, 211, 222, 237, 240
Attitudes toward Defense Reorganization 147, 148, 150, 152, 158, 160, 163, 168
Brain Trust 58-61; rejects Washington assignment 70
Judaism: family 3, 4; at Columbia University 5, 233; as Assembly candidate 8; Supreme Court 108; refugees 139, 140; Israel 233-238
Law Practice: early 5, 17, 18; proposed with FDR 51, 126; early New Deal 71-74; post-Washington 222, 227, 228, 238, 239

Presidential Counsel: Roosevelt 96, 173; last meeting 194; political conflict 174, 178-80, 191; FDR political deman retains 200; general duties 209, 210; Truman deputy 213, 214; Rosenman Mission 190-96, 201-203, 211; war crimes 190, 196, 197, 201, 203-205, 211; resigns 222-225

FDR speeches and messages: first efforts 22; 1930 campaign 33, 34; 1932 campaign 61, 62, 64; initial presidential efforts 100; 1936 campaign 101-106; Supreme Court 107-110; 1940 campaign 131-136; 1944 campaign 184-186; last message (Yalta) 193, 194; *Public Papers* 112-124, 132, 208; *Working with Roosevelt* 23, 118

Truman speeches and messages: contrast with FDR 208, 209, 215, 216, 228

Elder statesman: universal training 228, 229; collective bargaining 229-233; national politics 235, 239-41; New York politics 239, 241-243; City Bar 243, 244; judicial selection 244, 245; opposition to

Carswell 244, 245; death 246

Rosenman, Sol (father) 2, 4

Rosenman, Goldmark, Colin and Kaye 227, 238

Ross, Charlie 209, 218, 221, 237

"runaway employers" 85

Ryan, Monsignor John A. 187

"Sacred Cow" 197, 198

St. Lawrence Power Authority 34, 35

St. Lawrence River 30

St. Lawrence River Development Commission 33, 34

St. Lawrence power project 220, 241

Salant, Richard 118

San Francisco Conference 196, 201-203

Sanger, Margaret 15

Saturday Review of Literature 116

Seabury, Samuel 43-45, 48, 49, 52, 65, 76, 77, 79, 82, 244

Seagrams 227

Selective Service System 167

SHAEF 195

Shafer, Paul W. 173

Shalleck, Joseph 7

Sheehan, William 37

Sheehy, John E. 54

Sheintag, Bernard 62

Sherman, Henry L. 74

Sherwood, Robert 135, 142, 144, 160, 163, 164, 185, 195

Silver, Rabbi Hillel 237
Sloan, James 138
Smith, Alfred E. 1, 9-12, 18, 19, 21, 24, 30, 33, 38, 40, 58, 59, 61, 62, 69
Smith, Harold 153, 154, 159-161, 163, 219, 224
Snyder, John 217, 218
Sommerville, General Brehon 173
Stalin, Josef 203
Standard Oil Co. of Indiana 93
Stare decises 84-88
Steingut, Irwin 57
Stettinius, Edward 210
Steuer, Aron 67, 68
Steuer, Max 67
Stevenson, Adlai 239, 241
Stimson, Henry L. 93, 125, 127, 128, 244
Stone, Judge Harlan F. 6, 187
Stone, I.F. 152
Stout, Rex 161
Straus, Nathan Jr. 16, 17, 156, 157
Straus-Rosenman Bills 16
Strauss, Lewis 78
Supply Priorities Allocation Board (SPAB) 149, 151-53, 190
Swope, Herbert Bayard 79

Taft, William Howard 125
Taft-Hartley Act 230
Tammany Hall (New York County Democratic Committee) 8, 33, 37, 38, 53, 66, 76, 77, 227, 242

Teamsters Union 133
Tennessee Valley Authority 87
Thayer, Warren T. 30
Time 152
Townsend Harris High School 5, 95
Trosk, George 77, 79, 82
Truman, Harry S. 199, 208, 215-217, 221, 224, 236, 237
Tugwell, Rexford 60, 71, 99, 100
Tully, Grace 62, 123
Tuttle, Charles H. 33
Twentieth Century-Fox 227
Twenty-One Points 215-217

United Nations Organization 195, 197, 200, 210, 235
United Real Estate Owners Association 153, 155
United States Housing Authority 153, 155
Universal Military Training Advisory Commission 228, 229
Untermeyer, Samuel 79

Van Devanter, Willis 110
Vinson, Fred 213, 217

Walker, Frank 103
Walker, James J. 38, 41, 44, 45, 66, 67, 76
Wagner, Robert Jr. (Mayor) 242, 244, 245
Wagner, Robert Sr. (Senator) 102, 156
Wagner-Steagall Act 155

Wallace, Henry   132, 136,
  137, 152, 182, 187-190
war crimes trials   201-205,
  211
War Manpower Commission
  159-167
War Production Board   161
Ward, Hamilton   30, 31, 33,
  42, 43
Wardman Park Hotel   175
Warm Springs, Georgia   24
Wasservogel, Judge Isidore
  14
Water-Power development
  30-36
Watson, Edwin "Pa"   193
Webster, Bethuel M.   245
Weizmann, Chaim   236-238

Welles, Sumner   161
Wheeler, Burton J.   110
Wickard, Claude   165
Wickersham, George W.   244
Williamsburg (yacht)   223
Wilkie, Wendell   133, 136,
  143, 181
Winchell, Walter   126
Wise, Rabbi Stephen S.   44-
  46, 152, 237
Withrow v. *The Joint Legis-
  lative Committee*   92
Woods, Dr. Alan   171
Working with Roosevelt   23,
  118

Yalta Conference   189, 193,
  194